Christianity, Metaphor, and the Urge to Truth

Christianity, Metaphor, and the Urge to Truth

Unburdening from the Absolute

Barry Stephenson

CASCADE Books • Eugene, Oregon

CHRISTIANITY, METAPHOR, AND THE URGE TO TRUTH
Unburdening from the Absolute

Copyright © 2025 Barry Stephenson. All rights reserved. Except for brief quotations in critical publications or reviews, no part of this book may be reproduced in any manner without prior written permission from the publisher. Write: Permissions, Wipf and Stock Publishers, 199 W. 8th Ave., Suite 3, Eugene, OR 97401.

Cascade Books
An Imprint of Wipf and Stock Publishers
199 W. 8th Ave., Suite 3
Eugene, OR 97401

www.wipfandstock.com

PAPERBACK ISBN: 979-8-3852-1795-3
HARDCOVER ISBN: 979-8-3852-1796-0
EBOOK ISBN: 979-8-3852-1797-7

Cataloguing-in-Publication data:

Names: Stephenson, Barry [author].

Title: Christianity, metaphor, and the urge to truth : unburdening from the absolute / by Barry Stephenson.

Description: Eugene, OR: Cascade Books, 2025 | Includes bibliographical references and index.

Identifiers: ISBN 979-8-3852-1795-3 (paperback) | ISBN 979-8-3852-1796-0 (hardcover) | ISBN 979-8-3852-1797-7 (ebook)

Subjects: LCSH: Metaphor—Religious aspects—Christianity. | Language and languages—Religious aspects—Christianity. | Theology, Doctrinal. | Imagination—Religious aspects—Christianity. | Sin—Christianity. | Atonement.

Classification: BR115.I6 S74 2025 (paperback) | BR115.I6 (ebook)

VERSION NUMBER 09/17/25

Revised Standard Version of the Bible, copyright 1952 [2nd edition, 1971] by the Division of Christian Education of the National Council of the Churches of Christ in the United States of America. Used by permission. All rights reserved.

The next best thing to being really inside Christendom is to be really outside it. . . . The best relation to our spiritual home is to be near enough to love it. But the next best is to be far enough away not to hate it.

—G. K. Chesterton, *The Everlasting Man*

Metaphors are fossils that indicate an archaic stratum of the trail of theoretical curiosity—a stratum that is not rendered anachronistic just because there is no way back to the fullness of its stimulations and expectations of truth.

—Hans Blumenberg, *Shipwreck with Spectator*

Contents

Preface | ix

1. God Is an Absolute Metaphor | 1
2. Metaphor, All the Way Down | 14
3. Anthropogenesis and the Urge to Truth | 40
4. Sin and the Darwinism of Words | 59
5. The Metaphorics of Sin | 77
6. Christianity and Redemptive Violence | 116
7. God | 150
8. Jung's Mythic Gnosis: A Critique | 182
   Coda: "When Did We See Thee Hungry?" | 213

Bibliography | 219
Index | 229
Scripture Index | 237

Preface

PETER BERGER ONCE OBSERVED that with the secularization of society comes a secularization of consciousness. Among the entailments of this general shift in consciousness is an erosion of the capacity for symbolic thinking and a relegating of symbolic thought to inferior status. The trinity of literalism, historicism, and materialism rule the roost, a fact that makes teaching religion (or, as most of my colleagues would have it, teaching "about religion") a most difficult endeavor, since religious language and thought are thoroughly metaphorical, analogical, and symbolic. The ontological and epistemological assumptions of a secularized consciousness are hard nuts to crack.

The following chapters are representative of my efforts to frame an approach to Christian thought that emphasizes foundational metaphors. The organization is thematic, exploring such matters as sin and atonement, divine violence, the personalization of divinity, eschatology and Christology. Alongside aspects of Christian thought, readers are presented with an introduction to the fields of metaphor theory and philosophical anthropology, especially Hans Blumenberg's contributions to the history of ideas. In Blumenberg's adroit hands, the history of ideas in European culture becomes the story of various attempts to distance or unburden oneself from the demands of an oppressive absolute.

As "distancing" and "unburdening" are different activities from "pursuing truth," Blumenberg has affinities with Nietzsche, who questions the pursuit of truth as an absolute virtue. His view, that truth is a construct born out of human necessity and will to power, is seemingly at odds with traditional religious thought, the latter typically (though perhaps improperly) understood as a set of antiquated claims to truth; as such, Nietzsche is a progenitor of the secularization of consciousness. Somewhat surprisingly, however, this perspective reinscribes, or, to use Blumenberg's term, "reoccupies" the human need to create meaning in a seemingly indifferent universe. Nietzsche's exploration of the "urge to truth" and Blumenberg's focus on the necessity of myth for unburdening humanity from the absolutism of reality frame a worldview that transcends the confines of literalism, historicism, and materialism. Blumenberg's philosophical anthropology serves not only to illuminate the inherent tensions within secularized thought but also offers a pathway towards a nuanced engagement with religious ideas. Following his lead, this work aims to bridge the gap between the secular and the sacred, offering a fresh perspective on the enduring relevance of religious ideas in our secular age.

Chapter 1

God Is an Absolute Metaphor

> God is a concept.
> —John Lennon

VOLTAIRE ONCE QUIPPED, "IF God did not exist, it would be necessary to invent him." Voltaire was no friend to the church and despised priests; but he was unwilling to do away with God for fear morality would collapse. "I want my attorney, my tailor, my servants, even my wife, to believe in God," he wrote. Why? So that we might "suffer from less theft and less cuckoldry." Voltaire posits a functional existence for the Almighty, suggesting that if, when he arrived on the scene, the idea of God had been absent, he would have necessarily had to invent it, lest sociopolitical life be a free-for-all. Here, "God," is an idea, a non-physical "big Other," an ultimate conceptual or metaphysical reality that ensures a rational and moral basis or justification to our lives and actions. Belief in God is, argued Voltaire, a "useful creed."[1]

---

1. The oft-cited "If God did not exist" aphorism dates from 1768, in a letter Voltaire penned to the anonymous author of a popular atheistic work titled *The Three Imposters*. Voltaire took serious issue with the atheism of *The Three Imposters*; in denying God the book denied society and civil order a most useful, even necessary, framework. The full stanza reads, "If the heavens, stripped of his noble imprint, / Could ever cease to attest to his being, / If God did not exist, it would be necessary to invent him. / Let the wise man announce him and kings fear him. / Kings, if you oppress me, if your eminencies disdain / The tears of the innocent that you cause to flow, / My avenger is in the heavens: learn to tremble. / Such, at least, is the fruit of a useful creed." The "cuckoldry" passage is from a dialogue titled "The ABC" (also published in 1768), with each of the letters serving as a character. Though Voltaire is often identified with "B" and this quote is from

Between Invention and Discovery

To follow Voltaire and treat God as a useful, invented idea is to speak neither of fakery nor in favor of a facile relativism. We need not posit an absolute distinction between discovery and invention. Ideas are real existents, though they lack the thing-like quality of stones and corkscrews.[2] Without the idea of God, claims Voltaire, we would have no framework, no reason, no foundation to ground and inform our actions; we would merely do what we do—anything and everything our will and power may accomplish. Here we reach the crux of the matter: human beings have no inherent orientation to the world, but we need one if we are to survive, get along, and prosper. We are not merely creatures of stimulus-response reactions—we are creatures of intentional action, but we can only act purposively with foreknowledge of what the world is. For Immanuel Kant, "orientation" is the basic ground on which reason operates, and he observes the etymological origins of the term orientation in locating oneself in relation to sunrise. Orienting oneself in a landscape thus becomes the basis for a more figurative representation of the world we seek to know, a subjective stance that must be assumed to know anything at all.[3] An orientation (a matrix, a rule, a system, a faith) is not discursive knowledge, but a framework in and through which we "position" ourselves. Traditionally, this need for orientation has been met by religion, that "system of symbols," to invoke anthropologist Clifford Geertz's well-known definition, that nurses "moods and motivations," gives us a "conception of a general order of existence," and clothes this order "in an aura of factuality" so that those "moods and motivations seem uniquely realistic."[4] The sociologist Peter Berger imagines this symbolic system as a "sacred canopy," an overarching conceptual-spiritual framework that a people "constructs" to provide meaning, significance, and orientation.[5]

---

the mouth of the loquacious Englishman "A," it is nevertheless indicative of Voltaire's position: the idea of God has extraordinary social value. Voltaire was not, however, a mere functionalist; he also held that from rational argument and observation one could infer the existence of God.

2. Today, *reality* is largely defined in opposition to *ideality*: the "really real" is thought to be entirely physical, brute stuff, not mind or ideas or values or gods, which are taken as mere epiphenomena of matter. In my view, reality and ideality need not be separated.

3. Kant, *Religion Within the Boundaries*, 1–15.

4. Geertz, *Interpretation of Cultures*, 87–125.

5. Berger, *Sacred Canopy*.

Karl Barth railed against thinking about Christianity as a social construct that provides orientation. For Barth, infinite distance separates God and humanity (which is to say, the difference is not a matter of distance at all but of ontology). Constructivism, like natural theology, attempts to understand religion based on our human requirements and capacities; in so doing, it may well undercut the revelatory quality of Christianity. A robust faith is eroded if one adopts or adheres to it because it is merely useful. Christianity is not a "sacred canopy" we erect over ourselves, but a revelation given to us. While Barth may provide a useful rebuttal of liberal theology's overly optimistic account of human capacities and reason, he also runs the risks of underestimating the role of human reason and the natural world in theological reflection and ignoring, from an assumed position of unassailable safety, the intellectual and cultural developments of the modern world. Moreover, absolute revelation is a poor starting point from which to carry on a conversation about God with those unaccustomed with or unwilling to engage God-talk. There must be a middle way between the absolutism of a Barthian dialectical theology and the supposed proofs of natural theology, between the demand for faith and demands of reason.[6] My attempt to walk such a middle path is informed by metaphor theory, social-cultural history, and philosophical anthropology. The tension between discovering truths (or having them given to us) and inventing them, the difficulties in sorting out the innate and acquired, the trouble identifying what persists within the flux of change—these tensions are, in the end, irresolvable, and so must be embraced.

We are a species that poses and requires answers to big questions, and though the answers may differ across time and space, the questions are of a perennial sort. How are we to best live? Why do things go wrong? How are we to relate to strangers? Is the world a welcoming place? Are our actions freely undertaken, or determined by powers beyond ourselves? Is there an afterlife? What is truth? Why is there anything at all? What demands our condemnation, and what our love? What is the origin and source of this world? How is it that there is life, consciousness, self-consciousness? For the German philosopher and historian Hans Blumenberg, these types of questions are theoretically unanswerable but nevertheless must be answered, and we do so through what he terms "absolute metaphors," pragmatically oriented answers to the unanswerable.

---

6. See Küng, *On Being a Christian*, 64–67.

Human necessities extend beyond food and shelter. We need a roof over our heads, of course; but we also need a metaphysical home, a set of answers to fundamental questions. We may hold these answers in a rigid or a loose fashion, that style of holding itself being part of one's orientation. In phenomenology, a key term is *Lebenswelt* (lifeworld), which points to the dense nexus of intersubjective relationships (between people, nature, objects, values, and ideas) that we experience in their immediacy and givenness, long before reflection applies itself to the work of understanding, explaining, critiquing, abandoning, or justifying these relationships. Modernity has long been described as a process leading to the fracturing of shared, unifying, collective systems of symbols, sacred canopies, mythological narratives, and lifeworlds—an era lived under the sign of critique. The great disruption that is modernity has left us but mere fragments and whispers of once sacred orders. Locating, gathering, and fashioning these strewn pieces into some sort of quasi-stable whole has infused modern projects with a meaningful task grounded in an exhilarating sense of creative freedom, but the epoch was (and remains) an "age of anxiety."[7] That anxiety may well be heightened when one embraces a position holding that the stuff of culture is merely "made up." Our truths, our answers to perennial questions, are fictions, as Nietzsche powerfully emphasized. Of course, this does not mean all answers are equal; nor does it mean answers from other places and times have no bearing on the way we pose questions and give answers here and now.

Culture is the solution to a problem, the problem of being human; and culture is always a work-in-progress. Culture is everything we learn, in distinction from what we instinctively know and do. Shivering is not a practiced behavior, but an innate response to a decrease in body temperature. Wearing a warm coat on a frosty winter morning is a learned behavior—though, judging from how teenagers in my neck of the woods approach winter dress, not an easily learned one. Breathing comes naturally, but we can learn to control and modulate the breath. Blinking is

---

7. Auden, *Age of Anxiety*. The literature recounting the existential promises and tumult of modernity is, of course, vast. The allusion to cobbling strewn fragments comes from T. S. Eliot's *Wasteland*, where culture is imagined as existing in a state of ruins—but ruins capable of being put together in a such a fashion as to save one's soul from ruination. For a comprehensive historical overview of such themes, see Taylor, *Secular Age*. Postmodernity, which can be read as suspicious critique of modernity as well as a failure of nerve to engage in repairing the sacred canopy's torn fabric, tends, to my mind at least, in the direction of tossing out the baby with the bathwater. If foundations have their limits (and they do!) so, too, does suspiciousness of created orders.

an automated biological system; winking is proto-conspiracy. Culture consists of a system of symbolic conceptualizations ("There is frost on the grass this morning; it is cold out today, best wear a jacket"), tools that extend the body's relationship to and control of the environment (a jacket), and a repertoire of practices (taking off your jacket and hanging it up when entering the house). When my cats come in from outside on a rainy day, they proceed to dry and groom themselves; humans set out their umbrellas to dry and reach for a towel. Culture is nature by other means. Engaging in imperial conquest or performing puja in the morning are, as cultural forms, in principle no different from dress.

There is no need to posit a chasm between nature and culture, as some theorists do; a gap, yes; maybe even a crevice, but not so large we cannot leap it, though there is always potential danger in such jumps. Better still would be to build a bridge, in the full knowledge that maintenance, additions, reconstructions, even bridge replacements will be necessary over time. I should caution that my placing puja and hanging up one's jacket in the same sentence is not meant to reduce puja to a banal, habitual gesture. There is plenty of such nonsense already, the reaction to it in religious circles is understandable, and I have no wish to contribute to it. There is a depth and a subjectivity to human life that thwarts all attempts at a facile reductionism. I am all for defamiliarization, just not the sort that explains monotheism in terms of DNA.[8]

What I do hold dear is the need, after several centuries of an at times mean-spirited, reductive, materialistic naturalism (which congealed in the intellectually impoverished and unimaginative diatribes against religion penned by Richard Dawkins and Christopher Hitchens),[9] to contin-

---

8. As an example of reductive extremes, see Hamer, *God Gene*. Cognitivists make a similar move, as in the work of Newberg and d'Aquila, *Why God Won't Go*. That there is a genetic/neurological component or dimension to religion (and not just religion but of course *everything* human) is more than merely plausible—it is a fact. But such works tell us little about cultural difference and cultural change. How does an understanding of neurons help us understand why Yahweh first instituted animal sacrifice but then later asked his people to abandon it? A thousand years ago, Jews, Muslims, and Aztecs had the same biochemistry, the same brains, the same neurological wiring as each other, but quite different sets of beliefs and ritual practices. The hominid family of primates is a family precisely because of its invariant features, one of which is to generate out of those invariant capacities a dizzying variety of forms. Worldview analysis attempts to detail, make sense of, and, occasionally, when warranted, pass judgment on this variety.

9. Dawkins, *God Delusion*; Hitchens, *God Is Not Great*. The rise of the so-called "new atheism" exemplified in the figures of Dawkins and Hitchens has received considerable pushback, even from among atheists. As entry points into the debate, see Eagleton, *Reason, Faith, and Revolution*; LeDrew, *Evolution of Atheism*; Midgley, *Science as*

ue to develop an anthropological and evolutionary-informed naturalism that: (1) questions the very category of "religion" as an outmoded, no-longer-useful invention of modernity; (2) approaches the texts, ideas, and rites of nameable religious traditions as forms of practice and ways of knowing, variously and selectively worthy of conservation, modification, or the trash heap; and (3) eschews a simplistic, rationalistic atheism by making room for consideration of the reality of the non-physical and the experience of transcendence.[10]

Distancing, or "Self-Assertion"

Karl Marx developed and popularized a basic assumption of this book, namely, that "man produces man."[11] Marx was likely alluding to a line from Mark's Gospel: "The Sabbath," says Jesus, "was made for man, not man for the Sabbath" (Mark 2:27), perhaps the most concise critique we have of the limits of religious institutions, or of institutions generally. The insight also demonstrates that we have known for a long time that humans invent culture. We are the species that produces itself; we make stuff up, from sabbath days (leisure time, the fair distribution of rest, a great idea) to gasoline engines (at first, perhaps, a good idea, but

---

Salvation; Jones, *Can Science Explain Religion?*

10. As Noam Chomsky has recently observed, attempts to articulate a coherent notion of the "non-physical" ultimately fail, not because there is no such thing but because we lack a basic, coherent notion of the physical. The mind-body problem is as much the product of our not understanding the physical as it is perplexity over the mysterious nature of mind. In other words, in Chomsky's monistic view, there is no clear boundary to be drawn between body and mind, a view sometimes referred to as mysterianism, which holds that the problem of consciousness (among other problems) will never be solved, precisely because it isn't a problem but rather a mystery (see Chomsky, *What Kind of Creatures*, 27–30). Nietzsche made much the same point in his rejection of those sages who are "despisers of the body." "'Body am I, and soul'—thus speaks the child. And why should one not speak like children?" (See Nietzsche, *Portable Nietzsche*, 146). Nietzsche is aghast that religious-mystical types throughout history have despised the body; today, it tends to be materialist-rationalist types making the same logical move in despising the soul.

11. Marx focused on the role of labor in this production, but he recognized the life of the mind in generating subjectivities and social relations; he simply considered thinking as a form of activity as well as an inherently social act: "Just as society itself produces man as man, so it is produced by him.... Activity and mind are social activity and social mind.... The natural existence of man has here become his human existence and nature itself has become human for him. Thus society is the accomplished union of man with nature, the veritable resurrection of nature, the realized naturalism of man and the realized humanism of nature" (Fromm and Marx, *Marx's Concept of Man*, 128).

now, clearly, a colossal mistake). We make stuff up in response to challenges and threats, but also to nip potential threats in the bud before they arise. Another term for this activity of world-making[12] is *self-assertion*, a distancing and perspectival resistance to being subsumed by indifferent or hostile realities. We distance ourselves from nature (through, for example, the tending of fire and the creation of tools), but we also require distance from family members and consensus ways of life should they become ineffectual, harmful, or oppressive. Jesus recognizes that institutions and traditions are to serve our well-being; when they do not, they may be dismantled, reformed, or renewed. One can hardly find fault with someone who rejects 1 Cor 14:33–36, to say nothing of 1 Tim 2:12, neither having ever served women. Moreover, in these specific cases, we have good evidence of the made-up nature of Paul's silencing of women, the line arguably being inserted into a later version of 1 Corinthians and Timothy being penned not by Paul himself but by one of his later followers. In other words, Paul didn't even write those texts.[13] Thomas Jefferson wholeheartedly embraced this notion of self-assertion, audaciously creating his own version of the Bible, a cut-and-paste job he titled "The Life and Morals of Jesus of Nazareth." But even if we refuse to take scissors and gluestick to the Book, we nevertheless create versions of it in and through which parts of it we read (if we read it at all), via the implicit or overt interpretative frames we read through, and in relation to other ideas we have encountered. Often, the outcome of our reading the Book is firmly in hand before ever turning a page.

The intractable difficulty with practices, symbols, and ideas is the old conundrum, "we can't live with them, and we can't live without them." Ideas and institutions (including that of God, variously understood, and "his" churches, variously conceived and organized), though necessary (we can never operate outside of a posited, functioning network of symbolic systems, meanings, institutions, and social relations), are nevertheless laced with inherent paradoxes, gaps, inconsistencies, and antagonisms. That is the nature of the hand we have been dealt. Even a cursory reading of the Bible reveals deep contradictions. Deuteronomy warns that God will bring "rain" to the obedient and "dust" to the disobedient (28:12–24).

---

12. S. Brent Plate develops the idea of religion as a form of world-making in his *Religion and Film: Cinema and the Re-creation of the World*. Along these lines, Ann Taves, harkening back to Clifford Geertz, has suggested that religious studies rebrand and reorient itself as worldview analysis, in "From Religious Studies."

13. See Borg and Crossan, *First Paul*.

For Jesus, God "sends rain on the righteous and on the unrighteous" (Matt 5:45), a very different view than that expressed by the Deuteronomist, and one more in keeping with the prophetic tradition: "Is it not from the mouth of the Most High that good and evil come?" (Lam 3:38). It isn't that ideas are at first far from a truth that is "out there," as the *X-Files* has it, and we progressively wind our way towards it. Rather, ideas, meanings, significances stop working, because they exist in a world marked by contingency, a fact known even by God himself who, we read, after surveying the devastation he wrought with the great flood, decided apocalypse was not the best course of action after all, and gives himself a much needed talking-to: "I will never again curse the ground because of man, for the imagination of man's heart is evil from his youth; neither will I ever again destroy every living creature as I have done" (Gen 8:21). Even God, it seems, can own up to a mistake or two, and change his mind and methods from time to time. Can we imagine the complexity of the social, historical, and conceptual changes concentrated in this single sentence conjuring the ambiguous and paradoxical image of a self-correction on the part of the Absolute? Can we appreciate what was passed through, what was allowed, what was turned aside, what was risked, for God to come to this critical assessment of his ideas, his plans, his actions, and reorient himself, distance himself from himself?

Absolute Metaphors, Fundamental Myths

We tend to assume that ideas and concepts, doctrines and dogmas are to be evaluated based on their fit with an objective, empirical reality, and the way they can answer questions that we pose. But in the history of ideas, as practiced by Blumenberg, this assumption puts the cart before the horse. This is particularly the case with what Blumenberg terms "absolute metaphors" and "fundamental myths." According to Blumenberg, an absolute metaphor is a metaphor that cannot be easily or simply replaced by a literal or non-metaphorical equivalent without a significant loss of meaning. These metaphors are so deeply embedded in our language and thought that they transcend mere linguistic ornamentation and become fundamental to our conceptual framework. Blumenberg argues that absolute metaphors play a crucial role in human understanding, particularly in dealing with abstract, complex, or inaccessible realms of thought. They provide a way to conceptualize and communicate about aspects of reality that are otherwise difficult (if not impossible) to grasp. Absolute metaphors are not just tools of language but are integral to the process of human cognition and perception. Examples of absolute metaphors include concepts like "the stream of time" or "the light of truth," which Blumenberg discusses in detail. These metaphors are so ingrained in our discourse that they shape how we think about time and truth, respectively. They are not simply decorative language but foundational to our understanding.

Regarding John Lennon's line, "God is a concept," we approach the heart of the matter when we consider "God" as an absolute metaphor in Blumenberg's terms. The idea of God (and its equivalents in various cultures and religions) transcends the literal and enters the realm of the metaphorical, serving as a foundational concept through which people understand various aspects of existence, morality, purpose, and the universe. Attempts to describe and relate to God are so many bridges across the gap between the abstract, often incomprehensible nature of diverse phenomenon—life, death, self-awareness, existence as such—and more concrete, everyday human experience.

God, like other absolute metaphors, functions to make sense of the incomprehensible or the ineffable. It provides a way to articulate and engage with aspects of human experience that are otherwise beyond our immediate understanding, beyond logic, beyond conceptually clear clarifications: not the irrational side of ourselves but the a-rational or nonrational dimensions of existence. In this sense, "God" is understood as that absolute metaphor that helps us grapple with questions of existence, morality, purpose, and the unknown: God is the absolute metaphor of absolute metaphors. Blumenberg's approach is philosophical and not theological. He is not concerned with the literal existence or non-existence of an "entity" that an absolute metaphor (like truth or care or God) represents but with how these metaphors function in human thought and language.

Absolute metaphors carry a surplus of meaning that cannot be fully unpacked or translated into straightforward, non-metaphorical language. Myths are like absolute metaphors, only they operate at the level of narrative structures rather than isolated linguistic expressions. As linguistic expressions come to be embedded in a culture's answers to existential pressures or situations—"sin is crouching at the door" (Gen 4:7)—absolute metaphors become generative of efforts to articulate the question behind these answers, and this typically takes the form of a "fundamental myth." Blumenberg sees fundamental myths as narrative structures that give meaning and order to human experience. While Blumenberg's fundamental myths share some characteristics with traditional myths, his concept is broader and more abstract. It's not limited to specific stories or characters but encompasses underlying narrative structures that can manifest in various forms across different cultures and times. Examples of fundamental myths include narratives about the hero's journey, the quest for knowledge, or the struggle between good and evil. These are not just stories but are deep-seated ways of framing human experience and existence. The fundamental myth of Western philosophy, for example, is that in the progress of culture *logos replaces mythos*.

In the writings of Paul and the Gospels, redemption through Christ is a central theme. This answer of redemption—the idea that through the cross, humanity is offered salvation—is a foundational aspect of subsequent Christian theology. Following Blumenberg's method, this answer leads to the formulation of the questions, "From what have we been saved? From what have we been redeemed?" These questions probe the nature of the human condition and the reason why such redemption was necessary in the first place. For Christianity, the dominant fundamental myth linking answer and question was expressed by Augustine: the cross redeems us from original sin. One of today's pervasive ideas is that history is simply the road taken to get to where we are at now. But the history of the past, what Blumenberg calls "the past's past," entails more than merely tracking down the causes behind what is today; rather, it is the history of possibilities, conditions, and circumstances; roads taken and not taken, with the latter perhaps still walkable after all. Perhaps Christ redeemed humanity from being enslaved to demonic powers, a different, but popular fundamental myth than the Augustinian one that carried the day.

The history of the past has a normative dimension, rooted in what Blumenberg describes as "the elementary obligation of forsaking nothing that is human, . . . according respect to those who have fallen into obscurity."[14] If for several generations now we have been conceived and reared in a "secular age,"[15] such an obligation would lead us to consider religious thought, practice, and experience, that spectre-like, unassimilable, irritating "other" haunting the modern world's secular conception of itself—not for apologetic purposes, but, first, out of a measured respect and, second, as a potential resource for dealing with the current mess we

---

14. Blumenberg, *Wirklicheiten*, 170.
15. Taylor, *Secular Age*.

find ourselves in. Kierkegaard distinguished *remembrance* from *memory*; the former, the proper locus of his method of repetition, is ultimately forward-looking, while memory dwells in the past.

What follows then is a form of remembrance, an introduction to *aspects* of Christian thought, via metaphor and myth, which are the generative motors for religious ideas, doctrines, and dogmas. As Blumenberg describes our current philosophical and methodological situation, "the demise of metaphysics calls metaphorics back to its place."[16] One implication of this formula is that the provisional, imagistic, and perspectival will be given precedence over doctrine and dogma, and truth becomes a viewpoint rather than a substance. Truth cannot be identified with any one thing, but neither can truth be grasped apart from things. Truth here is medial, an intervening variable, an invisible thread stitching together pieces of fabric into whole cloth. In this sense, I can understand the potentially triumphalist and exclusivist words of Jesus, "I am the way, and the truth, and the life; no one comes to the Father, but by me" (John 14:6).

The word "aspect" is an astrological term, connoting the relative positions of the planets as they appear from earth, but also how the planets appear to or "look at" one another. An aspect is a way of viewing something, a countenance, an appearance. The rich etymology of this word suggests the activities of observation, contemplation, and examination: to figuratively consider, to ponder, to look upon and behold. What follows are words describing how Christianity looks to me, as viewed from a particular vantage point and through a certain set of optics; move to a neighboring hill, pick up another spyglass, and one will no doubt see differently and see different things. I am, however, looking at Christianity, not Buddhism or Premier League Football, so I refuse the charge that this book is merely a subjective, impressionistic, or relativistic account. And Jesus as the *truth* (as well as *way, lamb, door, vine, love,* and *life*) reveals the productive role of truth in making meaning possible, in turning happenings into experiences, in communicating religious concern, and delivered in love.

To focus on *metaphors* and *myths* rather than *beliefs* or *dogmas* is to approach Christianity as a perspectival world-viewing, rather than as a set of empirically testable propositions about the world (the inclination of scientific types, who often aim to debunk) or as a set of performative commitments in which one puts one's ultimate trust (the inclination of religious types, who generally take up apologetics). John Lennon was half right when he observed "God is a concept," but big concepts like God are in

---

16. Blumenberg, *Paradigms for a Metaphorology*, 132.

turn inescapably grounded in metaphor, and absolute metaphors are both fleshy and contextual, grounded in bodily experience of ourselves and our world. "Absolute" here does not mean eternal, universal, unchanging; rather, the term points to a zone of experience and thought that cannot be clarified into the clear, distinct concept without remainder. Contra Lennon, God is an absolute metaphor. To plumb the metaphorical, mythic, and fictive basis of Christian ideas is to follow the tracks of others who grant nonconceptual thinking (as found in myth, metaphor, gesture, parable, anecdote, gloss, jokes) a legitimacy it has sorely lacked since the rise of rationalism and positivism, tracks that lead the more abstract and conceptual language of theology back to *mythos* and an engagement with the *lifeworld*, that partly empirical, party theoretic idea so central to German hermeneutic and phenomenological traditions.

My inclinations are anthropological, historical, aesthetical, and philosophical, and this short study aims to be a contribution to the history of religious ideas, tacitly framed by the debate over the relationship between *mythos* and *logos* and motivated by frustration with the boring and sterile alternative between atheism and theism. Influences and conversation partners come from the fields of *philosophical anthropology* (especially the German philosopher Hans Blumenberg), *cognitive metaphor theory* (as developed by George Lakoff and Mark Johnson), an eclectic cluster of works that can be grouped under the rubric of *metaphorical theology* (the title of an important work by Sallie McFague).

We will take a few deep dives into the historical contexts informing biblical texts and early Christianity. This is not because the Gospels are biographical or historical in today's sense of these genres; rather, they are proclamations, committed testimonies, literary in form that, according to the genre conventions of the time, were received as biographies and histories honoring past events. But to understand them today, given our "historical consciousness," one must know something of the social-historical matrix within which these texts emerge. If the canonical Gospels, Paul's letters, and other early texts reveal the contents of the "post-Paschal" faith in the resurrected Christ within early Christian communities, written decades after the death of Jesus, do they tell us anything about what the earthly, historical Jesus did and said? They must, or they say nothing at all—and this is not only the basic position of historical-critical scholarship but of the heart of Christian faith as well, for the resurrected, living Christ is held to be the specific man Jesus of Nazareth. In today's theology, "the kerygma of the community simply cannot be understood unless we begin quite correctly with the historical Jesus of Nazareth."[17] Moreover, understanding the meaning of the constitutive metaphors of religious thought requires social-historical context, since metaphor maps a concept by transposing source domains (material conditions, the senses) into the target domain of ideas. Christ as a "good shepherd" (John 10:11) can makes no sense if you've not a clue about sheep and fields and dangerous predators.

Any attempt to say something about human "being-in-the-world"[18] will of necessity step beyond simple, objective description into the realms of the speculative and the normative. I am concerned with those efforts within Christian tradition to answer basic problems (perhaps reducible to a fundamental problem) faced by our species. This is not to propose a fixed human nature or essence but to describe Christian thought as a response and contribution to dealing with our anthropological situation, a situation incisively described by anthropologist Roy Rappaport: we humans are "a species that lives and can only live, in terms of meanings it itself must fabricate in a world devoid of intrinsic meaning but subject to physical law."[19] In slightly different language, we have the power, the autonomy, to fabricate "worlds" (and we must do this), but this autonomy and its fabrications are constrained and put under pressure both by various anthropological limits and the intercourse between those very fabricated worlds. Or, put another way, human beings live in the tension of radical contingency. Just as getting to work on time is contingent on all sorts of people and machines and plans functioning in unison, so, too, existence itself is contingent: We can take neither getting to work nor being here in the first place for granted. Our contingency, our being on the edge of not being at all, is existentially etched in our souls. The T-Rex slipped off that edge; we, so far, have not. Unlike the T-Rex, however, we are aware of the edge. We anticipate the edge, reflect on it, deny it, run from it, embrace it—we adopt any number of strategies for dealing with contingency, including the invention and discovery of religious ideas.

---

17. Küng, *On Being a Christian*, 157.

18. The phrase here was introduced into philosophical and religious conversations by Martin Heidegger. It suggests something like an interpretation or reflexive reinterpretation of the activity of existing.

19. Rappaport, *Ritual and Religion*, 451.

Chapter 2

Metaphor, All the Way Down

> Poetry begins in trivial metaphors, pretty metaphors, "grace" metaphors, and goes on to the profoundest thinking that we have. Poetry provides the one permissible way of saying one thing and meaning another. . . . People say, "Why don't you say what you mean?" We never do that, do we, being all of us too much poets. We like to talk in parables and in hints and in indirections—whether from diffidence or from some other instinct. . . . Unless you are at home in the metaphor, unless you have had your proper poetical education in the metaphor, you are not safe anywhere.
>
> —Robert Frost, "Education by Poetry"

> As an ornament, the metaphor is of no interest to us, because, if it says more pleasantly that which can be said otherwise, then it could be explained wholly within the scope of a semantics of denotation. We are interested in the metaphor as an additive, not a substitutive, instrument of knowledge.
>
> —Umberto Eco, *Semiotics and the Philosophy of Language*

How are we to approach Christian thought? "Approach" here means something like the route one visualizes to the summit of a peak, or, less high and mighty, the steps to be taken across a muddied, puddled section of a forest path. My assumption, my approach, following Robert Frost, is that poetic, metaphorical speech constitutes "the profoundest thinking we have." The first steps in this approach are to defend metaphor as a legitimate mode of thought and to locate the genre of religious texts in the world of metaphor, symbol, and myth. These are moves that neither relegate religious thought to an inferior status, nor simply let religion off the hook of critique by way of a facile gesture towards the symbolic. The move into metaphor demands historical understanding, often deep historical understanding, since metaphors are rooted in the thick textures of social-cultural life. Metaphor has something of a bad reputation, and this reputation needs to be overcome. Metaphor is not simply a figure of speech but is constitutive of understanding. Even mathematics relies on metaphor to communicate its understandings, so the metaphorical nature of religious thought need not be an obstacle to analysis, appreciation, or commitment. It is the entailments and implications of a metaphor that need to be explored and, ultimately, assessed.

Secondly, my approach to studying religious thought is framed by "philosophical anthropology," and in the following chapter I outline the basic features of this school of thought. What philosophical anthropology makes possible is a naturalistic way of understanding religion, one that takes religious ideas, beliefs, and practices as legitimate attempts at world-making, without abdicating the need to possibly critique or distance oneself from those ideas. My approach to studying Christian ideas is akin to that used in, say, the history of science, where one views a scientific model as paralleling, simulating, or mirroring that which it models. Religious thought is an attempt to describe, explain, and live in the world, though one that relies heavily and (usually) self-consciously on metaphoric, mythic, and fictive modes.

The Genre of Religious Texts

> Can one really be "religiously unmusical" if one is working on religion?
>
> —Hans Joas, *The Power of the Sacred*

> Pilate said to him, "So you are a king?" Jesus answered, "You say that I am a king. For this I was born, and for this I have come into the world, to bear witness to the truth. Every one who is of the truth hears my voice." Pilate said to him, "What is truth?"
>
> —The Gospel According to John

Jesus preaches the "kingdom of heaven." In doing so, he deploys a series of comparisons. In Matthew's Gospel (13:24–47), Jesus, in rapid fashion, sketches his vision:

> *The kingdom of heaven may be compared to a man who sowed good seed in his field.*
>
> *The kingdom of heaven is like a grain of mustard seed that a man took and sowed in his field.*
>
> *The kingdom of heaven is like leaven that a woman took and hid in three measures of flour.*
>
> *The kingdom of heaven is like treasure hidden in a field.*
>
> *The kingdom of heaven is like a merchant in search of fine pearls.*
>
> *The kingdom of heaven is like a net that was thrown into the sea and gathered fish of every kind.*

Unable to say precisely what (to say nothing of where) the kingdom of heaven is, Jesus develops his sense, his intuition, of what it is like, or to what it may be compared. Obviously, the kingdom of heaven is not a place, in the same sense that the Kingdom of Saudi Arabia or the various Magical Kingdoms of Disney are places. Rather, Jesus uses his day's form of social governance (a kingdom) to describe a state of being and to project a vision of a social world better than that of Roman-occupied Palestine. Jesus works analogically, as a metaphorician, employing the basic move of metaphorical thought: this is that—heaven is a hidden treasure, or a mustard seed, or a fish net. Jesus offers a set of suggestive images. A nascent concept/theology of the kingdom of heaven is nestled within Jesus's constant recourse to images drawn from the lived social world of kings and fields, fishing nets and bread, to a hopeful vision of a world different from the day-to-day life of those to whom he preached and ministered. To be fair, Jesus also deploys a good deal of fear. Not achieving the kingdom is described as experiencing an "outer darkness," or being a cast in a "furnace of fire" where in their sufferings "men will weep and gnash their teeth" (Luke 13). Of course, such a celestial furnace of fire is not a physical place.

Many will sit with the patriarchs at table in the kingdom of heaven, says Jesus (Matt 8:11); but it would be ridiculous to inquire about the table's dimensions, the name of its builder, or whether it is of oak, acacia, or marble. The teachings of the Catholic Church have long emphasized that heaven is a state not a place, as Pope John Paul II explained:

> Metaphorically speaking, heaven is understood as the dwelling-place of God . . . heaven becomes an image of life in God. . . . To describe this reality Sacred Scripture uses a symbolical language which will gradually be explained. . . . "Heaven" or "happiness" in which we will find ourselves is neither an abstraction nor a physical place in the clouds, but a living, personal relationship with the Holy Trinity.[1]

Most religious ideas are expressed in terms of metaphors, symbols, and images; they are not usually empirical claims of literal things or historical accounts of events—which is not to say religious texts contain no empirical claims or historical content. "They bound him and led him away and delivered him to Pilate the governor" (Matt 27:2) is straightforward description of a historical event (the arrest of Jesus), and one in principle open to verification.[2] The arrest-torture-humiliation-crucifixion of Jesus is not in itself a religious idea but a historical event, though an event of supreme importance in formulating an idea of the nature, significance, and meaning of the person of Jesus, as well as the nature and character of God. In biblical texts, we also encounter descriptions of events that could have happened but didn't. A man named Cain could have killed a man named Abel; here, historical veracity is both difficult to come by and far less important than thinking about the problems of sibling rivalry, envy, and murder. There are also biblical "events" that could not have happened, historically speaking, because they are contradicted by another biblical account of the same event. Did the daughter of Jairus (whom Jesus resurrected) die before or after Jairus asked Jesus for aid?[3] Of course, there are challenging cases: Was Moses a historical figure? Was there a battle that brought down the walls of Jericho? Did Peter three times deny he was a follower of Jesus? Often, it is impossible to answer such questions with historical certainty. In a more straightforward sense, of course Peter denied Jesus, since that it is what is written. Peter's denial does not require historicity to be meaningful, to be part of creating and projecting a world. If there is no betrayal and denial, there no trust and faith.

1. John Paul II, "General Audience."
2. There are always some outliers, but there is a broad consensus among historians that Jesus was a historical figure and that he was executed by crucifixion during the governorship of Pilate, in part because independent sources make the same claim as the Gospels. See Ehrman, *Did Jesus Exist?*
3. This is one of many contradictions discussed in detail by Ehrman in his *Jesus Interrupted*, 41.

Getting the history right is one thing; needing the potentially historical to be definitively historical is another. Determining historical veracity can be important, but it is not always paramount; regardless of whether the murder of Abel is empirical history, the point is to pursue the meaning of the story—murder, after all, is real enough. Historically speaking, it is unlikely there was an exodus of Israelites from Egypt such as that described in the book of Exodus, if there was an exodus at all. Two million people marching for forty years in the Sinai desert would have left physical traces. There may well be historical events behind the exodus: people moved about in the ancient Near East, for a variety of reasons (famine, war, captivity, escape), so an Israelite exodus from Egypt is not implausible, but likely not verifiable. A more pressing question for our purposes here is understanding the need some people feel to have each detail of the book of Exodus to be thoroughly historical. My position is that this need is a mix of one part history (the modern mind is infused with historicism) and one part psychology (people tend to want certainty). But Maimonides, the influential twelfth-century Jewish philosopher-theologian, did not ground the holiness of the Torah in the historicity of the "events" described therein.[4] Neither did the Christian theologian Origen (d. 254 C.E.). Origen was at pains to educate Christians on how to read Scripture, and he would have scoffed at today's literalism; we know this because he scoffed at it in his day:

> Who is so foolish as to suppose that God, after the manner of a husbandman, planted a paradise in Eden, towards the east, and placed in it a tree of life, visible and palpable, so that one tasting of the fruit by the bodily teeth obtained life? And again, that one was a partaker of good and evil by masticating what was taken from the tree? And if God is said to walk in the paradise in the evening, and Adam to hide himself under a tree, I do not suppose that anyone doubts that these things figuratively indicate certain mysteries, the history having taken place in appearance, and not literally. . . . And what need is there to say more, since those who are not altogether blind can collect countless instances of a similar kind recorded as having occurred, but which did not literally take place? Nay, the Gospels themselves are filled with the same kind of narratives; e.g., the devil leading Jesus up into a high mountain, in order to show him from thence the kingdoms of the whole world, and the glory of them. . . . The attentive reader may notice in the

---

4. See Roberts-Zauderer's *Metaphor and Imagination*.

Gospels innumerable other passages like these, so that he will be convinced that in the histories that are literally recorded, circumstances that did not occur are inserted.[5]

That Origen rails against what we would today call "biblical literalism" is a sign that the tendency to concretize symbols and metaphors as literal things and events seems a universal proclivity. Some people are positively allergic to fuzzy uncertainty, and certainty today is usually yoked to empirically verifiable facts, including the facts of history. Clearly, a felt need for certainty also has a social dimension; in times marked by insecurity and instability certainty is understandably longed for. Psychologically speaking, extremisms and fundamentalisms are rooted, among other things, in a near total aversion to ambiguities and uncertainties, and to the confusions of social upheaval or potential upheaval.[6]

We have quickly waded into deep and troubled waters. For nearly two centuries the historicity of biblical texts has been a frontline in various culture wars, a bone of contention within and across denominations and congregations, and (for those who feel they've arrived) the litmus test for joining or refusing entry into the modern world. Again, my position is that the meaningfulness of, say, the parables or miracles of Jesus does not rest on their being descriptions of historical happenings. Most everyone is comfortable with the fact that Jesus taught and preached in and through stories; but the suggestion that the authors of the Gospels told "stories" about Jesus is deemed by some scandalous.[7] Yet, if stories were good enough Jesus . . . .

Lastly, there are "events" that lie outside of history altogether: snakes do not speak to people, Jesus and Satan did not walk up a mountain together, Jonah was not swallowed by a big fish and then spat out—scenes that, precisely because they are not historical accounts, cry out for interpretation, not historical verification. While most reasonable people (I hope!) agree that snakes cannot talk, some reasonable people might hold on to the belief that Jesus fed five thousand people with just five loaves of bread and two fish or that he walked on water. I have no desire to disabuse

---

5. Origen, *De Principiis*, bk. 4.

6. See Hogg and Blaylock, eds., *Extremism*, vx: "Uncertainty and extremism often appear to go together. There are many examples. The best documented is probably the global rise of national-political extremism during the Great Depression of the 1930s—developing into a shift toward fascism, communism, and nationalism that culminated in genocide and a world war that killed between 62 and 78 million people."

7. Crossan argues that the Gospels are "parabloized history." See *Power of Parable*.

them of their credulity; in such cases, a way through the impasse might be to agree to disagree and then move on to the matter of what such acts might mean: What ideas, what entailments, are embedded in the story/event about the distribution of food? Of course, sociocultural history is crucial to answering such questions, as meaning depends upon context. In the Palestine of Jesus, hunger (today called food scarcity) and famine were common, even pervasive, problems.[8]

When discourse moves in the realm of myth, symbol, and metaphor, as religious discourse generally does, we have not left the world of reason or thinking for flights of fancy. Margaret Atwood's *The Handmaid's Tale* or George Orwell's *1984* are not scientific or philosophical treatises. They are perhaps best categorized as *allegories*, though, given their prescience, the designation of *prophecy* wouldn't be amiss. Regardless of their genre, these works most certainly exemplify thinking, and they tell us much about totalitarianism. Thomas Aquinas, owing to the philosophical style of his work, is readily reckoned as a thinker; but so, too, was the author of the book of Job, one of the most complex stories ever told. Auguste Rodin's "Thinker" is a thinker, and Rodin is too. It is a gross prejudice to think that religious texts, simply because of their form and style, contain no ideas. We may distinguish between conceptual and non-conceptual thought, but the latter is still thought. Stories, not just science, pursue ideas and truths.

Talk of "heaven" uses a language of place to speak of states and relationships, but heaven itself is not a physical place. For Aquinas, "Incorporeal things are not in *place* after a manner known and familiar to us, in which way we say that bodies are properly in *place*; but they are in *place* after a manner befitting spiritual substances, a manner that cannot be fully manifest to us."[9] Aquinas can't help but use the language of thingness, of materiality, to describe non-material reals ("spiritual substances"), and he also recognizes here the difficulties in articulating with precision the nature of non-material things, precisely because they are non-material and we are limited to using matter (sounds, gestures, ink on paper) to gesture towards that which is beyond matter. Only a strident physicalism seeks to reduce, for example, all talk of the mind to the brain. Conscious, phenomenal experiences may well correlate to measurable brain states, but it is a huge (and philosophically troubled) leap to claim

---

8. See Jensen, "Climate, Droughts, Wars."

9. Aquinas, *Summa Theologiae*, supplement, q69, a1, reply 1.

these experiences are therefore nothing more than brain states.[10] You can lose your soul, says Jesus, but not in the same fashion that you might lose your car keys, for the soul is not a thing but rather an idea or image describing some constitutive aspect of ourselves as subjects. When Thomas Paine wrote, "These are the times that try men's souls," only the incurable materialist would respond with, "But we have no soul." Of course, we have no soul, as the soul is no-thing; it is not located slightly to the left of the appendix; it isn't locatable at all—but this absence of taking up space or having weight is no strike against the soul's reality, just as the absence of historicity is not a strike against the reality, meaning, and significance of events in the Bible. The rules of chess are real, but entirely immaterial. No one has ever tossed around a piece of logic like a football, but logic is real. Here, I agree with C. G. Jung, who observed that it "is an almost absurd prejudice to suppose that existence can only be physical."[11] And yet, especially in the modern era, the prejudice is rampant that minds are nothing but brains, that in saying "Jesus is the son of God" we somehow imply God has testicles, and that free will is an illusion, reducible to firing neurons. There are more robust and valuable versions of materialism, to be sure, and we will get to them; but the brittle, rationalistic reduction of anything and everything to "nothing but" material stuff or else nothing at all is absurd, and not a little boring.

Christian and Jewish texts, theologies, and commentaries across the centuries have had to tend to metaphor and myth, precisely because, as John Paul II states, Scripture is a "symbolical language." When Jesus announces, "I am the door" (John 10:9), we should not picture a rectangular hewn block of wood with a handle and hinges wandering the roads of Palestine with twelve apostles; biblical literalism is an impossible position to maintain for very long. Jesus is of course speaking here metaphorically; he is figuring an image of himself. On the other hand, the Christian tradition developed an uneasy relationship with myth and metaphor, preferring doctrinal and dogmatic positions, aspiring to replace stories with philosophically rigorous universal, eternal truths, creedal and confessional statements, and systematic theologies. Systems are meant to satisfy a need for order and longevity, and hence they must be airtight and complete. Building a system of ambiguous traffic signals and signs is ill-advised. But eventually systems (or paradigms) break

---

10. See, for example, Velmans, "Introduction to Monist Alternatives."
11. Jung, *Psychology and Religion*, CW 11, par. 16.

down, sometimes owing to their oppressive nature and the resistant hammering from within, but more often simply due to erosion working away at the pillars of the structure, which needs to be abandoned before complete collapse. Systems, structures, truths—these are built to last, and hence relatively inflexible in the face of strong winds or shifting soils. Stories, on the other hand, are closer to the soils themselves; they may lay fallow for a time, but they can be tilled, reworked, fertilized, allowing for a variant of crops to emerge. The myths of Prometheus or Odysseus are archaic, appearing in manifold forms across the ages. One reason for a myth's longevity may be strong institutional support, even life support, to keep the story from dying; but more crucially is myth's power to access a felt sense of significance and familiarity. Myth (metaphors strung together in narrative form) resists the label of "art" or "fiction" precisely because of an archaic, archetypal nature making myth available for aesthetic reception and reworking. A mythical way of looking at things is different from theoretic, dogmatic, or mystical perspectives; myth fails to compete with the explanatory power of science, the certainty of dogma, and the oneness of mystical experience. And yet, the mythic/metaphoric option persists. Why?

Blumenberg argues that though holding "reduced claims to reliability, certainty, faith, realism, and intersubjectivity," myth nevertheless "constitutes satisfaction of intelligent expectations." To these expectations, Blumenberg assigns the label "significance," which is the proper register for myth.[12] Significance cannot, in a strict sense, be defined; rather, it is a lived, felt experience of fittingness, fecundity, involvement: There goes Sisyphus yet again, pushing that same damn rock up that same damn hill. I know this story. I've seen and felt this before. Though recognizing that we make history, there is a dimension of this history that eludes constructivism; parts of the world we inhabit come to us charged with a valence or density. In science, space and time are Newtonian, which is to say, flat, uniform, and homogeneous. But in culture, there are places and times, figures and objects that are charged with meaning and significance—such is the realm of myth. Sisyphus is a figure of futility, but in what this futility consists and where it is to be found needs reworking from one epoch to the next; there is something compelling in the image of Sisyphus pushing that stone uphill, over and over again; in modernity, the futility of Sisyphus is found in grasping

---

12. Blumenberg, *Work on Myth*, 67–70.

the futility of being yoked to a single reality, the same stone, rather than trying another stone, or a different hill, or both.

Despite the Bible being full to bursting with metaphor and mythic motifs, the contemporary study of biblical metaphor was slow to take root. Robert Alter, writing in 1996, observed a persistent "metaphor avoidance" in biblical studies.[13] Why does the obvious observation that religious language is thoroughly metaphorical and mythic often lead to a wringing of hands in religious circles and denigration from the positivists? If we can agree that Jesus is a not a literal door, why the gasps or anger at the suggestion that walking on water or resurrection move as much in the realm of symbol and metaphor as they do in empirical history? For certain religious folks (let's call them *literalists*), if something is metaphorical, then it is not "really real"; to the mind of the literalist, the labels "metaphor," "symbol," and "myth" reduce the fullness, the power, the efficacy, the *reality* of the matter at hand. For the positivists, on the other hand, the "metaphor" label points to the presence of emotive rhetoric and logical ambiguity, both of which, in their minds, lead away from a clear analysis and the dogged pursuit of truth. Both camps are secretly yoked to an epistemological and ontological harness that views deploying the word metaphor to speak of religion as either a slur or a signal of intellectual impotence. But what if metaphor, far from being a denuded reality or obstacle to knowledge is our only route to understanding ourselves and the world? What if we take "nothing but metaphor" as not a polemical attack but as an entirely accurate description of the basis of language and thought?

The Evils of Metaphor?

Reflection on the nature and meaning of metaphor is part of the intellectual history of the West. Aristotle and Aquinas, among many others, gave the matter considerable attention. Part of this history is normative assessment of the value of symbolic, metaphorical language. Aristotle was not exactly a fan; he generally eschewed ambiguity in language, and therefore held that symbolic language was inferior to plain prose and an obstacle to logical clarity; he did, however, reserve the right for properly used, persuasive, figurative, rhetorical speech. Aquinas, in contrast, recognized the need for language modes beyond the univocal—especially

---

13. Alter, *Genesis*, xiii.

analogy and metaphor—in articulating religious life and aesthetic experience. In the modern era, with the rise of science, the Enlightenment, and rational positivism, figurative language generally came to be viewed with suspicion. Christianity made its own contributions to the erosion of a positive assessment of figurative language, exemplified in the insistence of Luther and other Protestant reformers on a literal approach to Scripture.

One of the more hilarious critiques of the "evil" of metaphor was offered by Thomas Sprat, a bishop of the Church of England and a founding member of the Royal Society:

> Who can behold, without indignation, how many Mists and Uncertainties, these specious *Tropes* and *Figures* have brought on our knowledge? For now I am warm'd with this just Anger, I cannot with hold my self, from betraying the Shallowness of all these seeming Mysteries; upon which, we *Writers*, and *Speakers*, look so big. And in few Words, I dare say, that of all the Studies of Men, nothing may be sooner obtain'd, than this vicious Abundance of *Phrase*, this Trick of *Metaphors*, this Vocabulary of *Tongue*, which makes so great a Noise in the World. But I spend Words in Vain; for the Evil is now so inveterate, that it is hard to know whom to blame, or where to begin to *reform*.[14]

For Sprat, metaphor is positively demonic. Clearly, Sprat would have no truck with the flowery language, rhetorical flourishes, imagery, and allegories of poetic types. He was among those who called for the banning of figurative language from scientific publications and talks sponsored by the Royal Society. John Locke thought metaphor was a "powerful instrument of Lies and Deceit."[15] In the same vein, Thomas Hobbes considered the seductive power of metaphor to be a political liability. Metaphor, according to Hobbes, couples the power to arouse the passions with illusion, making metaphor an acute danger for the stability of the commonwealth: "[Metaphors] openly profess deceit; to admit them into counsel, or reasoning, [is] manifest folly."[16] Where Hobbes is more judicious in his

---

14. Sprat, *History of the Royal Society*, 12.
15. Locke, *Essay Concerning Human Understanding*, 508.
16. Hobbes, *Leviathan*, 47. The metaphorical dimensions of Hobbes's thought and writing warrant considerable attention. Hobbes was a critic of metaphor, but that certainly did not stop him from using it. That Hobbes had a more nuanced view of metaphor than these brief comments indicate is true enough (see Feldman, *Binding Words*, 20–26). My point, however, is the negative epistemological assessment of metaphor that is characteristic of Enlightenment (and later positivist) thought.

evaluation of "rhetoric" and "eloquence," his comments reveal an underlying negative epistemological assessment:

> Reason and eloquence, though not perhaps in the natural sciences, yet, in the moral, may stand very well together. For wheresoever there is place for adorning and preferring of error, there is much more place for adorning and preferring of truth, if they have it to adorn.[17]

Hobbes understands metaphor to be potentially useful; it may "adorn" a known truth claim to promote moral instruction—but it is not and never could be in itself an instrument of truth. Figurative language must be separated from reason, and reason elevated to a place of pre-eminence.

The epistemic primacy of literal speech is definitive of modernity. As a by no means trivial example, because of what it reveals, consider recent commentary on the story of Jonah and the whale, by the rationalist atheist Richard Dawkins and the biblical literalist Robert Allan. Their respective positions turn out to be two sides of the same epistemological coin. Dawkins sees appeals to "symbolism" a sign of religion's "fatuousness," designed to save phenomenon that science has shown to be ridiculous,[18] the implication being that religious folks used to really believe Jonah was in a whale, and many still do; for those who don't, they turn to symbolism as a way around the problem rather than tossing the book in the dustbin of failed history. For blogger and ordained minister Robert Allan, if Jonah was not literally inside a whale, the "story is quite meaningless."[19] In the *Harper's Bible Dictionary* from 1952, the entry on the book of Jonah takes it for granted that "many Jews and Christians . . . have accepted the story as historical. In the pre-scientific era this literal interpretation was acceptable."[20] Really? The authors of this entry simply assume literalism as the default position of pre-modern, "pre-scientific" societies, but they certainly do not demonstrate the position; my sense is

---

17. Hobbes, *Leviathan*, 467–68.

18. Richard Dawkins (@RichardDawkins), "'Jonah's story is symbolic of Christ's death & resurrection , , ,' And there you have it. The religious mind in all its symbolic fatuousness" Twitter (now X), Jan. 23, 2015, https://twitter.com/RichardDawkins/status/558535568041463808

19. To cite one of many examples, blogger and ordained minister Robert Allan is "convinced by the available evidence that Jonah should be interpreted as literal history, including all of its more remarkable aspects such as Jonah being swallowed by a large fish or whale. If it is not literal, then the story is quite meaningless." See King, "Story of Jonah."

20. Miller and Miller, eds., *Harper's Bible Dictionary*, 345.

that the assumption here has history backwards. Biblical literalism as we know it today is a response to the rise and victory of scientific rationalism and historicism, which biblical literalists take on board as arbiters of truth, forcing themselves into a corner where symbolic, allegorical, and metaphor language must necessarily be misread as literal claims if they are to possess any value. Within a rationalist worldview that divides fact from fiction, object from subject, history from myth, and the real from the false, people of all stripes explicitly or implicitly place a "merely," or an "only," or a "nothing but" in front of metaphor, thereby denying the epistemic value and potential of figurative language.

The well-worn tracks of metaphor theory have been beaten by the so-called "substitution" and "emotive" models, which deny metaphor cognitive importance. Language, in this view, has both cognitive and emotive powers, the former supplied by the clarity of factual prose, the later by the flights of metaphor. Metaphor, in these schools of thought, can never be true, in the sense of supplying new propositional content or knowledge of the world, but only more or less effective, for good or ill, in moving people to think or act in a certain way. Literal speech is first-order knowing, metaphorical speech second-order evocation. The broad critique of metaphor reached its pinnacle in the influential school of logical positivism, as described by Andrew Ortony:

> A basic notion of positivism was that reality could be precisely described through the medium of language in a manner that was clear, unambiguous, and, in principle, testable—reality could, and should, be literally describable. Other uses of language were meaningless for they violated the empiricist criteria of meaning. During the heyday of logical positivism, literal language reigned supreme.[21]

The positivist attack on metaphor rests on two key assumptions: First, we can, in fact, separate the cognitive and emotional dimensions of language; second, the best kind of language for pursuing truth and cultivating understanding is the literal and empirically verifiable propositional statement. The first assumption is dubious; the second is denies all forms of understanding beyond (or other than) the scientific. Within such a framework, the sentence "Augustus is the son of God" can possess no truth value as it in no way helps us understand the actual world. The notion that metaphor is a vehicle of knowledge was never broadly popular,

---

21. Ortony, *Metaphor and Thought*, 1.

but as Paul de Man has observed, any remnants of such a notion were all but erased through the malignant attacks of Enlightenment and post-Enlightenment rationality.[22] In any case, I doubt a card-carrying positivist would have had the nerve to stride up to Caesar Augustus and inform him his title was merely a metaphor.

Metaphor operates beyond a logic of identity. The Aristotelian principle of logic has it that two things cannot be the same thing (the kingdom of heaven cannot be a precious pearl), but a poetic mind uses "primitive, archaic forms of thought in the most uninhibited way, because his job is not to describe nature, but to show you a world completely absorbed and possessed by the human mind."[23] These words, from literary critic Northrop Frye, implicitly suggest a division of labor: physics and other sciences describe nature, but when it comes to "a world" and our situatedness in it science comes up short and we rely on metaphorical language to articulate understandings, meanings, and significances. If we can bracket out the pejorative sense of the terms "primitive" and "archaic," which encodes a tacit developmental narrative in which thought progressively moves from *mythos* to *logos*, Frye is suggesting that metaphor is foundational: archaic not in the temporal sense of old fashioned, or out of date, but in the sense of the word's etymological root: *archon*, "the ruler," "to be first," "the first principle" of things. What if the supposedly non-metaphorical, clear cut, hard-nosed realms of science and mathematics also rely on metaphor?

It's a Metaphorical World

Writing in the 1950s, C. P. Snow described a divide in intellectual life in the modern era between the sciences and humanities, a mutual disregard that often tipped into disdain.[24] Such obliviousness and disdain still exist, to be sure, but there are increasing points of contact and an ethos of interdisciplinarity uncharacteristic of Snow's era. One step to rapprochement

22. De Man, "Epistemology of Metaphor." The emotive theory of metaphor is part of the broader tradition of logocentric thought, analyzed and critiqued by Jacques Derrida. Derrida makes a persuasive argument that the history of philosophy is one of attempting to "dominate" metaphor with the concept. He recognizes that the tradition of philosophical thinking in the West both relies on metaphor and yet desires understanding not premised upon or rooted in metaphor. See his "White Mythology: Metaphor in the Text of Philosophy," in *Margins of Philosophy*.

23. Frye, *Educated Imagination*, 32.

24. Snow, *Two Cultures*.

was physicist Thomas Kuhn's work on the way scientific revolutions take place. A straightforward, broadly accepted view of science is that as time goes on, science finds out more and more facts about the world, and devises ever better theories to explain those facts; science, in other words, makes progress. In contrast, Kuhn argued science is conducted inside of an existing *paradigm*, a set of assumptions and practices, a worldview. Rather than a long march of progress towards a true understanding of things, science develops in fits and starts, in relation to the decline of an old way of seeing and doing things and the emergence of the new. When paradigms change, it isn't simply that theories change; rather, there is a transformation of the entire set of grounding assumptions and practices that define what constitutes good science. If we accept Kuhn's concept of the paradigm shift, we face the difficulty of how to justify the notion of scientific progress. Kuhn suggested that two different paradigms each have internal integrity and they are "incommensurable," meaning that you cannot compare the merits, say, of Newtonian physics with quantum mechanics, as they operate in radically different physical and even social worlds, responding to very different sets of questions premised on very different sets of assumptions. In addition to challenging a linear notion of scientific progress, Kuhn highlighted that science, too, exists inside of a conditioned way of seeing and interacting with the world. In other words, science is also cultural—an observation that is itself part of a paradigm shift in how we understand the world, the rise of social constructivism, which brings science and other activities such as religion and art into, if not the same orbit, at least the same galaxy. For those who prefer their science neat, Kuhn tossed some troubling ideas into the drink.[25]

Since Kuhn, we've also come to a greater understanding of the role of metaphor in science, which, when it turns to matters of understanding, endlessly traffics in metaphor. Is light a "wave" or a "particle"? Light is neither; light is both. Or, consider that it is very difficult to think about evolution without the image of a family (or ancestral) "tree." Is evolution a tree, as Darwin thought, with branches, some dead, some alive, roots deep in the ground and trunk extending ever upwards to the heavens? Or is it a "ladder," with discontinuous steps, as Aristotle thought? Is the brain a "computer," performing "computations?" Was the brain a computer before there were computers, and we just didn't know it? Does DNA consist of "letters" that form "code," as Francis Crick and James Watson proposed? Is

---

25. Kuhn, *Structure of Scientific Revolutions*.

DNA alphabet soup? Is the atom "plumb pudding," as Ernest Rutherford imagined? Or a mini "solar system," as Neils Bohr thought? Are subatomic "particles" actually "strings?" Is gravity "curved" spacetime, as Einstein proposed? Is space-time curvaceous? Even mathematics, which supposedly exemplifies abstract conceptual thought in its purest form, requires metaphor to be conceptualized at all. "Coordinates, fluxions, symbolic logic and Riemann surfaces are all metaphors, extending the meanings of words from familiar to unfamiliar contexts."[26]

Austrian mathematician Kurt Gödel developed his incompleteness theorems in the 1930s, and they are generally acknowledged as among the most important in the entire history of mathematics. One dimension of these theorems is that though there may well be true statements in mathematics, that truth cannot itself be proven. Every formal system of axioms has a limit, a gap that shoots through it. Imagine an index card. On side A we read "The statement on the other side of this card is true." Now, turn the card over to side B, which reads, "The statement on the other side of this card is false." I will let the reader's mind twist to reconcile the logical knot created by this scenario. Gödel managed to spin the minds of mathematicians in a similar fashion, showing that mathematical language has at its core a paradoxical and self-referential structure that makes proving the axioms of a given, formal system impossible; mathematical systems cannot demonstrate or prove their own validity. As one commentator puts it, "Gödel's theorem is a metaphor for the fact that no logical program can hope, even in the limit, to answer all the questions."[27] One of the major complaints brought against metaphor across the centuries is its "equivocal" nature; it turns out that even mathematics, that most conceptually precise and rigorous of disciplines, equivocates.

Is "the heart, but a spring; and the nerves, so many strings; and the joints, but so many wheels, giving motion to the whole body, such as was intended by the artificer," as Thomas Hobbes proposed in his *Leviathan*?[28]

---

26. Dyson, *Birds and Frogs*. Dyson commends to his readers a book by the Russian mathematician Yuri Manin, *Mathematics as Metaphor*, noting that Manin understands the "deepest concepts in mathematics [as] those which link one world of ideas with another" and "sees the future of mathematics as an exploration of metaphors that are already visible but not yet understood." In other words, buried within mathematical concepts are metaphors, and the task involves walking these concepts back to their metaphorical roots, much as I am doing in this book with respect to Christian concepts or ideas.

27. Rucker, *Mind Tools*, 247.

28. Hobbes, *Leviathan*, 7.

Is the human body a "machine"? Science makes progress within a given paradigm, but when paradigms shift, an entirely different set of conceptual and evaluative criteria emerge. Inside the conception of the metaphor of the body as machine, western biomedicine has done wonders. But the machine metaphor seems impotent to deal with the felt experience that the body is more than the sum of its parts, a basic principle of holistic medicine. In a Hebrew medical treatise published in Vienna in the early eighteenth century, the human body is portrayed as a house.[29] The house metaphor is not, in some objective sense, less accurate than the machine metaphor. Rather, each image (body as machine, body as house) discloses/creates the body and sets the table for certain ways of interacting and engaging the body, each with accompanying assets and liabilities. "All the world's a stage," says Shakespeare: the world as a drama. Other metaphors for the cosmos deploy the language of game, dance, clockwork, organism, and an expanding and contracting balloon, among others. Is the universe a balloon? As biologist Stephen Jay Gould noted, "We reveal ourselves in the metaphors we choose for depicting the cosmos in miniature,"[30] and this is as true of science as religion.[31] Metaphysical conjectures such as these are metaphorical shots in the dark, they are unfounded, in the sense that they cannot be verified; but neither can they be falsified, which is to say that they are founding of a world, they create and disclose the possibilities for acting in and on a given world. In the eighteenth century, the world was a sophisticated "clockwork"; now, it is a sophisticated "network." What it will be tomorrow is anyone's guess.

Metaphors carry with them entailments, relations, consequences—and they require evaluation. Metaphors are crucial for understanding, but they can be found wanting. They can harden into things and lose their lifeblood. Sometimes, we forget we are using metaphors, as they become naturalized, second nature, concretized. Cosmology readily understands the expanding universe through the image of a balloon or a bubble, but we are unlikely to mistake the universe for a balloon. With the body as machine, things are different, because of the grounding, pervasive nature of the metaphor. But metaphors can lose efficacy. "Of course, one cannot think without metaphors," writes Susan Sontag, "but that does not mean

---

29. Lepicard, "Alternative to the Cosmic."
30. Gould, *Full House*, 7.
31. See Hesse, *Models and Analogies*, on use of metaphor in science as valid means to depict reality.

there aren't some metaphors we might well abstain from or try to retire."[32] Counterintuitively, much work in metaphor theory is not undertaken to tease out further meanings from figurative speech, but, as Sontag intends, to extract or remove meaning. For example, "virgin birth" is a metaphor, so what needs extracting is the idea that the phrase describes a literal conception. For her part, Sontag lamented the harm done to people by the "war on cancer" metaphor. Disease is, of course, no metaphor; but how we imagine, understand, relate to, treat, and talk about disease most certainly is. Since Sontag's early analysis, considerable work has been done on the harm done by imagining cancer through militaristic metaphors.[33] Science, mathematics, medicine—these fields also employ metaphor, and people working in them sometimes fall prey to literalism just as religious people do. A cardinal example is the brain-as-computer metaphor.[34]

The upshot of this survey is that we can no longer write off religious language owing to its metaphorical nature. To the extent that religious thought is (or becomes) problematic, it isn't by virtue of being rooted in metaphors, but rather the entailments of a set of dominant metaphors. Metaphors are necessary for understanding, but they have assets and liabilities, and they have a kind of lifecycle: they are born, they mature, they die; they may also live on indefinitely, encrusted and hidden in our words and concepts—when this happens, we may well miss the point or insight of the original metaphor.

In the world of metaphor, a man can be fully a god and a god fully a man: this is not irrational thinking, but a form of magical thinking. The gift of "metaphor is perhaps one of man's most fruitful potentialities. Its efficacy verges on magic, and it seems a tool for creation which God forgot inside one of His creatures when He made him."[35] In metaphor, the properties or features (or, at least a portion of these) of one object are transferred or applied to another. Metaphor contains both identity and difference, comparison and contrast, like and unlike. There is a fuzziness to metaphor (as with analogy and comparison) that irks people who demand univocal meaning. Metaphor is suggestive and slippery, not certain and sticky. In some fashion, rejection of the epistemological value of metaphor owing to its ambiguity is a form of fundamentalism,

---

32. Sontag, *Illness as Metaphor*, 93.

33. See Hauser and Schwarz, "War on Prevention"; Kruijff and Van Zweden, "Harmful Impact"; Flusberg et al., "War Metaphors."

34. See Dupuy, *On the Origins*.

35. Gasset, *Dehumanization of Art*, 33.

a posture, a frame of mind that can only tolerate singleness of meaning, refusing to accept the rough textured and changing nature of our knowledge of the world. If postmodernists are positively allergic to certainty, positivists and fundamentalists demand nothing less. There is a good deal of psychology at play in metaphor theory. The post-Jungian psychologist James Hillman observes that we use ideas "to see the idea cloaked in the passing parade." Ideas have archetypal propensities; ideation, concepts, theories—these are free creations of the mind but are nevertheless patterned. Hillman emphasizes that we do not merely "see" patterns or structures in data; ideas are the very means in and through which we discern the patterns to begin with. "We are always in the embrace of an idea."[36] The passing parade to notice here is the persistent tendency in western philosophical and scientific traditions, traceable to their beginnings in ancient Greece, to rid language and understanding of figurative speech. The idea that allows us to perceive this "parade" is what Hillman calls a "monotheistic consciousness," a style or posture of consciousness characterized by concern for consistency and unity on one hand, and, on the other, with a lack of tolerance for paradox and ambiguity; another term for it is "fundamentalism." Jacques Derrida wrote of "logocentricm." Hans Blumenberg's term for this phenomenon is "absolutism," a topic to which we will return.

Cultural historian Peter Burke argues that from the late Middle Ages through the Enlightenment we can detect in Western culture a rise in "literal-mindedness," described as "a propensity to reject or at any rate to devalue symbolism, whether in the interpretation of texts, rituals, other human behavior, or the natural world." With this upswing in literalism comes a corresponding decline in "symbol-mindedness." Burke cites a passage from anthropologist Clifford Geertz, who complains about the theoretical prejudice that "'symbolic' opposes to 'real' as fanciful to sober, figurative to literal, obscure to plain, aesthetic to practical, mystical to mundane, and decorative to substantial. . . . The real is as imagined as the imaginary."[37] Geertz locates this change in attitude that devalued the symbolic in the nineteenth century; Burke pushes this date back, providing numerous examples of a shifting worldview in early-modern Europe in the wake of Catholic and Protestant Reformations. Burke acknowledges that his efforts are but a piece of a "grand narrative" of an ongoing

---

36. Hillman, *Re-Visioning Psychology*, 121.

37. Geertz, *Negara*, 134. Jacques Derrida (in *White Mythology*) makes much the same point in his discussion of "proper" and the "non-proper."

shift that would reach at least back to classical Greece, and he outlines several potentially fruitful avenues of research.

One potential problem with Burke's argument is that he approaches this grand narrative in waiting with a tacit from-mythos-to-logos frame, though avoiding the strong normative claim that logos is an advance. Burke himself realizes this limitation when he comments that "the story told so far is implausibly unilinear, implying that people have been becoming more and more literal-minded over the centuries. . . . The crosscurrents of what might be called 'reactive symbol-mindedness' deserve further investigation." A possibility here is that given so many instances of tension between literal-mindedness and symbol-mindedness through the centuries, perhaps we are dealing more with an archetypal propensity than an unfolding story. That the church fathers had to write instructions on how to read the Bible, in which they are often at pains to burst the literalist's bubble, points to a persistent tendency to concretize metaphors and symbols into hardened, literal things, to historicize allegories, anecdotes, and myths into events. At any rate, Burke is on to a historical dynamic when he writes that, in its "nineteenth- and twentieth-century manifestations," literal-mindedness is best defined as "a sophisticated (or trained) incapacity to understand symbolism."[38]

Metaphor still has its detractors, largely the legacy of forms of Anglo-American commonsense empiricism and positivism, which does indeed seem to cultivate a "trained incapacity" for symbolic thought. In my field, religious studies, worry about the symbolic is often akin to that voiced by Dawkins. Russell McCutcheon, for example, sees metaphor and symbol as circumspect because they are all too easily invoked by the religious whenever there is a need to find a way around the force of rational critique, or to accommodate modern sensibilities, but with no clear rationale as to when passages are to be read literally, rather than allegorically. Who could argue with McCutcheon when he writes, "It should be apparent that, when reading a document that reflects the entrenched cultural and historical context of people half a world away and reaching back thousands of years, it is utterly impossible to take the entire document literally."[39] True enough. But did those people way over there and way back then take their texts literally, as McCutcheon implies? It is by no means clear that this is the case. Who reads literally? The general

---

38. Burke, "Rise of Literal-Mindedness," 364–66.
39. McCutcheon, *Critics Not Caretakers*, 51.

population? The uneducated? The educated? Those with a psychological need for certainty? What is read literally, and why? That the figurative language in religious texts might offer insight, perspective, distance, reflexivity, fresh ideas—all this receives little of McCutcheon's attention.

Metaphorical Openings in Thought

Umberto Eco observes that metaphor "has been the object of philosophical, linguistic, aesthetic, and psychological reflection since the beginning of time."[40] Eco's historical omniscience aside, the textual record does reveal a fascination not just with using metaphor but understanding it. Despite remaining suspicions about the motive for metaphor we have witnessed a sea-change since the days of Thomas Sprat. The understanding and assessment of metaphor picked up steam in the 1950s and shows no sign of abating. Already in 1978, Wayne C. Booth wryly commented, "I have in fact extrapolated with my pocket calculator to the year 2039; at that point there will be more students of metaphor than people."[41]

The nature and function of metaphor are complex topics; amidst the controversies and multitude of approaches and theories, many would agree with the simple definition offered by Kenneth Burke: "Metaphor is a device for seeing something in terms of something else. It brings out the thisness of that, or the thatness of a this."[42] Where matters become more interesting is with what appears a fateful choice about this most precious of figures of speech. Either metaphor is constitutive of linguistic activity as such or language is a rule-governed activity and metaphor is a nonsensical abuse of these rules. If the former, then any effort to define metaphor must rely on metaphor, a case of definitional tail chasing at its finest. If the latter—that is, if linguistic capacity is akin to a machine that generates sensible statements—how is it that nonsensical language nevertheless communicates something understandable? To follow all attempts to resolve the conundrum would take us too far afield, though I would note that one such attempt, made by Umberto Eco, ends with the (metaphorical!) claim that metaphor is a "tool that permits us to understand the encyclopedia better. This is the type of knowledge that the metaphor stakes out for us." And what is the *encyclopedia*? In Eco's semiotics, the

---

40. Eco, *Semiotics*, 87.
41. Booth, "Metaphor as Rhetoric," 49.
42. Burke, *Grammar of Motives*, 503.

concept *encyclopedia* refers to the vast and complex social-cultural-historical field inside of which semiosis (the shared use and interpretation of signs and symbols) takes place. Here, the role of metaphor is cognitive and pragmatic, a tool to test, explore, expose, re-think, re-work, and play with existing meanings and significations. Eco likens the use of metaphor to an "excitation" of one's cognitive state. Beyond communicating meanings, the aim of metaphor is a kind of extension of ourselves into the surrounding lifeworld. Eco calls a metaphor "good" (valuable, efficacious, powerful) when it "does not allow the work of interpretation to grind to a halt . . . but . . . permits inspections that are diverse, complementary and contradictory." Metaphor creates an opening, a space for thinking, digesting, assimilating ideas. Fecund metaphors trigger a process and "once the process of unlimited semiosis has started, it is difficult to say where and when the metaphorical interpretation stops."[43] Metaphors, in other words, don't mean; rather, they open a space for probing meanings and establishing significances.

The modern philosophical tradition—especially, the Anglo-American tradition—has generally considered metaphor an aberrant or ineffectual use of language for pursuing matters of truth. One of the more recent trenchant critiques of metaphor's capacity for meaning is that of Donald Davidson, who holds that words mean simply what they mean. Romeo's line, "Juliet is the sun," just means that Juliet is the sun. Of course, Juliet is not the sun; hence the phrase is meaningless or, even worse, misleading. In seeking out how metaphor works, invoking the notion of a metaphorical meaning just sends one around in circles. Better, suggests Davidson, to focus on the effect of metaphor on the hearer, which is to nudge one towards making sense of the senseless. Any real information that someone might derive from this phrase requires some amount of translation or interpretation: the sun makes me happy, so Shakespeare is saying that Juliet makes Romeo happy. But the sun may well be experienced and understood in all sorts of ways; hence, Shakespeare is not communicating any positive content, but merely providing an occasion for interpretation.

Whether the sun metaphor really can be experienced and interpreted in the infinite variety of ways is open for debate. There is perhaps more universality in metaphor than Davidson and other positivists realize.[44] As William Lycan puts it, "If Davidson is right [about metaphor]

---

43. Eco, *Semiotics*, 120–24.
44. See Ma and Liu, "Universal Approach to Metaphors."

one can never misinterpret a metaphor."[45] That Shakespeare can be interpreted in a variety of ways does not necessitate an infinite variety of ways. I have the creative power to claim that Romeo means "Juliet is a boundless source of renewable energy," but this interpretive leap cannot hold; matters of interpretation and meaning are thoroughly social processes; moreover, regardless of the interpretation, surely Romeo is trying to assert something about Juliet, and not just anything; and, one nested frame out, Shakespeare was trying to assert something in his drama of the strife between the Montagues and the Capulets.

This is not to do justice to Davidson's views, to be sure. His work on metaphor has been part of the analysis and debate for more than three decades. But there is enough rigorous critique of his position (sometimes referred to as the standard communication model, SCM) that exploring the meaningful, truth-directed dimensions of metaphorical language itself (rather than simply what is provoked) cannot be written off as a fool's errand.[46] Perhaps the line that has been so crucial in linguistics between what words *mean* and what they *convey* has been far too thickly drawn.

There is now a broad acceptance that metaphor is so thoroughly entwined with our capacities for language, reflection, and symbolization that it has deeper implications than simply being a figure of speech with rhetorical potential for good or ill. The beginnings of a change in attitude towards non-conceptual thought are perhaps traceable to the work of I. A. Richards, in his influential *The Philosophy of Rhetoric*, published in 1936. "Metaphor," writes Richards, "is the omnipresent principle of language" and the "pretence to do without metaphor is never more than a bluff waiting to be called."[47] The thought of George Lakoff and Mark Johnson, the well-known architects of conceptual metaphor theory, represents the fruits of the new direction launched by Richards. They hold that "subjective experience," "forming judgments," and "abstract thought" *require* the use of metaphor, it being "virtually impossible" to reckon such process occurring without metaphor:

> Even if nonmetaphorical thought about subjective experience and judgment is occasionally possible, it almost never happens. We do not have a choice as to whether to acquire and use primary metaphor. Just by functioning normally in the world, we

---

45. Lycan, *Philosophy of Language*, 178.

46. Critiques of Davidson's work on metaphor have been given by Lycan, *Philosophy of Language* and Taylor, *Language Animal*.

47. Richards, *Philosophy of Rhetoric*, 92.

automatically and unconsciously acquire and use a vast number of such metaphors.[48]

Thales of Miletus proposed that the "all things are full of gods." Today, we might say, "all language is full of metaphor."

Metaphor does more than "pretty-up" language. It is implicated in acts of cognition. There is more truth in "I'm feeling down today," than a positivist is willing to acknowledge. What could possibly replace this sentence? "I have a negative mood"? Part of the truth-bearing capacity of metaphor is that it weds thought and experience to corporeality, to the fleshiness of the body. Slumped shoulders and head down are not "symbolic" of a "depressed" state: they are the thing itself.[49] Following Lakoff and Johnson, a basic assumption of this book is that metaphor is central to how we express ourselves and understand our world. We can think and speak without metaphor, but not for long. "Richard has the heart of a lion" does not mean the man is a freak of nature; but neither is it merely a fancy way of saying "the king is brave." Aside from losing evocative power, the reduction to "he's brave" overlooks that the word "brave" means "having or showing mental or moral strength to face danger."[50] Here, "moral strength" is itself a metaphor, drawing on our experience of muscular strength to say something about one's character. And what about "facing" danger? Metaphors all the way down.

Philosopher William G. Lycan advances a similar view to that of Lakoff and Johnson:

> Virtually every sentence produced by any human being contains importantly metaphorical or other figurative elements. My use just now of the word "element" was at least in part metaphorical. Or consider the number of times in a day that someone utters the word "level." "Level" is almost invariably metaphor, unless the speaker is actually talking about a horizontal layering of some physical thing. Nonliteral usage is the rule, not the exception.[51]

---

48. Lakoff and Johnson, *Philosophy in the Flesh*, 59.

49. Kövecses has explored in detail both the question of metaphor's universality (*Metaphor in Culture*) and its rootedness in bodily experience (*Where Metaphors Come From*).

50. *Webster's Third New International Dictionary of the English Language Unabridged*.

51. Lycan, *Philosophy of Language*, 210. Along these lines, see Taylor, *Language Animal*.

Metaphor is the means to talk about anything that really matters: to develop our ideas, to express our emotions, to reflect on experience, to articulate our desires, to offer our hopes—in the end, metaphor is all we have, the *archon* of language and thought. More than a linguistic device, metaphor, as a "cognitive activity of the mind,"[52] is how we know the world.

Descartes helped inaugurate the modern methodological program bent on the full objectification of truth by means of perfectly precise concepts, the model for which was the logic of mathematics. Within this program, "all forms and elements of figurative speech, in the broadest sense of the term, prove to have been makeshifts destined to be superseded by logic," by the purity of the concept. Again, in such a worldview, the best we can ascribe to metaphor is that it may contribute to the "effect of a statement, the 'punchiness' with which it gets through to its . . . addressees."[53] Today, it is widely (though not universally) recognized that the turn inaugurated by Descartes—developed by Enlightenment thinkers, and later reinforced by positivism to generate what Merlin Donald calls "theoretic culture," marking a sharp break from "oral-mythic"[54] culture in order to rid ourselves of myth and metaphor in favor of clear, distinct, mathematically precise ideas, supposedly in service of a truly proper understanding of things—was perhaps not such a sharp turn after all (since scientific discourse is rife with metaphor), but was a wrong turn.

I. A. Richards was an early voice defending metaphor as an instrument not only of rhetoric but of thought, asking that we disabuse ourselves of the idea that metaphor is merely "a grace or ornament or added power of language, not its constitutive form."[55] Twenty years after Richards, Max Black published a groundbreaking study of metaphor, marking a sea change in conceptions of metaphor, the starting point for which was rejecting the "commandment" that "metaphor is incompatible with serious thought."[56] Today, it is entirely defensible to "insist that thought is essentially metaphoric, that metaphors are cognitively

---

52. Cormac, *Cognitive Theory of Metaphor*, 127.
53. Blumenberg, *Paradigms for a Metaphorology*, 2.
54. Donald, *Origins*.
55. Richards, *Philosophy of Rhetoric*, 90.
56. Black, *Models and Metaphors*, 25. For Black's groundbreaking essay, see Black, "Metaphor."

irreducible and indispensable, and that any adequate account of meaning and truth must give a central place to metaphor."[57]

Richard Rorty analyzes the shortcomings of the West's philosophical and scientific ability to understand metaphor as the outcome of the dominance of a metaphor. The mind as the "mirror of nature" is an image that imagines understanding as the mind's efforts to produce ever more accurate representations of an external reality. My allegiances are far closer to Richards or Rorty or Charles Taylor than to the position represented by, say, Donald Davidson. Taylor's aim in *The Language Animal* is to defend what he terms "constitutive-expressive" theories of language against the supremacy in the modern era of "designative-instrumental" theories. Language, argues Taylor, does not simply describe what is there but plays an active role in creating what we are capable of perceiving. If metaphor allows us to "see" something we wouldn't otherwise see, and if religious language (like the language of science and mathematics) is inherently metaphorical, then religious language is not rudimentary and incorrect science but also a vehicle of insight, knowledge, and understanding.

---

57. Johnson, ed., *Philosophical Perspectives on Metaphor*, 19.

Chapter 3

Anthropogenesis and the Urge to Truth

> What, then, is truth? A mobile army of metaphors, metonyms, and anthropomorphisms—in short, a sum of human relations which have been enhanced, transposed, and embellished poetically and rhetorically, and which after long use seem firm, canonical, and obligatory to a people: truths are illusions about which one has forgotten that this is what they are; metaphors which are worn out and without sensuous power; coins which have lost their pictures and now matter only as metal, no longer as coins.
>
> We still do not know where the urge for truth comes from.
>
> —Friedrich Nietzsche, *On Truth and Lies in an Extra-Moral Sense*

THE FIELD OF PHILOSOPHICAL anthropology works to unearth the phenomenological and existential significances in what we know about anthropogenesis, the evolutionary process of hominization, of becoming human. The term "philosophical anthropology" refers to a school of thought associated with figures such as Max Scheler, Helmuth Plessner, Arnold Gehlen, and Paul Alsberg, who were influenced by advances in evolutionary theory, the biological sciences, and currents of German philosophy stemming from the thought of Johann Gottfried Herder, Wilhelm Dilthey, and Edmund Husserl. The fruition of this tradition is the work of Hans Blumenberg, whose work cuts a wide swath, examining the place of metaphor and myth in both the process of hominization and the trajectory of Judeo-Christian and European intellectual history. Several of Blumenberg's framing assumptions and ideas dovetail nicely with British and North American traditions of cultural and symbolic anthropology, in the work of, among others, Clifford Geertz and Roy Rappaport, theorists who, so far as I can tell, were not familiar with Blumenberg's work.

The Evolution of Humanity

One of the key premises of philosophical anthropology is that the human being, as the least instinctually determined of all animals, requires culture to make up for a deficit in genetic "programming" to guide behavior. Unable to survive solely on the back of innate instinctual mechanisms, the proto-human stumbles upon culture as an adaptive response to an existentially threatening situation. Culture then is something of a leap out of or a leap beyond nature, a second skin or phantom body, making up for what biology is unable to supply. Human beings do not simply react to the world, but act on and in the world, through language, symbolization, tools, ritual, and the entire range of cultural/institutional forms we have created. As Geertz puts it, "Our capacity to speak is surely innate; our capacity to speak English is surely cultural."[1] Culture, consisting of "systems or complexes of symbols," lies outside the "boundaries of the individual organism" in the "intersubjective world of common understandings into which all human individuals are born." It is precisely because "genetically programmed processes are so highly generalized" in humans that we need "culturally programmed ones."[2] Geertz's research focused mainly on existing intersubjective worlds, that is, on the way an active culture creates relatively passive subjectivities. But those cultures are, in the first place, created by people in and through language and labor. Geertz wasn't particularly interested in anthropogenesis, though he does offer reflection on the relationships between mind, body, and culture.

Only the most reductive proponents of sociobiology attempt to unite biological and cultural evolution as a single process. My assumption, a widely shared one, is that biological and cultural evolution cannot be explained by the same theoretical orientation. Biological evolution proceeds by genetic mutations, natural selection, and the inheritance

1. Geertz, *Interpretation of Cultures*, 50.
2. Geertz, *Interpretation of Cultures*, 92–93.

of adaptively valuable traits. Cultural evolution involves memories, institutions, languages, tools—and these are created, invented. The two types of evolution, however, parallel one another and do interact. Certainly, our biology (which includes our mind) constrains or channels culture. As Terry Eagleton notes, "It is hard to find anyone who thinks that tickling the starving is ever preferable to feeding them."[3] The kind of body we are sets limits on cultural patterns. It is difficult to know for certain whether culture can influence biological change, because biological evolution takes place over such a long period of time; the least that can be said is that researchers and theorists are increasingly willing to think through the interchange of biology and culture, as well as reflect on the philosophical and ethical entailments of such interplay.[4] As a limit scenario, given that culture has produced nuclear weapons, which could end biological evolution altogether, it seems reasonable to suppose culture impacts biological evolution.[5]

There is broad support in evolutionary biology for the idea of homo sapiens being biologically under-determined. The more complex an organism is, the more detached or distanced it is from being seamlessly integrated into its habitat and the more flexible and involved it thereby becomes in shaping a niche in which to live. Humans figure as the most detached organism, which is another way of saying humans possess the highest degree of internal freedom for self-generated adaptive processes; humans are the most cultural of all organisms. Another way to put this is that the loss of simple genetic determination results in a greater capacity for phenotypic innovation, which means that evolutionary theory has to account for "the generative capacity of the organism" to play "an active role in the production of novel phenotypic expressions."[6] Some researchers are exploring the idea that, in humans, a gene-culture process (rather than simply genetic process) is now the dominant mode of evolution.

---

3. Eagleton, *Why Marx Was Right*, 109.

4. As entry points to a complex discussion, see Moss, "Representational Preformationism"; Moss, "Redundancy, Plasticity, and Detachment"; and Moss and Pavesich, "Science, Normativity and Skill."

5. See Laland et al., "How Culture Shaped." As one example, the authors mention the impact of dairy farming on favoring the spread of adult lactose tolerance. Along another line of inquiry, Catherine Malabou has applied new research in examining how trauma can be passed on genetically in revisiting Freud's discussion in *Moses and Monotheism* (1939), of the issue of phylogenesis and transgenerational inheritance. See Malabou, "Psychic Phylogenesis."

6. See Moss, "Redundancy, Plasticity, and Detachment."

In his study of the "evolution of humanity," anthropologist Roy Rappaport dives deep into questions of hominization, examining the role of religion and ritual in relation to those unique capacities that distinguish human being in the world from that of our animal kin, capacities such as the possession of language and ability to employ symbols. The evolutionary advent of language gave our earliest ancestors enormous advantages. Language provided the capacity to provide more detailed information about one's world, but, significantly, the ability to extract oneself from the immediacy of the here and now to conceive the past and the future. Through language and symbolism, writes Rappaport, "discourse not only can escape from the confines of the here and now to recapture the concrete past and distant or to approach the foreseeable future. It could also eventually escape from the concrete altogether." For Rappaport, humanity is characterized by the capacity to live in subjunctive spaces. Discourse, "empowered by grammar ... becomes free to search for worlds parallel to the actual as those of 'the might have been,' 'the should be,' 'the could be,' 'the never will be,' 'the may always be.'" To enter subjunctive spaces—"the realms of the desirable, the moral, the proper, the fortuitous, the imaginary, the general, and their negation, the undesirable, the immoral, the impossible"—means humanity does "not simply discover what is there. It is to create what is there." We might imagine a new idea or practice as the cultural equivalent of a random genetic mutation; like genetic mutations, some ideas are valuable, some are harmful.

For Rappaport, the origin of religion and cultural systems is not found simply in the need for social order and organization; nor is the origin of religion to be understood as the emergence of nascent rational thought, as primitive or pseudo-science. Rather, religion emerges out of a subjunctive space of questions and meanings: "Humanity is a species that lives and can only live in terms of meanings it itself must invent. These meanings and understandings not only reflect or approximate an independently existing world but participate in its very construction."[7] In the debate between epistemologies of discovery and invention, we need *both* perspectives. We invent—and must invent—the worlds in which we live, but we also discover their limits, their assets and liabilities in meeting bodily needs and capacities while dealing with changes to the physical environment, and through encounters with other cultural systems. Crucially, Rappaport argues, the rise of ritual (and, more broadly,

---

7. Rappaport, *Ritual and Religion*, 5–8.

religion) is aimed at dealing with a potentially destructive feature of language. The same powers of language to deploy symbols and conceive alternatives also generates the ability to lie and lying can become a threat to the viability of not only personal relations but group dynamics and social systems; the work of ritual action, in Rappaport's view, is to stabilize or delimit the danger of the lie.[8]

Blumenberg worked in a different intellectual tradition from that of Geertz and Rappaport, but his philosophical anthropology shares their conception of the human being as a "creature of deficiency," or what is sometimes referred to as a "negative anthropology," which distinguishes itself from more "positive" attempts to build a philosophical anthropology on the back of a premised human essence, such as the human being as a tool-making animal (*homo faber*) or as the animal that plays (*homo ludens*). "Man's deficiency in specific dispositions for reactive behavior vis-à-vis reality—that is, his poverty of instincts—is the starting point for the central anthropological question as to how this creature is able to exist in spite of his lack of fixed biological disposition."[9] Blumenberg, like Hannah Arendt, develops an anti-essentialist perspective on the human being, emphasizing contingency and a suspicion of attempts to define a universal, eternal human essence. Human beings lack a fixed essence (though we do have unique capacities associated with language), but we can, nevertheless, reflect on the conditions under which we live—securing from nature food and shelter, interacting with groups organized around ways of life different from our own, and dealing with the advantages and dangers associated with self-awareness. For Blumenberg, no matter what "essence" we ascribe to humanity, that capacity does not account for our being here in the first place. Rather, our existence is a result of certain "accomplishments," which are in hindsight ascribed to us as "belonging to [our] nature. The first proposition of an anthropology would then be, it cannot be taken for granted that man is able to exist."[10]

Blumenberg adopts an evolutionary perspective that speculates in naturalistic terms about a watershed situation in the evolution of humanity when early man became unfit to adaptively survive changing environmental circumstances. Blumenberg is puzzled by the simple fact that we exist. He does not take this existence for granted. All creatures that exist do so because they have survived through adaptive processes;

8. See Stephenson, "Liminality, Structures."
9. Blumenberg, "Anthropological Approach," 189.
10. Blumenberg, *Beschreibung des Menschen*, 535.

the human being is no different. Adaptation is slippery concept, used in a variety of ways. In its basic form, the concept describes the capacities of living systems to respond to perturbations that threaten disruption, death, or extinction. Adaptive response includes both short-term changes in state (say, the "fight or flight" mechanism), as well as longer-term changes to structure (say, the development of the dorsal fin or a bipedal gait). Though Blumenberg is loath to pursue what he calls the "mania" for origins, and finds theorizing origins an "idle" activity, he nevertheless roots his metaphorology in an anthropological story, though one in keeping with the conclusions of contemporary science, a story of the near failure of adaptive processes.

Under some external environmental pressure, some 2.5 million years ago, our ancestors left the forested regions of Africa—the biotope for which they were adaptively fit—to take up life on the open savannah, adopting an upright posture and exposing themselves to the biological and existential benefits and "risks of the widened horizon of perception, which were also those of its perceivability."[11] Unprotected, exposed, open to threats from all sides, and adaptively unsuited to life in a new environment was, narrates Blumenberg, the anthropogenic traumatic experience the successful navigation of which set the course for our becoming the kind of creature we are. As Arnold Gehlen puts it,

> Humans have no natural protection against inclement weather; we have no natural organs for defence and attack but yet neither are our bodies designed for flight. Most animals surpass man as far as acuity of the senses is concerned. Man has what could even be termed a dangerous lack of true instincts and needs an unusually long period of protection and care during his infancy and childhood. In other words, under natural conditions, among dangerous predators, man would long ago have died out.[12]

How is that we didn't? How is a creature without a fixed nature possible in nature? Kant asked, "What is man?" Blumenberg shifts the question, asking, "How is the human possible?"

In this school of thought, those unique capacities of the human species, chief among them language and the power of symbolization, must be the answer: because these powers are unique to human beings, they must be the adaptive powers that fill-in the gap opened by our biological

---

11. Blumenberg, *Work on Myth*, 4.
12. Gehlen, *Man*, 26.

shortcomings. Staying within the "confines of our current conceptual apparatus, vocabulary, research, and inference" we "posit that some such problem [the failure of instincts] induced the 'prehuman creature' to adapt by forming what we would call a culture."[13] Culture fills in our missing instinctual determination; we adapt ourselves to the environment via language and symbols, which hold at bay the overwhelming, self-aware encounter with reality as such, while also making ourselves adequate to the environments (which include other cultures) that we encounter. Blumenberg posits the "necessity of picturing an initial situation that serves the purpose of the old *status naturalis*," a theoretical "limit towards which the extrapolation of tangible, historical features into the archaic tends."[14] Our instinctual deficiency makes us vulnerable, exposing us to threats; paradoxically, not being tied to any particular ecological niche or rigid and complete instinctual program offers "world openness," a dynamic flexibility and power to transcend nature, make it object of thought, and adapt it to our needs.

The Absolutism of Reality

Blumenberg's narration of anthropogenesis fits quite well with accepted science, but what he is really after is a phenomenological description of the experience that accompanies hominization, an experience he distills in his concept of the "absolutism of reality." Blumenberg calls this effort a "thought model," and realizes full well that in its pure form, the absolutism of reality is a "limit concept" that may never have been fully realized in history. Blumenberg invites us to imagine our way into the experience of a creature poised between animal and human. His account of that experience sheds light on a range of phenomenon such as the function of myth and metaphor, and cultural, epochal change (Blumenberg's chief concerns), but also early childhood development and the nature of anxiety. The concept of the "absolutism of reality" describes a core existential dilemma. The transition from forests to savanna was a double-edged sword; we solved an evolutionary problem, surviving by taking advantage of a new biotope and developing language—especially the power to access personal and group memories and subjunctive anticipatory states through myths; but this newfound openness to

---

13. Blumenberg, *Work on Myth*, 4.
14. Blumenberg, *Work on Myth*, 3.

the world was also one filled with anxiety. Our *plasticity*—our ability to anticipate, reflect, change, and act—is both source of strength and constitutional weakness. Unlike other animals, humans don't straightforwardly react to the world through a stimulus-response process. As Gehlen observers (above), fight or flight is not a viable species strategy for human beings. Rather than rely on innate responses, instinctual *reactions*, we must intentionally *act* in and on the world through language and culture. But, imagining ourselves back to this foundational moment of anthropogenesis, how do we act, if we don't know how to act? There is no sufficient biological program controlling the situation, and the cultural program has yet to be written. Instinct doesn't work, while culture, that substitution for the loss of instinct, has yet to be fully formed. What do we do? We must act; we don't know how to act.

The concept of the "absolutism of reality" then describes a situational moment in evolutionary history when early hominids "came close to not having control of the conditions of [their] existence and, what is more important, believed that [they] simply lacked control of them."[15] If this situation was not answered, the accompanying anxiety would have generated a panic or a paralysis threatening survival. The response was culture, eventuating in language and the symbolic world of myth and ritual. Unlike other theories of symbolism, which take language and the power to generate symbols as part of an essential human nature, Blumenberg sees these as solutions to a problem, the danger of the absolutism of reality. Importantly, this response to the experience of the absolutism of reality is a "spontaneous generation," a shot in the dark, as it were, a dimension of the ur-myth of anthropogenesis that remains central to subsequent cultural and intellectual history. In approaching the history of ideas, and the history of Christian thought in particular, a key position Blumenberg often adopts is in the observation that "questions do not always precede their answers. There is a spontaneous generation, from the authority of nonrational annunciations, of great and acutely active assertions such as those of eschatological immediate expectation, the doctrine of the Creation, or original sin."[16] Yahweh's counsel to Cain, be aware, "sin is crouching at the door," is another such assertion. Only after the fact do we come to pose the question, What is sin?

---

15. Blumenberg, *Work on Myth*, 3–4.
16. Blumenberg, *Legitimacy*, 66.

Blumenberg's key conceptual framework, responding to the absolutism of reality in the process of hominization, is crucial to Blumenberg's overall philosophy, and may be fleshed out with a few analogous situations. We tell young people that they can be anything they want to be, but this radical, exhilarating openness often generates intense anxiety, because it is a too immediate, vast, and undefined relationship to the world. Finding one's way involves making decisions, extracting oneself from the excess of available options, and creating a horizon, a frame inside of which one has a sense of direction, an orientation, a path. It used to be that routes into the adult world were well defined; the freedom to choose one's path in life was more circumscribed, if available at all. I am all for the freedom to choose one's vocation and, more broadly, one's path. But we should acknowledge the price of increased freedom is heightened anxiety, and young people often face enormous hurdles when they can't see a path to their future. Coming of age is but a particular example of the basic problem humans face—the openness that constitutes human being in the world, the need to fence off a piece of that openness in which to live, as well as the potential harm that fence may do should it become a constricting, limiting, unclimbable wall.

Another example. Psychologists are beginning to identity a new syndrome: eco-anxiety. Faced with the dissemination of the scientific evidence of rapid warming, the shift from the language of "climate change" to "climate emergency," the increasing number of severe weather events, the endless debates among the political class, the dire warnings about the future—in the face of all this, many people, especially young people, are experiencing something far beyond being scarred. We are only beginning to understand the mental-health impacts of our rapidly changing climate and the various cultural responses to this fact, among which include disinformation and denial. The language of "anxiety," "dread," "terror" is being used to describe the response, and one can understand why. A tornado is threat, but a definable, locatable one; but "the climate," "extinction," or "the planet" are concepts of such scale they threaten our ability to comprehend and capacity to act. The scale of the climate crisis, a new reality demanding an immediate and collective response, to is so vast, so amorphous, and the threat posed by that reality so total and complete, it is not difficult to understand why it arouses intense anxiety. "Fix the climate" is not unlike "be anything you want"—both involve swallowing (or being swallowed by) an excess of reality; as finite, limited beings, we need bite-sized pieces.

These kinds of experiences are more generalized in the literature and philosophy of existentialism. The catch phrase of existentialism is "existence precedes essence." Before you are anyone in particular, before you form an essence, a core identity—a teacher, an electrician, a poet— you simply are. Raw encounters with being, with reality as such, is the hallmark of existentialism; the experience is generally overwhelming. Here is how one proto-existentialist thinker described encountering the universe:

> When I consider the short duration of my life, swallowed up in an eternity before and after, the little space I fill engulfed in the infinite immensity of spaces whereof I know nothing, and which know nothing of me, I am terrified. The eternal silence of these infinite spaces frightens me.[17]

Blaise Pascal is terrified by nothing, by no-thing, which is characteristic of anxiety. Pascal offers here a hair-raising description of Blumenberg's absolutism of reality. Nietzsche, more than two centuries later, described much the same experience. Nietzsche's madman depicts the "death of God" that marks modern culture as a wiping away of the horizon with a sponge, as the unchaining of the earth from its sun, as a plunging in all directions, as a "straying through an infinite nothing."[18]

As a last example, consider the so-called "startle response," a pre-emotional, involuntary reaction to an unexpected sensation. A gunshot is heard: we duck slightly, flex our fingers, contract the abdominals, bend the knees, and turn to observe what is happening. Of course, we don't do this, in the sense of *deciding* to do it; the startle pattern is *primal*, universal, innate; we share it with animals. Many researchers describe the startle pattern experience in infancy as the first indication that a gap exists between the individual and the world. This isn't the experience of fear, but what we do to ready ourselves to assess the situation that gave rise to being startled. We may conclude it is nothing and go about our business; we may prepare to fight; we may run. So long as the situation can be assessed, several emotional and physical responses may play out. Emotively, we might feel curious, perturbed, or fearful.

But what happens when we are startled, not by catching a glimpse of a bear in the woods but by something too conceptually enormous to comprehend, something like climate change. Or, one step further, what

17. Pascal, *Pensées and Other Writings*, 26.
18. Nietzsche, *Gay Science*, 181–82.

happens when we are intransitively startled, startled by the simple fact of existence itself? For neurologist Kurt Goldstein, such a situation of objectless startle is generative of anxiety. Unlike fear, anxiety has no precise object. On the path from fear to anxiety (which is also the path from animal to human, as a well as the ontogenesis of subjectivity and self-awareness) a "qualitative change is occurring—that is, a change from the perception of the threat as coming from a specific object to an apprehension which engulfs the whole personality so that the person feels his very existence is endangered."[19] This engulfment of the whole person is what Blumenberg means to communicate in his key concept of "the absolutism of reality." Far from merely a threat, such experiences underlie the metaphysical experience of reality, a limit experience of the power and presence of the unseen and the uncognizable, which drives the quest for knowledge of and connection to that ultimate reality, as found in the traditions of mystical thought and practice the world over. The absolutism of reality is the basis for the effort to name and relate to the "sacred," the name given to the source of fear and fascination, threat and blessing, evil and good.

Myth in Light of Contingency and Distancing

Core experiences informing Blumenberg's thought are those of *contingency* and *distancing*. We are unfit for the world, and existence cannot be taken for granted. As creatures of contingency, we require orientation. The vulnerability that attends awareness of contingency, for which there is never any final solution, paradoxically means we have a certain openness to the world. We counter our vulnerability with various absolutes, with a system of symbols, stating, "This is the way things are"—while our openness means these absolutes are not necessarily how things have to be. Contingency mints a coin: the obverse is possibility generating threat; the reverse, exigency generating possibility: this is our existential economy. The contingent nature of things means we can (unlike other animals), within certain limits, intentionally change and adapt; we can assert ourselves on and in the world. The dizzying side of contingency, experienced as threat, means that we must find ways to remove or distance ourselves from the world as such, reality in its raw form, lest we become overwhelmed with the objectless anxiety. In the saying "You need

---

19. May, *Meaning of Anxiety*, 58–59.

to take a step back," we find condensed a key dimension of Blumenberg's insight that humans are creatures that need to create "distance." We are creatures of action-at-a-distance. Our upright posture and visual acuity allow us to interact with our environment from a distance. Our capacity to fashion a spear and throw it creates space between ourselves and the dangerous animals we hunt. Our capacity to transmit cultural memory allows for perceiving our world from the distance of the past. Concepts, indeed, words themselves, are also a form of distancing. The experience of entering a culture very different from one's own is often overwhelming. To prevent being swallowed-up, we learn the names of important items and the words required for the niceties of social interaction, and thereby begin to parcel out this new world, and find our way around. We can detect distancing in the need, say, to have a diagnosis of an illness, and the comfort such diagnosis can bring, even if the prognosis is poor. Naming is a form of gaining some measure of understanding and hence control over nebulous, amorphous reality. It is no accident that creation myths from around globe typically involve the giving of names.

Culture—again, a catch-all term for human capacities, discoveries, and inventions such as language, symbolization, customs, self-reflection, intentionality, art, science, religion—this is all a stop gap, an adaptation tacked on to biology devised by a creature's anxiety-filled confrontation with an indifferent, hostile, and, in the beginning, nameless universe that cares not whether the human survives. Culture is "an urgently needed program for countering our specifically biological deficiencies."[20] Culture distances us from problems and contingencies that threaten to overwhelm. Distancing is also a matter of self-assertion. When a child begins to "push-off" from the parent, distancing themselves, by crawling, then riding a bike, then leaving home, this is a species of the more general class of acts needed to resist being subsumed by an indifferent or overwhelming reality.

Of course, we are not merely locked in a struggle for existence, but also a struggle for happiness. Our needs for self- and group-preservation do not make the desire for enjoyment an unnecessary folly. The desire for happiness, for opportunities to express oneself, to realize capacities and talents, seems to be an emergent property. Abraham Maslow describes human needs as a pyramid-shaped hierarchy. A solid base of food, shelter, and security leads upwards through communion

---

20. Blumenberg, *Beschreibung*, 552.

with others and "self-actualization," the drive to become what one is capable of becoming.[21] Blumenberg, though his starting point is a negative anthropology, makes room for such an understanding. Concisely summing up the efforts in the field of philosophical anthropology to formulate a basic understanding of the powers that drove anthropogenesis, Blumenberg sees two trains of thought:

> Man is viewed either as a poor or as a rich creature. The fact that man is not fixed, biologically, to a specific environment can be understood as either a basic lack of proper equipment for self-preservation or as openness to the fullness of a world that is no longer accentuated only in terms of vital necessities. Man is made creative either by the urgency of his needs or by the playful dealings with his surplus talents.[22]

We are more than organisms toiling away to ensure our survival; we struggle on two fronts, for survival but also for happiness and significance. The struggle or search for happiness (John Paul II's synonym for "heaven," we recall) is not "superfluous." Meeting our basic needs is not enough to make us happy; the self-awareness and creative powers we possess clamor for use. Reason, language, culture—these may have originated in the need to deal with a reality all too directly experienced; but once these powers come in to play, they may distance us enough from the exigencies of nature to allow for a more free, undirected play and self-presentation.[23] Jesus perhaps said something similar when he noted that "man shall not live by bread alone" (Matt 4:4).

Blumenberg is at pains to develop an understanding of anthropogenesis as part of his effort to correct our theories of metaphor and myth. Myth has long been theorized in terms of the dominant mode of thought that replaced it, namely, science, from a perspective that narrativizes intellectual history as movement a *from mythos to logos*. For Blumenberg, myth is to be considered not in terms of what came after it, but from the perspective of what problems myth worked to overcome, namely, the experience of the absolutism of reality, our need for consolation, significance, to distance ourselves from anxieties and vulnerabilities. It is a mistake to think that in the twenty-first century such needs are no longer with us. Instead of teleology, Blumenberg "proposes an interpretation of

---

21. Maslow, *Toward a Psychology*.
22. Blumenberg, *Wirklichkeiten*, 104.
23. See Wertz, "On the Possibility."

human 'symbolic forms' as factors that all contribute, simultaneously, to the single comprehensive endeavor of making human existence possible by overcoming the problem of our biological nonadaptation, our constitutional deficit of instinct."[24] Philosophical anthropology, as Blumenberg practices it, is not based on an assumed human nature or essence, but on—or better, inside of—a root human problem. Cultures are to be viewed not as steps on a path of progress but as responses to a universal, common predicament. We deal with the absolutism of reality by creating culture—more manageable, smaller scale, named absolutes.

The Fossil-Like, Truth-Oriented Nature of Metaphor

The New Testament image of a "kingdom of heaven" emerges in the context of and in contrast to the existing and experienced kingdom, the Empire of Rome, which conquered Syria-Palestine in 66 B.C.E., roughly sixty years before the birth of Jesus. Jesus proposes an alternative to this kingdom—an option, a variation, a potential—which will come to variously serve Christians and the church as consolation, program, and coercive tool. The kingdom of heaven preached by Jesus can be readily understood as an answer to a problem, namely, the Roman Empire; perhaps it is an answer to the entire history of empires.[25] And what was the problem with the Roman Empire?[26] In a word, survival: biological survival (the poor, the sick, the marginal lived permanently precarious lives); psychological survival (the pressures of domination and exploitation on one's sense of well-being demanded compensatory hope); cultural survival (the empire under Augustus, who came to power in the years just prior to the birth of Jesus, launched an intensive program of Romanization); religious survival (the temple in Jerusalem, the heart of religious life, was under threat

---

24. Wallace, "Introduction," xii.

25. The "kingdom of heaven" is yet another example of how established "answer positions" receive, in the context of changing circumstances, the formulation of new questions the position is said to answer. For example, the question—Where do souls go after death?—and its answer—heaven.

26. I am aware of the effort of Monty Python, in their film, *The Life of Brian*, to comedically answer the question of what the Roman accomplished for us by listing the achievements of that empire, which are numerous. The problem remains, though, whether these achievements justify slavery, dispossession, and imperial conquests. It is doubtful that aqueducts, roads, and libraries require empire.

and would eventually be entirely destroyed, and hundreds of thousands of Jews killed or displaced from their territory).[27]

The situation on the ground in Roman Palestine was not entirely different from the experience of colonized peoples in modernity. Indigenous groups have faced and continue to face challenges to survival on multiple fronts—indeed, some tribes (the Beothuk of Newfoundland, the Ona of Tierra del Fuego, the Yahi of California) suffered extinction.[28] Frank L. Baum, author of *The Wizard of Oz*, editorialized on solving the "Indian problem" by advocating genocide.[29] In face of the existential threats faced by Jewish communities in first-century Palestine or Native communities on the plains in the mid-nineteenth century, we should not be surprised to see creative adaptations and changes to worldviews, as individuals and groups responded to the pressures of their respective colonial situations. In the Ghost Dance movement of Wokova, in the syncretism of Black Elk, in the emergence of new movements such as the Native American Church, we witness creative cultural responses to the devastating impacts of an aggressive conquest, dispossession, and control of Indigenous lands and traditions. Finding ways to conserve, protect, and transmit traditions and institutions that colonial authorities always seek to variously control, undermine, outlaw, or eradicate is also part of the history of colonization. One of the features of Judaism in the era of Jesus is its fragmentation into factions taking various responses to the pressures of Romanization: violent resistance, rebellion, and war; non-violent resistance; collaboration; withdrawal, flight, and seclusion. Without normatively assessing any of these moves, we could perhaps imagine them as a set of variations, cultural experiments in withstanding external pressures in service of survival.

Thinking and reflection take place in the context of a problem, puzzlement, confusion, or uncertainty. The "urge to truth," to finally move towards an answer to Nietzsche's question, stems from the sense that something is awry, and the first foray into making sense of the senseless is metaphor: to get a handle on something new (a new

---

27. In first-century Palestine, most of the population consisted of the peasantry—tenant farmers, sharecroppers, and hired labor. There was no middle class. Two-thirds of the population lived in severe poverty; 90 percent faced daily struggles for sufficient sustenance. See Häkkinen, "Poverty."

28. Biblical books chronicle (and sometimes enthusiastically revel in) the genocide of entire peoples.

29. See Bunch, *Oz and the Musical*.

experience, idea, concern) we liken it to what we know.[30] This is not to say we set out to put reason in service of answering clear questions; rather, we respond to existential situations to dispel fear, discomfort, dread. Nietzsche condenses an extreme version of this basic experience and strategy in his observation that in the face of extreme disorientation and distress, "If we [nevertheless] have our own *why* of life, we shall get along with almost any *how*."[31] The human animal is unique in requiring not only food and security but also a system of meaning that can forestall confusion or neutralize cognitive threats—or, to say the same thing, to provide orientation. The unfamiliar, the potentially threatening, a disruptive experience—these mark the onset of the effort to understand, to think, an effort that unfolds initially through non-conceptual thought, through metaphor.

Metaphor, in combining linguistic (and non-linguistic) "anomalies" into a unit, is a "knowledge process that describes a form of evolutionary epistemology." We come to know the world by combining concepts that are not normally connected, to form new concepts, new ideas; of crucial importance is the fact that these ideas are thoroughly embedded in our sensory and kinetic body, and our social world. "I am stuck in the mud" is an example of the way "metaphors construct a linguistic bridge from the embodied mind to culture. New metaphors change the culture in which we live, thereby affecting the ways in which humans interact with their environment."[32] As Blumenberg puts the matter, into "the functional transition from merely supposing something to having it fulfilled in intuition, metaphor interposes a heterogenous element that points towards a different context from the actual one." Metaphor aims to "repair" a disturbance of consciousness, which seeks a harmony of experience, by transferring or assigning the new experience or idea "to the inventory of a human life-world in which not only words and signs but also things themselves have 'meanings.'"[33]

Jesus proposes not life in this Roman kingdom (the disturbance) but rather the kingdom of heaven, which is like a sown grain of mustard seed (the resolution). If the response or intuition takes root, the assertion or idea embedded in the metaphor is often subsequently understood as

---

30. There are other tools at our disposal in dealing with situations in which our reason and will tend to fall short: jokes, anecdotes, gestures, and ritual are among them.
31. Nietzsche, *Portable Nietzsche*, 468.
32. Cormac, *Cognitive Theory of Metaphor*, 128.
33. Blumenberg, *Shipwreck with Spectator*, 83–84.

the answer to a preceding question, though it is at least as often the case that the question comes to be formulated after the answer has taken hold, as that to which the answer responded. Paul repeatedly, consistently, and spontaneously preaches and writes of Christ in the language of redemption (*apolytrōsis*).[34] The social-cultural background is the practice of freeing (manumission) slaves, which generally included a temple ceremony, casting manumission as a sacred act. Typically, when a slave was to be freed, "redeemers" would deposit a sum of money at a local temple. The slave owner would bring his slave to the temple, where the slave would be "sold" to the god of the temple. Paul, in adopting this language and practice for the event of Calvary thereby identified the executed body of Christ as a "price" paid for our freedom. But freedom from what, exactly? It is this way that answers often precede questions, and the subsequent task of post-Pauline theology will be to make explicit the question to which redemption through crucifixion is the agreed-upon answer. The core Christian doctrine expressing this question is that of "original sin," consolidated—and, as it were, consecrated—in the thought of Augustine, whose life and writings have had an "incalculable" influence on Christian thought and Christian institutions.[35] It is not clear, however, that Paul (and even more so the historical Jesus) would have necessarily understood the redemptive event as an answer to the question of what to do about the problem original sin.

Some of truth-oriented metaphors and narratives come to ground entire cultural systems while also, over time, as Nietzsche observes, lose their "sensuous power," becoming reified and hardened as things, places, or lifeless abstractions. This reification is the reason we need what Blumenberg calls *metaphorology* and *work on myth*, which show the limits of conceptual discourse while also loosening and unpacking the hardened concept. Metaphorology "allows the univocal end result to be recognized as an impoverishment of the imaginative background and the threads leading back to the lifeworld."[36] Blumenberg follows Nietzsche here, preferring the insights embedded in a sensuous if more ambiguous "mobile army of metaphors" than the crystal clarity of a pure concept. One way of reading the Bible is as a series of responses to existential problems, which makes the Bible (or at least strands of it) readable as a profound critique of religion, since religious beliefs and practices, like political or

---

34. See Rom 3:24 and 8:23; 1 Cor 1:30; Eph 1:7, 14; 4:30; Col 1:14.
35. Wiley, *Original Sin*, 56.
36. Blumenberg, "Beobachtungen an Metaphor," 163.

economic systems, can become problematic. As such, we should not be surprised that biblical language is fundamentally metaphorical. Read in one direction, Jesus's intuitions of heaven will come to be elaborated, across centuries, in sophisticated dogmatics and theologies, a process through which the everyday language of fields and fish is increasingly swallowed by abstract, conceptual, taken-for-granted, believed in ideas, as is the case with the term "heaven" itself. Read in the other direction, Jesus's efforts to express his vision are not to be viewed as the building blocks of a systematic theology, but in terms of his using facts on the ground and the capacity of metaphor to give shape and form to the lived experience of people in early first-century Palestine.

Blumenberg metaphorically describes the metaphors we encounter in historical texts as "fossils" revealing "an archaic stratum of the trial of theoretical curiosity—a stratum that is not rendered anachronistic just because there is no way back to the fullness of its stimulations and expectations of truth."[37] Jesus could not have formulated such a metaphor as Blumenberg uses here; Jesus lived in a world without an awareness of fossils or fossil records. For Blumenberg, the metaphorics of a text or a body of texts "read" as fossils allow us to work like a paleontologist, where the reconstructed living creature is the "lifeworld"—or, closer to Blumenberg's concerns, to that which disturbs or interrupts the lifeworld, understood as the matter of fact, day-to-day, taken for granted set of shared values, beliefs, and practices. Blumenberg was a theorist of the non-conceptual: myth, metaphor, anecdote, gloss—but he recognized these as fully legitimate modes of thought.

In his early work, Blumenberg proposed that students of the history of ideas should tend to metaphors, as they are transitional steps between an intuition and the rigorous development of a clear and accurate concept. For example, in molecular biology, the images of letters, codes, and information served the development of the concept and discovery of DNA—but the genome is not a text, and we can perhaps dispense of the textual metaphor. But Blumenberg also drew attention to what he termed "absolute metaphors"—those metaphors that provide a bedrock on which conceptual thinking is built and therefore cannot be reduced to or expressed in conceptual language without remainder. Our notions of truth, for example, are so deeply intertwined with metaphors of light and vision that it is virtually impossible to think about truth without these

---

37. Blumenberg, *Shipwreck with Spectator*, 82.

metaphors. Toward the end of his career, Blumenberg further developed his appreciation for how work on myth and metaphorics orients us towards those features of the lifeworld that sparked the "theoretical curiosity" that produced them in the first place; metaphors, in other words, alert us to the presence of a problem, and the effort to overcome it. Metaphor and myth are signs of creativity at work; the former endeavoring to get at something by innovatively expressing it in terms of whatever happens to be on hand (this new thing is that already known thing), the latter weaving sets of metaphors into a narrative, a story. Metaphor and myth are non-conceptual ways of thinking, but they most certainly are thinking, a move by which Blumberg undercuts the long-standing *mythos-logos* binary, along with its accompanying narrative of a progressive movement away from the primitivity of myth towards the maturity of reason. "Reason," writes Blumenberg, "means just being able to deal with something,"[38] and myth and metaphor are among the principal tools we have at our disposal for dealing with life.

What the "fossil"-like nature of metaphor points to is not, in the case before us here, simply the concerns and language of Jesus and his contemporaries but rather Jesus's "theoretical curiosity"—that is, the outcome of his thinking about what disturbed his being comfortably situated in his lifeworld. And though there is "no way back" to the "fullness" of how Jesus's metaphorics generated "stimulations" and "expectations of truth," neither are these two-thousand-year-old parables, images, and metaphors "anachronistic." Metaphors can and do speak across time, and "a historical phenomenology must . . . tend to decayed forms, which appear after speech is taken literally, as embarrassment in the face of the demands of realism."[39] Heaven, of course, is not a place in the same sense that Cairo is a place (that would be a "decayed form" of the notion of heaven)—but Christianity has always known this, if also from time to time embarrassingly forgotten what it knows and hopes to know in the fullness of time.

---

38. Blumenberg, *Work on Myth*, 63.
39. Blumenberg, *Shipwreck with Spectator*, 93.

Chapter 4

Sin and the Darwinism of Words

> The LORD said to Cain, "Why are you angry, and why has your countenance fallen? If you do well, will you not be accepted? And if you do not do well, sin is couching at the door; its desire is for you, but you must master it."
>
> —Genesis 4:6–7

THE CONCEPT OF SIN describes our propensity to violence and our seemingly endless capacity to deceive, oppress, betray, and humiliate others. Among all theological concepts, it alone has a solid empirical foundation, as the nightly news reveals. Why is there bad in the world? Why so much suffering? These are pressing questions in Jewish and Christian traditions, which take a reduction in the overall amount of suffering as a kind of progress. One might take a step further and suggest that some form of theodicy—an account of the how and why of death and suffering—is basic to all cultural forms. Another central constituent of culture is the need for legitimacy. Adam Kotsko takes these two central cultural problems (suffering and legitimacy) as the basis for all political theology, for the traffic back and forth between religion and politics, which amounts to "an inquiry into the ways that human communities try to justify their structures of governance (the political problem of legitimacy) and to make sense of their experience of suffering and injustice (the theological problem of evil)."[1]

---

1. Kotsko, *Neoliberalism's Demons*, 127.

It would be wrong to reduce Christianity to a system of morality, a move that the church itself has often made, especially its Protestant varieties, which often emphasize moral life over dogma, sacraments, and liturgy. Nevertheless, it is the moral vision of Judaism and Christianity that has resonated loudly cross the centuries, and percolated into modern, secular society. If the Greeks bequeathed to the West science, and the Romans law, Judeo-Christianity promoted social welfare, the sanctity of life, and peace (while also often radically straying from a path it laid down).[2] Though clearly possessing qualities of affirmation, Christian culture across the centuries is in many respects an indictment of the world. If we can realize with Louis Armstrong "what a wonderful world" we live in, we can also point to the squalor of children in Bangladesh working in grueling and toxic conditions stripping and dismantling decommissioned oil tankers. The modern world's discourse of human rights, our concern for victims, our desire to alleviate suffering—these owe a great deal to Jewish and Christian morality. Ever since Karl Löwith's *Meaning and History* (1949), considerable work has been devoted to arguing for or against the idea that Judaism and Christianity, and especially the biblical legacy, are loadstones for understanding and advancing contemporary political thought. "Thy kingdom come, Thy will be done, on earth as is it is heaven" (Matt 6:10) is the progenitor of modern social-justice movements.

That the bad exists is a simple, phenomenological observation. But the question remains, Why is there so much bad? And, at a psychological level, why, as the apostle Paul asks, do we often wind up doing (and perhaps even take perverse pleasure in doing) the very things we know we should hate? "I do not understand my own actions," admits Paul (Rom 7:15). By the time of Augustine's death, in 430 C.E., Christian dogmatic theology had arrived at an answer that would in large measure dominate Christian tradition and culture for centuries to come, especially in western, Latin Christendom: the suffering in the world is the result of *sin*, even more, of *original sin*. This was a move that intimately tied our

---

2. Julian the Apostate, emperor from 313 to 363 C.E., in a letter written in 362 C.E. to Arsacius, the high-priest of Galatia, specifies "measures to be taken for the relief of the poor" (hostels for strangers, food and drink for the poor servants of the priests and beggars); he goes on to say, "I order that one-fifth of this be used for the poor who serve the priests, and the remainder distributed by us to strangers and beggars. For it is disgraceful that, when no Jew ever has to beg, and the impious Galilaeans support not only their own poor but ours as well, all men see that our people lack aid from us." (Stern, *Greek and Latin Authors*, 1549–50).

experience of the bad to both freewill and a conception of an utterly depraved, innate disposition passed on through sexual reproduction. Sin, says, Paul, "dwells within me. For I know that nothing good dwells within me, that is, in my flesh. I can will what is right, but I cannot do it" (Rom 7:17–8). Often, we are unable to even will what is right. Because of sin's "hard-wired" quality, pulling ourselves up by our bootstraps cannot be the answer to sin: only an "unmerited" grace, delivered from on high, can deliver us from ills of our own creation.

For Buddhists, desire is the cause of suffering in the world; for Christians, the culprit is sin. It is only because the notion of sin has been, as I shall argue, thingified in a way that the notion of desire has not that we perceive the Buddhist and Christian perspectives as radically different. In many respects, subsequent iterations in Western culture describing what ails us can be viewed as secular formulations of the religious idea of sin. Social contract theorists such as John Locke and Thomas Hobbes propose a political theory based on an anthropology of a state of nature, a selfish war of all against all. For Freudians, unruly, unconscious drives are the wellspring of human suffering. For Marxists, the private ownership of the means of production is the source of disordered relationships and suffering. For some geneticists, genes are the source of aggressively violent, selfish behavior. For neoliberals, individual failures of will and refusal of hard work are the source of hardship and trouble. Any comprehensive system of thought needs to wrestle with why the world is "out of joint."[3]

Linking sin with the will, as do Paul and Augustine, makes us responsible for the world. "I didn't know," cannot get us off the hook. Sin is both the state we are in and the cause of that state. We are the reason for the bad we experience and witness. We send those children into the bowels of a ship to wade in oil-logged water to retrieve steel. Universalizing suffering in relation to the human will indicts and implicates us all. When Jesus accosts the group ready to stone to death an adulterous

---

3. The phrase "out of joint" is most famously associated with Shakespeare's *Hamlet* (Act I, Scene V). Upon encountering the ghost of his father and learning of the treachery behind his father's death, Hamlet exclaims: "O cursed spite, / That ever I was born to set it right! / The time is out of joint." The idea of the world or time being "out of joint" or misaligned can be found in various forms across different cultures and epochs. It's a powerful metaphor that captures a sense of disarray, chaos, or things not being as they should be. The etymology of the Pali term *dukkha* is often related to the image of a wheel that is off its axis or a potter's wheel that's out of balance. The term is commonly translated as "suffering," "unsatisfactoriness," "discontent," or "stress" in the context of Buddhist teachings. Life is akin to a misaligned or off-balanced wheel: it's going to be a bumpy ride.

woman (an act fully in keeping with the laws of the day) with the rightly famous words, "Let him who is without sin among you be the first to throw a stone at her" (John 8:7), we readily feel the power of this Jewish-Christian understanding of sin to modulate our behavior.[4] But there are many potential problems. Is the absolutist claim that there is "nothing good" about our flesh not a step too far? Moreover, Christian theology tends to implicate us in events that seem less sinful than simply sad. Is death itself, as Paul thought, the product of human sin? And what of the pain and suffering associated with a natural disaster? We may exploit the cheap labor of children, launch ground wars, and commit domestic violence, but we do not unleash a tornado on a trailer park or cancer cells on an infant.[5] We can separate these kinds of bad into the human-caused and the naturally occurring, but Christian thought, beginning with Paul, wants to yoke them together through ambitious interpretations of the implications of Adam's fall. Not just acts of the will or human nature but the entire cosmos stands in need of redemption.

A most serious difficultly with the Christian idea of sin is that experienced suffering, even of the accidental sort, is often interpreted as the result of the outcome of a sinful act or an inherent sinfulness. If sin leads to hurt and suffering, then when we witness someone or some group suffering, we may infer they must be in a state of sin or are being punished for past sins. This faulty reasoning, coupled with the notion that suffering is a way of making up for or correcting sin, leads Christian thought and culture down the tempting garden path of redemption through violence known as the doctrine of atonement—but we are getting way out in front of our skis.

---

4. This passage in the Gospel of John (7:53—8:11) is often referred to as the "Pericope Adulterae." It is one of the most debated passages in the New Testament regarding its authenticity. The earliest and most reliable Greek manuscripts of the Gospel of John do not contain this passage, and it is absent from many early translations and commentaries on John. These facts, plus stylistic differences and changes in the location of the pericope across different manuscripts, have led to the consensus that the story was not in John's original Gospel, though it's eventual appearance may reflect the oral transmission of a historical event. In any case, our approach must not ask whether it happened but, What does it mean? That the story found its way into tradition is historical and factual enough.

5. Of course, life in the Anthropocene, where our interventions in the natural world are generative of a climate emergency, complicates this simple distinction.

John Carpenter's *The Thing*

Critics instantly panned John Carpenter's 1982 horror film, *The Thing*, but time has been more discerning. The film has found a following, regularly making lists of the top horror films of all time, drawing the attention of film critics and cultural theorists, and garnering the sought-after status of cult classic.[6] The setting for the story is a scientific research station in Antarctica, a hostile environment condensing and amplifying the basic struggle to survive against natural forces that threaten to overwhelm us. The extreme conditions of Antarctica contextualize the film's questions about the lengths humans will go in a struggle for survival and at what point the cost to one's humanity becomes too great. As outside, so in—the research station is a pressure-cooked micro-society, though a strange one: no women are present, and the men are exclusively scientists or military personnel. As the internal pressure builds in the face of an unknown danger, the ties binding the men together (if they ever existed in the first place) quickly fray and snap. The film is grim, to say the least, which was a reason for its initial dismissal, but also its staying power. In its relentless drive to, as one critic puts it, expose "the fragility of our bodies, our identities, our relationships, and our system(s) of meaning,"[7] the film repels and fascinates. Rejected in part because out of step with the Reagan era's projection of hope—the efforts to strike a more positive and hopeful tone in the wake of the paranoia, violence, disorder, and cultural upheavals associated with the civil rights movement, the Vietnam War, and Watergate—*The Thing* would eventually find its audience among those who felt that Steven Spielberg's *E.T.* and *Forest Gump* were perhaps not the final word on human nature or human relations. In these regards, the film is not unlike the topic of this chapter, the notion of *sin*: despite a rough ride and attempts at outright dismissal by hopelessly upbeat optimists, sin has staying power.

Carpenter's *The Thing* may seem a stretch for a discussion of sin, but it is worth exploring. For one, film analysis casts us into an interpretive, symbolic, and narrative mindset, reminding us that before it was *doctrine* of the church, sin was thought about in terms of a *story*. Many assume the first appearance of sin in the Bible is in the tale of the garden of Eden, though this is not the case. Later Christian theologizing would apply the language of sin to the primal scene of

---

6. For a reception history, see Conolly, *Thing*.
7. Addison, "Film's Darkest Vision," 157.

prohibition-temptation-transgression-expulsion in the garden, but the first encounter in the Bible with the word/concept "sin" is the story of Cain and Abel, the story of a murder, a fratricide. Second, the film's themes are related to biblical and theological ideas about sin, exploring the vulnerability of the flesh and disordered human relations. Lastly, one of the foci of metaphor theory is the study of how metaphors become concretized or literalized; that is, how they become thing-like. Just what is "the thing," in the film? An "alien," yes. But seeing as there are no aliens, the film prompts us to ask, what is this alien being? A dangerous "animal"? A "foreign' body"? An "infection"? It isn't easy to put our finger on exactly what "the thing" wreaking havoc is, which is why we need metaphor. The "thing" calls out for interpretation, as does "sin."

The film opens with a prologue, a shot of empty space, panning from the stars to a spacecraft sailing towards the earth's southern pole: raise foreboding soundtrack and looming film title, *The Thing*, which erases the earth before transitioning to white title credits on black background. The second scene shifts to a helicopter erratically pursuing a husky across the frozen landscape of Antarctica, as a gunman fires wildly at the dog. The helicopter lands at an American research station, Station 4, the gunman moving from rifle to grenade in his crazed effort to kill the animal. In the ensuing chaos, a member of the research team is wounded, the gunman and pilot (members of a nearby Norwegian station) are killed, the helicopter set on fire, and the dog taken inside the station. There begins the detective work to determine the reasons behind the crazed effort to kill the dog.

A trip to the Norwegian station reveals a gruesome scene with contorted, violently killed bodily remains, and what appears to be a large ice sarcophagus, minus whatever creature it once housed. Back at the home station, the husky undergoes a disturbing transmogrification into an alien creature, while a second trip to the Norwegian site reveals an excavated spacecraft, buried under a hundred thousand years of ice, and a nearby second site where the Norwegians, we surmise, had discovered the creature encased in ice after it had been ejected from the craft as it crashed. The pieces can now be put together: the Norwegians had discovered the remains of an alien, brought the alien back to the camp, whereon upon it warmed up, became animated, and began assimilating human bodies by transmogrifying itself into the semblance of its hosts. One of the station's scientists conducts computer modelling, revealing some members of the crew are likely already infected and, further, that should the creature make it off the continent and reach a populated area, apocalypse is near certain.

The second half the film is a descent into paranoiac madness and death, framed around the effort to use a blood test to identify those people who had (either knowingly or unknowingly) become hosts for the creature. Mistrust, fear, isolation, a Hobbesian-like war of all against all follows. In the final scene, as the station burns, the remaining two team members eye each suspiciously, not knowing whether either has been infected, or knowing whether the creature has been killed. The only certainty is death (or, if they are infected, another long hibernation for the victor) as they sit suspiciously across from one other, waiting to "see what happens." The two are reduced to a state of complete inaction; inert, they sit and await their fate.

Just what is "the thing"? What does it represent or suggest? Elena Glasberg has drawn attention to the colonial dimensions of the story, reading it as a commentary on the role of state-sponsored science-military programs to inhospitable regions. The narrative contains an element of colonial contest between Norwegian and American stations, informed by desires not entirely different from the alien, whose presence and aims precede by several millennia the European and American efforts to occupy and control the frozen wasteland. The motif of war games informing the story quickly slides into irrationality and apocalyptic-scale destruction, fueled by an obsession with "the instrumentality of science to the state concerned with power, capital, and purely symbolic forms of colonization."[8] For many viewers, the film suggests a case of seeing the enemy, and realizing it is us.[9]

For Eric White, *The Thing* is an evolutionary narrative, the alien "thing" standing in for our face-to-face encounter with raw life, with that which relentlessly and endlessly morphs and devours in service of nothing but bare life, eliding attribution of any sort of meaning. The polymorphic "thing" is "capable of absorbing the human as but one among other morphological possibilities in its seemingly infinite repertoire." As such, it lives as

---

8. Glasberg, "Who Goes There?," 654.

9. A US Naval commander, Oliver Hazard Perry, in a battle against the Royal Navy in 1813, sent the communique "We have met the enemy, and they are ours." Years later, during the Vietnam War, the saying was used by cartoonist Walt Kelly in his comic strip *Pogo*, as a critique of American involvement in Vietnam.

> the embodiment of evolution. Hideously metamorphic, compounded of tentacles, insect and crustacean-like appendages, dismembered mammalian and especially human bodies, and covered in slime, this unclassifiable presence transgresses every attempt to impose a rational structure upon experience.[10]

Evolution as such cares not for us; it simply does what it does. Of course, in the film, we see "the thing," but it is meant to represent that which we can't see, name, label, or define, that which in its totality we are unable to comprehend. Mark Fisher, in contrast, drawing on Gilles Deleuze and Félix Guattari, interprets the film in relation to "a dark potentiality" inherent within the capitalist system. Here, the alien "thing" is taken to be capital and the idea of capital, which, like the creature, is a "monstrous, infinitely plastic entity, capable of metabolizing and absorbing anything with which it comes into contract."[11] The film can be read in terms of globalization, evolution, and capitalism, yes, but there are number of parallels between the film and the biblical story of first sin in Cain's murder of Abel.

In Genesis, the brothers are moved for some unnamed reason to make an offering to their God, Yahweh. Cain offers "the fruit of the ground" (that is, grain, meaning Cain is a farmer), while Abel offers "the firstling of his flock" (Abel, a herder, offers a slaughtered/sacrificed sheep). Yahweh, for no stated reason, approves of Abel's offering, but rejects Cain's, an act that angers Cain and generates fraternal envy. Yahweh then counsels Cain:

> Why are you angry, and why has your countenance fallen? If you do well, will you not be accepted? And if you do not do well, sin is crouching at the door; its desire is for you, but you must master it.

It is something of mystery as to why Cain's offering is viewed as a case of not "doing well," but likely has to do with Yahweh's perception of Cain's motivation, his intention to outdo his brother.

As with the research station, the action in Genesis occurs in an isolated setting, distanced from any obvious social institutions or broader cultural milieu. The cast in each is all male. The driver of each microdrama is strained relationships: in the film, fear of the other, in Genesis, envy or jealously of the other. In each story there is a competition.

---

10. White, "Erotics of Becoming," 399.
11. Fisher, *Capitalist Realism*, 6.

In the film, a colonial effort to control land descends into a war of all against all; in Genesis, the brothers compete for the approval and affection of Yahweh. In Genesis, sin is imaged as a feral animal that threatens to attack and overpower Cain. Sin, crouching at the door of Cain's tent, waits to pounce, moving from outside in, to inhabit body and soul, causing Cain to commit murder. In the film, "the thing" is imagined as a beastly figure that, after infecting its host, generates a contagion of disorder and violence. Yahweh, anticipating that Cain's act will trigger a similar violent contagion, vows heavy repercussions should anyone lay a hand on Cain: violence begets violence, and vengeance is best left in God's hands, not ours.

The "thing"/sin is imagined in these stories not so much as something we are but as something foreign to us to which we might fall prey, or perhaps a regression to an animal state from which we have emerged. Once the attack or regression occurs, the outcome is a transmogrification of the individual. As Yahweh states, sin "desires you," an image of carnality that fuses bodies; does the alien thing take on the visible body of its host, or the host that of the alien thing? Sin, in desiring Cain, is imagined as possessing a kind of agency bent on erasing one's humanity. Once "sin" or "it" or the "thing" manifests, two distinct bodies (Cain in the tent, the beast outside) becomes one unified "thingly" creature. The "thing's" ability to assimilate and corrupt individuals can be likened to the concept of sin. Just as sin can spread and corrupt the soul, the "thing" infiltrates and corrupts the body. The pervasive fear of contamination in the film can be seen as a reflection of the fear of moral corruption in religious terms.

Of course, there are differences in these similarities that resist any complete mapping of the stories. The film, for example, connects "the thing" to a blood infection. Though blood is a potent metaphor in the Bible and will become crucial to the Augustinian understanding of "original sin," in the Cain and Abel story sin is only indirectly linked to blood, in Abel's slaying of a sheep, and in Cain's murder of Abel. Still, the move in the film to images of infection and tainted blood point to a powerful, age-old metaphoric framework intertwining race and biology: difference and otherness are signified and marked by tainted blood or disease.[12]

Another significant difference is that the Genesis story is embedded in a promising moral framework, while the film is basically nihilistic about our possibilities. Film critics rightly emphasize the nature of the

---

12. In ancient texts, plagues and disease such as leprosy are commonly used to identify religious otherness and the source/origin of personal, moral, and social afflictions.

relationships among the crew as a key to the film. Even before the creature arrives at the station, the "team" members are anything but a team: they are highly isolated, atomistic individuals; we know little to nothing of their personal backgrounds or character; their interactions betray no level of friendship, affection, or intimacy. R. J. MacReady (played by Kurt Russell) is the film's protagonist, a helicopter pilot who is less the de facto leader of the group than the focus of the narrative as the crisis unfolds. It may be tempting to frame the film in terms of sacrifice and redemption. Characters in the film make sacrifices for the greater good, mildly reminiscent of Christian themes of sacrifice, especially the sacrifice of Jesus for humanity's sins. MacReady's leadership and his willingness to risk his life could be seen in a Christ-like light, though the film's darker tone and ambiguous ending complicate any straightforward allegorical reading. The pressure of the situation does not lead to the development of character; character study seems far from Carpenter's aim, which is, rather, to depict a "growing indistinguishability of the monstrous from the human."[13] The film works to erase the personality of each crew member. No one emerges as the clear leader of the group—a status acquired by whoever happens to hold the gun or flamethrower; no aspirations to loyalty or care emerge in the face of chaos. The blood test used to identify those infected by "the thing" reduces humanness to merely genetically shared tissue—seemingly different from that of the creature, but still nothing more than "98 cents worth of chemicals,"[14] chemicals bent (as is the creature) on nothing more than survival. Civilization and culture are revealed to be thin and fragile; monstrousness first lurks, then springs; when it does, it becomes us, and we it.

Genesis is more hopeful. Yahweh calls upon Cain to "master" the beast's desire for him, a sign that such mastery may be possible. In the fratricide, sin is anticipated, a command issued, and a plea made for an act of will and a spirit of care to ward off murder. Moreover, Abel's blood "cries out" to Yahweh from the ground. Cain's unanswered question—"Am I my brother's keeper?"—leads the reader to ponder the inevitable misery of lives when our acts are detached from an ethos of care. A

13. Cumbow, *Order in the Universe*, 111.

14. This estimate of the value of the chemicals comprising the human body is discussed in a 1922 issue (May 6) of *The Journal of the American Medical Association*. The ninety-eight-cent value was also famously repeated in a 1924 lecture delivered by Charles Mayo to the American College of Surgeons in New York. The matter was discussed in a *TIME* magazine article from November, 8, 1926, titled "Ninety-Eight Cents."

through line in the history of Christian theology are debates over whether and how Yahweh's words can be embraced: Can sin be mastered? The generally accepted answer from Christian theology has been, No—at least, not without the grace of God. The very move to attempt to meet God on his own level, to rise to his call—"You shall be holy because I am holy" (1 Pet 1:16, echoing earlier Jewish texts)—has been mostly viewed as hubris, especially in western, Catholic Christianity. In the eastern, Orthodox tradition, the formula has been: God became man so that man could become God. The western, Augustinian-inspired tradition of Christian thought has been more reticent (even though Augustine, too, makes room for the notion of divinization). For Luther, salvation is the free gift of grace, entirely independent of one's holiness (or works). For Calvin, our nature is so corrupted that we are incapable of even faith, which means that our salvation is predetermined. Of course, the distance between not rising in anger to strike one's brother dead and the salvation of an eternal soul stained by a contracted congenital defect are quite some cognitive distance apart.

Carpenter's film winds us back to the monstrousness that resides at the core of human being. Blumenberg observes how logocentric thinking—in philosophy, art, and science—is grounded in "leisure and dispassion in viewing the world," but such a disposition toward the world is "already [the] result of that millenniums-long work of myth itself, which told of the monstrous as something that is far is the past and has been forced back to the edge of the world."[15] In Carpenter's hands, the monstrous thing returns: monstrousness is the experience of the inability to recognize, identify, and name the unnameable thing. Stories, claims Blumenberg, are told to kill—to kill time, but mostly, they kill fear. But Carpenter aims to scare us, and the chief reason the film is scary is because, as Blumenberg notes, "All trust in the world begins with names, in connection with which stories can be told."[16] All we have here is a nameless "thing" and naming it sin (or colonialism or capitalism or evolution) is but a weak attempt to denude the "thing's" power to erase humanity (figuratively and literally). But weak attempts are all we have.

---

15. Blumenberg, *Work on Myth*, 26.
16. Blumenberg, *Work on Myth*, 35.

"Darwinism of Words"

The story of Cain and Abel is fixed in a text, but, however surprising it may be—in Mesopotamian stories the shepherd kills the farmer—we must presume this story of fratricide rests upon a thoroughly worked-over set of images and metaphors, thousands or tens of thousands of years old that, after a long (and irretrievable) history, distilled into the naming of the thing so powerful as to lead to the murdering of one's brother. In the story, we find a zoomorphism, with sin *crouching* at Cain's tent door, an image that suggest the earliest conceptualization of sin drew upon the evolutionary experience of fearing and evading dangerous predators, coupled with the notion that to harm someone is to regress from the state of human to animal (even though animals generally do not harm or kill conspecifics).

The abstract word/concept "sin" is an example of what Blumenberg calls the "Darwinsim of words." For Blumenberg, the stories and images that have come down to us are as much the result of a mind-bendingly long process of cultural testing, optimization, and selection as they are the result of a priestly class protectively handing down revered tales (this view should not be confused with "social Darwinism," which purports to describe the selection for survival of specific social groups). Unlike science from antiquity, age-old myths can be fruitfully read today because they retain the relevance and significance that encouraged their survival in the first place. The story of Cain and Abel seems as fresh as when it was invented—and this is because it wasn't invented in the way that a work of art is invented, by an inspired artist. As Blumenberg observes, "If there is anything at all that deserves the attribution of the phrase 'It stays with me,' it is the archaic imagination, whatever it may have been that provided its initial material."[17] The story is simply there, in the cultural record, the result of a long period of reception and transmission taking place long before the age of writing.

Blumenberg recognizes there exists a plurality of ways of looking at or considering the world, and he differentiates among the theoretical/scientific, dogmatic, mystical, and mythological modes. That the myths spread across geography and time contain a standard corpus of stock images and themes points to a relatively consistent set of challenges and responses facing the human being. As Blumenberg notes, if myths were

---

17. Blumenberg, *Work on Myth*, 60.

merely early and poor attempts at scientific rationality, as Enlightenment rationalists old and new presume,

> they would have been disposed of automatically at the latest when science, with its increasing sense of accomplishment, made its entrance. The opposite was the case. Nothing surprised the promoters of the Enlightenment more, and left them standing more incredulously before the failure of what they thought were their ultimate exertions, than the survival of the contemptible old stories—the continuation of work on myth.[18]

Myth has its own sphere of legitimacy and relevance. While the theoretical attitude aims to reduce or extract subjective valuation down to zero, myth recognizes that the world has "valences," its images may be fantastical, but they possess the "status of reality," as well as inexhaustible depths. Enlightenment rationalism failed to "appreciate these intellectual and emotional needs"[19] informing the rise of and ongoing work on myth. Myth possesses "pregnance, as opposed to indifference," and, like the aesthetic object, part of the definition of significance includes "the way it emerges from the diffuse surrounding field of possibilities."[20] We can almost feel a tension in our muscles as Cain prepares to spring into violent action.

Here is a scientific approach to murder: "In humans, abnormal aggression is a hallmark of neuropsychiatric disorders and can be elicited by environmental factors acting on an underlying genetic susceptibility."[21] It isn't clear to me that this is a better understanding of, say, domestic violence than that offered in Cain and Abel. I seriously doubt the existence of a "murder gene." Certainly, I think, the story of the brothers can move us to reflection more than this genetic theory of aggression. Genetics is a classic case of what Graham Harman terms "undermining," the attempt to explain a thing by reference to that thing's elemental stuff. It has long been a principle in philosophic and religious traditions that things cannot (in some instances, should not!) be reduced to their parts without remainder: the whole is greater than the sum of its parts. A

---

18. Blumenberg, *Work on Myth*, 274. Among today's prominent rationalists are Richard Dawkins and Sam Harris, each of whom seem constitutionally unable to think symbolically or mythologically (and this in spite of Dawkin's advancing the view of "selfish" genes, clearly a metaphorical and mythological idea).
19. Blumenberg, *Work on Myth*, 287.
20. Blumenberg, *Work on Myth*, 69.
21. Anholt and Mackay, "Genetics of Aggression."

second approach to knowledge Harman dubs "overmining," the attempt to understand a thing in terms of its function and effects in an environment. Again, there is often a tendency to reduce things upwards to their effects and functions. A hammer is a tool; and tools are used to make us more comfortable; so, a hammer is that device that assists humans in being more comfortable. Idealism and social constructivism, which hold, in effect, that there is no independent reality outside of thought or systems of language, discourse and power are classic examples of overmining. Each approach, argues Harman, slips past the reality of the object itself, one moving "downward" to bits of stuff, the other moving "upwards" to the total environment. Undermining has trouble understanding emergent properties (a molecule of H_2O isn't wet, yet water—a large collection of H_2O molecules—is), and it tends to reduce complex things to merely simple parts. A most extreme case would be reducing the human being to a collection of atoms. Overmining has difficulties making sense of change; if there is nothing but events and processes "everything would be identical with its current and actual state of relations with everything else." Overmining also tends to overlook that though each object is related to the total environment, it nevertheless has its own internal integrity and consistency.

A table, writes Harman, is "neither the pieces of which it is made nor its effect on its users." Rather, it is a table. If knowledge, writes Harman, "is an attempt to reduce the table either downward or upward, then we can approach the table [itself] only through something that is not a form of knowledge." This "something," suggests Harman, is "art," by which he means we cannot know the world directly, but "must approach it obliquely in the manner of Socrates or Picasso."[22] Undermining (considering what a thing is) and overmining (considering what a thing does) are two valuable approaches to knowledge, yet they leave out a good deal of our cognitive and affective life. Philosophy, art, religion, music, ritual—these are not knowledge pursuits but activities: philosophy is not knowledge or wisdom but the love of wisdom; religion is not positive knowledge of the world but the effort to "bind together" sorrow and joy, meaning and significance, as the Latin roots of the word suggest. A corpus of stories (myths) is an object in Harman's enlarged sense of the term. Stories cannot be entirely reduced downwards to the words comprising them, or upwards to the forces or effects the story produces. The stories themselves

---

22. See Harman, "Undermining, Overmining and Duomining."

remain. Though Blumenberg does not use the term *archetypal*, he clearly shares something of C. G. Jung's notion of myth's universal proclivities: "The fundamental patterns of myths are simply so sharply defined, so valid, so binding, so gripping in every sense that they convince us again and again and still present themselves as the most useful material for any search for how matters stand, on a basic level, with human existence."[23] Myth speaks to us because it has served and continues to serve basic needs. Archetypes, such as the pursuit of wisdom or descent into madness or the experience of deep loss may not be physical components of the brain, but they are objects of thought and experience.

Blumenberg's historical presentation has mythic dimensions: in the beginning, facing overwhelming existential objectless anxiety, myth stepped in to contract the world into valences of significance, marked initially by the "fearsome," materializing, concretizing, distilling the anxiety inducing absolutism of reality into smaller bite-sized pieces. In contracting and parceling out reality as such into nameable "things"—kami, spirits, jinns, demons, angels, pixies, karma, chi, mana, furies, eros, sin—we were then able to develop techniques (stories, rites, taboos, spells) with which we could wrestle, avoid, tame, and, if not master, at least relate to these objects, powers, or quasi-persons. As Blumenberg describes the process, "something is 'put forward' to make what is not present into an object of averting, conjuring up, mollifying, or power-depleting action."[24] What we experience as superior power, we understand as particular powers (as entities, beings, substances, forces) generating those experiences. And, as it was in the beginning, so shall it ever be—the absolutism of reality rests at the core of the human experience—hence the persistence and legitimacy of the mythological way of regarding the world.[25] One of the powers that the received wisdom of myth advises us to watch out for is *sin*.

Sin in the Cain and Abel tale is akin to a root power or potential against which we must attain some level of mastery, lest that power undo all that we have or may become. Struggle against a force that threatens to overwhelm us is a basic, though highly generalized motif, capable of

---

23. Blumenberg, *Work on Myth*, 150–51.
24. Blumenberg, *Work on Myth*, 6–7.
25. No none has ever, and no one will ever, cast their eyes upon the "libido," though this is no argument against its reality. Lest one think such thinking is far in the past, consider the fetishized, anthropomorphic nature of talk about "the economy" and "market forces."

re-presentation in a variety of ways: an alien invasion, a pandemic, a natural disaster. In the foundational story of Cain and Abel, the word/concept *sin* is already there, part of the past's past, a cultural inheritance, a way of taking hold of the world and responding to it. Sin, in finding its way into the canonical text, is the visible remainder of a long historical-cultural process. The notion of an "ancient sin" is common in biblical cultures, pointing to a fracture in the unity of human and natural worlds, a dislocation marking, in effect, the beginning of human time.

Is sin then invented or discovered? Is it a real thing? Does it exist? Or is it merely an idea, maybe even a bad idea? It ought to be obvious by now that I reject such an approach. I am endeavoring to break down the tried and trusted move to bifurcate reality into the "really real" and the "merely imagined." It isn't that there are only ideas, only concepts, only words. Indeed, there is an extra-linguistic reality, but we know it through language. This is as true of the word "sin" as the word "God." Sin is a named thing/factor/power in a story, later it becomes an isolated idea, concept, theory, and piece of dogma. Sin, in other words, becomes ontologized, it becomes thingified—but even abstract, metaphysical ideas require metaphors if they are to be conceptualized at all. Here, language can lead us forward but also astray, for sin is no "it," no "thing." Sin cannot be weighed, though it can be imagined as a weight bearing down on us; you cannot detect sin in our blood, though it can be imagined as an infection; you cannot cut sin out like a tumor, but it can be imagined as a cancer; you cannot hedge sin with barbed wire, though it can be imagined as trespass; you cannot count sin like counting coins, but it can be imagined as a debt. If sin is a metaphor for some constitutive, though ultimately unnameable, thing, it is not a substantive, material reality but more of a virtual reality, though no less real for being so (the *mind* too cannot be localized in space, weighed, or measured, but neither—to my mind—can *mind* be reduced to merely another word for *brain*). Part of the history of thinking about and practically dealing with sin is its reification or concretizing into an abstract concept that aims to corral a related set of behaviors into a kind of substantive, material-thing-like entity, so that it can be engaged in some fashion.

Much the same can be said of the word, "God." Critics might incline to argue there is no God, just historically differing ideas about God. This quasi-nominalist point of view holds that words and concepts are nothing but names, with no connection to actual reality—only physical matter exists, and a word without a corresponding material object is nothing at all. The caution is worth keeping in mind, but the concept or word *God* nevertheless possesses, at the very least, a pragmatic reality; it is the absolute metaphor through which a significant portion of humanity—even the atheist!—has understood itself for the past several thousand years. What is the relationship between phenomenology and ontology, between the varied conceptions of God across several millennia and a more robust reality for those conceptions, beyond being mere inventions of imagination and language? To say this is a difficult question is to point to the entire history of western metaphysics; a comprehensive account of this story lies outside these pages, but we will take-up the name of God in a later chapter. What I would suggest is that one possible route to is to acknowledge the nominalist critique, while at the same time developing a more comprehensive sense of what constitutes an object, as with the recent forms of speculative realism and object-oriented ontologies. To this way of thinking, gender, democracy, fascism, traffic, and sin are as much objects as are stones, sailboats, hammers, parakeets, and envelopes. Again, with a nod to Jung and to cite Graham Harman, one of the leading proponents of object-oriented ontology, it is a false assumption to suppose that "everything that exists must be physical."[26] Sin is at least as real as "the general will" or the "invisible hand," the mysterious entities upon which modern democracy and the free market rest.

Sin's Trajectory

In biblical tradition, sin is first a potential waiting to spring and erase our humanity. Later, sin is mapped onto the macro forces of war, conquest, and poverty, with a logic that connects suffering and sin. For Paul, the author of the earliest Christian writings, sin takes on anthropological and cosmic dimensions, understood as the general or prime cause of what ails us: sin comes to be embedded in the very fleshiness of our existence. A few centuries later, Augustine would add to Paul's thought, identifying sex as the vehicle for the transmission of sin (this move would mold the Catholic Church's later distinction between sin as a personal act and sin as something contracted through procreation). In the trajectory of sin as a concept we see the development of not only theology but of robust

26. Harman, *Object-Oriented Ontology*, 25. Harman understands "objects" to include more than hard, substantive, physical reality. Democracy, God, and the Dutch East India Company (the latter a focus of Harman's inquiries) are each objects in Harman's sense.

social institutions to deal with the problematic presence of both sin and sin's wake. In the Hebrew Bible, protective fences around sin take the form of law, educative stories of transgression, and the ritual sacrifice of animals. Though Christianity will reject animal sacrifice, the problem of sin is paramount to the development of Christianity. A dominant thread in Christian theology will come to see the entire complex of incarnation-crucifixion-resurrection as an answer to the problem of original sin, the fundamental myth of a good portion of the Christian world, while ascetic practices of self-harm and generally negative attitudes towards the body will replace efforts of mastering and sublimating beastly propensities with their extirpation or extermination, a move that Friedrich Nietzsche would, centuries later, critique and reject with the utmost passion.

Again, we recall the words of Blumenberg: "The demise of metaphysics calls metaphorics back to its place." The invention of a general term, the concept, is the line dividing mythological and metaphysical thinking. Faust is a character in Goethe's play of that name. But the adjective "faustian" is now part of the English language. The move entails a certain rationalization and abstracting from a character in a lengthy and complex narrative to a potential personality trait, definable in less than a dozen words. Blumenberg first set himself the task of investigating the role of metaphor in the construction of concepts, with the latter being viewed as more rigorously demanding and precise, and hence, closer to the truth. But he soon realized that key concepts are never truly free of their metaphorical substrates and that, should the concept become troubled or ineffectual, it can regain a second life through our digging into the soils out of which it grew. This is our task here with the notion of sin. Sin as thing or state (the doctrinal/metaphysical view) is different from sin as impetus or act (the moral/mythological view). The formation of beliefs (dogmas, ontologies, metaphysical substances) transpires by their replacing stories, but also in the viewing of those stories as inferior, because stories cannot be validated in the same fashion as can a proposition. Ideas involve a reduction of the ambiguities and complexities of narrative, anecdote, and myth. Christian dogma and doctrine (such as original sin) combine philosophy and myth, but the work of the philosophical mind eventually dissolves myth into the pure idea: not Faust but the Faustian, not beings but Being, not sinners but Sin. To get at the meanings, as well as the assets and liabilities of a concept or doctrine, we need to unpack its metaphorical basis and its implications and entailments.

Chapter 5

The Metaphorics of Sin

> You shall do no wrong in judgment, in measures of length or weight or quantity. You shall have just balances, just weights, a just ephah, and a just hin:[1] I am the LORD your God, who brought you out of the land of Egypt. And you shall observe all my statutes and all my ordinances, and do them: I am the LORD.
>
> —Leviticus 19:35–37

> For my iniquities have gone over my head;
> they weigh like a burden too heavy for me.
>
> —Psalm 38:4

THE CHRISTIAN UNDERSTANDING OF sin is deeply indebted to the elaboration of the concept in the books of the Hebrew Bible. The English "sin" is a translation of the Hebrew word האטח (*hat'ah*), which means something like "to miss the mark." Etymological analysis connects the word to orienteering. We are to imagine setting off on foot to some location, but not arriving at the proper spot. In this simple etymology we have a rather comprehensive worldview. Life is understood as a journey, with a destination in mind, but we get sidetracked, take the wrong path, lose our way, fall in with troublemakers, and so on—the story of Pinocchio: *sin as waywardness*. In keeping with the journey metaphor, one implication is that

---

1. In biblical Hebrew, an *epah* is a unit of measuring grain, like a bushel. A *hin* is a fluid measurement of around four liters. The point is fair measurement and exchange of goods.

wrong paths can be retraced or abandoned, and the right path located or relocated.[2] Waywardness is developed within biblical texts through the images of being "a stranger in a strange land" (Exod 2:22) and wilderness wanderings in search of possessing the land promised to Abram's descendants (Gen 12:7), "a land which flows with milk and honey" (Num 14:8). The "milk and honey" imagery is also found in Exodus, where it is observed that this rich land is home to "Canaanites, Hittites, Amorites, Perizzites, Hivites and Jebusites" (Exod 3:8). The end to wandering and homelessness will come at the cost of ethnic cleansing with the aid of the covenantal "God of the fathers" (Exod 3:15).

Covenant

But sin as waywardness is seldom used in the Hebrew Bible. Sin typically refers to an offence committed against someone with whom the offender has a relationship; more broadly, the term covers violations of the 613 commandments of Jewish law. The idea of sin exists in relation to a norm, a law, a principle that is violated. The norm of these norms is the people's covenant relationship with God. Cain and Abel, Joseph and his brothers, and other stories—these can be read on multiple levels, including as metaphors of covenant, with "reliability, faithfulness, and believability" being "the [main] attributes of the God of the Covenant of the Old Testament."[3] Overwhelmingly, the key rhetorical mode of the Hebrew Bible as whole revolves around a people's covenant with the God of Abraham, Isaac, and Jacob (the "fathers") and their descendants. Joseph's last words reiterate to his brothers the covenant relationship: "And Joseph said to his brothers, 'I am about to die; but God will visit you, and bring you up out of this land to the land which he swore to Abraham, to Isaac, and to Jacob'" (Gen 50:24). Appearing to Moses at (or as) a burning bush, the Lord announces his provenance: "And he said, 'I am the God of your father, the

---

2. I cannot resist here a passage from C. S. Lewis's *Case for Christianity*, 24, where he writes: "We all want progress. But progress means getting nearer to the place where you want to be. And if you have taken a wrong turning then to go forward does not get you any nearer. If you are on the wrong road progress means doing an about-turn and walking back to the right road and in that case the man who turns back soonest is the most progressive man."

3. Blumenberg, *St. Matthew Passion*, 231.

God of Abraham, the God of Isaac, and the God of Jacob.' And Moses hid his face, for he was afraid to look at God" (Exod 3:6).[4]

Covenant, Yahweh, and Elohim

Etymologically, "covenant" means a "coming together"; in practical usage, the context was a formal legal and political agreement, with its incumbent duties, rights, and privileges. A common type was the suzerainty treaty, a formal agreement in the ancient Near East between a dominant power (the suzerain) and a lesser, dependent state or vassal. These treaties were common during the second millennium B.C.E. and were used to establish and regulate relationships between powerful empires and their subordinate regions or states. The suzerainty treaty outlined the obligations and responsibilities of both parties, typically emphasizing the vassal's loyalty and service to the suzerain in exchange for protection and benefits. These types of treaties and contracts became profound metaphors for the relationship between God and his people. By drawing on familiar structures from their everyday lives, the Israelites could grasp the nature of their relationship to the divine in concrete, relatable terms. The covenantal dimension remains central to Judaism,[5] and has a place in Christianity and Islam.

John Dominic Crossan delves into the concept of covenant relationships, paying special attention to the dynamic tension between divine promises and human obligations. In the Bible, God makes significant promises to his people, pledging blessings, protection, and a hopeful future. If they are bound to him, he is also bound to them. Divine promises are not unilateral; they demand a response from humanity. The covenant requires that God's people live in accordance with his laws and principles. This includes moral behavior, worship practices, and a commitment to social justice. Thus, the covenant is a two-way relationship, with both God and humanity having responsibilities to uphold. Central

---

4. This is not to ignore that there is a powerful universal dimension of the Hebrew Bible, with a concern to transcend narrow, ethnic particularisms.

5. There exists a range of interpretations of covenant within Judaism; the worst, in my view, are those that literalize the covenant relationship with respect to the possession of land. With the rise of rabbinic Judaism following the destruction of the second temple, the great "achievement the rabbinic imagination protected God's covenant from the destruction that befell his holy land and temple and permitted the process of covenantal revision, that is, *halakhah*, that has continued down to our own day" (Eisen, "Covenant," 109).

to Crossan's discussion is the concept of *sanction*, which encompasses both positive and negative consequences based on adherence to the covenant. Positive sanctions refer to the blessings and rewards promised by God for faithfulness and obedience. On the other hand, negative sanctions involve curses and punishments resulting from disobedience and breach of the covenant. These sanctions underscore the seriousness of the covenant, serving as powerful motivators for the Israelites to adhere to their commitments.[6] The concept of sin, then, most specifically applies to covenantal infractions, and an infraction, a violation, requires a response, which can range from the violence of physical punishment to the generation of a contrite and reoriented heart.

The English "the LORD God" is a translation of the phrase "Yahweh Elohim" (יְהוָה אֱלֹהִים), where "Yahweh" (יְהוָה) is the personal name of God. Yahweh Elohim is a name and, as it were, a job description, having the same grammatical structure as "John the Baker." The *Tetragrammaton* (four letters) "Yahweh" is the most sacred word in the Hebrew Bible and is not to be voiced. Pious Jews then (as now) when reading these letters replace "Yahweh" with "Adonai," from which is derived the English "Lord." Elohim (אֱלֹהִים) is a more general term for God or gods.

Yahweh and Elohim are used to refer to God in the literature of ancient Israel, with each carrying distinct connotations and contexts. Yahweh, the personal and chiefly covenantal name of God, appears approximately 6,800 times and is deeply intertwined with the direct, practical relationship between God and the Israelites. It is with respect to this covenantal relationship that Yahweh and his people interact; often, these exchanges entail violence on the part of Yahweh, either participating in violence on behalf of his people or using violence as a form of corrective action to educate or discipline his wayward people. The plagues in Egypt, the conquest of Canaan, and various divine judgments against Israel and its enemies are all narrated with Yahweh as the agential force. These acts of violence are typically framed within the context of enforcing the covenant, defending the chosen people, and ensuring the fulfillment of divine promises.

In contrast, Elohim, used around 2,600 times, emphasizes God's universal power and majesty. This term is often associated with broader and more abstract concepts of divinity, such as in the creation narrative of Gen 1, where Elohim is depicted as the powerful, transcendent

---

6. See Crossan, *How to Read*.

creator ordering chaos in fashioning the world. Whereas the heavenly bodies are, in Hellenistic cosmology, divine beings or objects, these are de-divinized in Genesis, with Elohim as the transcendent source of all things. The use of Elohim tends to be less personal and less covenantal compared to Yahweh, as well tending to highlight God's overarching sovereignty and justice. While Elohim is involved in acts of judgment, the narratives typically emphasize divine majesty and creative power rather than explicit violence. In the realm of historical biblical criticism, scholars generally agree that the different names of God (Yahweh and Elohim) reflect distinct textual strata, each with its own theological and political nuances. This understanding is central to the classical Documentary Hypothesis, which proposes that the Pentateuch—the first five books of the Hebrew Bible—is a compilation of four main sources, each contributing unique perspectives and styles.

The Yahwist (J) source, identified by its use of the name Yahweh, is characterized by vivid, anthropomorphic portrayals of God. This source derives from the southern Israelite kingdom of Judah. The Yahwist source tends to reflect the theological and political concerns of Judah, embedding narratives that underscore the significance of Jerusalem and its religious practices focused on sacrificial temple worship. In contrast, the Elohist (E) source predominantly uses the name Elohim until the divine name Yahweh is revealed in Exod 3. This source is marked by a more abstract depiction of God, who communicates through dreams, visions, and angels. It is associated geographically and politically with the northern kingdom of Israel and highlights the role of prophets and the critique of centralized power. The Deuteronomist (D) source also uses the name Yahweh, and has an emphasis on covenant, law, and centralized worship in Jerusalem. Found primarily in the book of Deuteronomy, this source advocates for the centralization of worship and adherence to a covenantal code, mirroring the religious reforms of King Josiah in the seventh century B.C.E. Finally, the Priestly (P) source, which uses Elohim in the early chapters of Genesis and switches to Yahweh after the divine name is revealed in Exodus 6, is noted for its formal, liturgical style. This source focuses on genealogies, dates, and ritual laws, underscoring the centrality of the Jerusalem temple and the priesthood. Yahweh is more commonly linked with explicit acts of violence due to the covenantal context, partly because the term appears far more frequently than Elohim. Elohim tends to represent the universal and majestic aspects of God, emphasizing creation and sovereign power.[7]

If we refract the prominent covenantal dimension of the Hebrew Bible through Blumenberg's philosophical anthropology, what might we observe? A covenant relationship entails mutual duties and responsibilities, but the underlying interest is in matters of reliability, trust, and stability. As Blumenberg notes in his *St. Matthew Passion*, those familiar with their Bible recognize "the LORD" (Yahweh) as the unfailing rescuer, embodying the ultimate source of security and reliability. This divine name is not merely a title but a profound assertion of God's enduring presence and faithfulness. In a world fraught with uncertainty and existential threats, the invocation of the LORD reassures believers of a dependable, steadfast divine presence.

The genius and terror of this conception of the divine-human relationship is that it opens avenues for interaction and negotiation:

> The *mysterium tremendum* is thereby [through covenant] rendered accessible and, to a degree, comprehensible. Israel cannot penetrate the fire and cloud of God's presence, but the people can know what God wants of them. Even more remarkably, they can rest confident that God will submit to the seeming indignity of human conversation. He will negotiate, with Abraham, over the destruction of Sodom, and agree, after the pleading of Moses, to pardon the transgressions of Israel.[8]

The problem is what happens when God appears to be in no hurry to fulfill his side of the contract, especially in the context of defeat in war, conquest, and colonization, as we find in numerous psalms.

> How long, O LORD? Will you forget me for ever?
> How long will you hide your face from me?
> How long must I bear pain in my soul,
> and have sorrow in my heart all the day?
> How long shall my enemy be exalted over me? (Ps 13:1–2)

---

7. These distinctions are broadly accepted. As an introduction, see Richard Elliott Friedman's *Who Wrote the Bible?* Moshe Weinfeld argues that the ethical monotheism present in the Elohist (E) source, with its focus on moral behavior and the ethical and social justice implications of the covenant relationship, represent a significant theological development in the history of religions in the ancient Near Eastern and Mediterranean worlds. See Weinfeld's *Social Justice*.

8. Eisen, "Covenant," 108.

> How long, O Lord, wilt thou look on?
> Rescue me from their ravages,
> my life from the lions! (Ps 35:17)

Such psalms narrate a people's suffering and steadfast hope, but also introduce a worry. "How long" will it be until God fulfills his side of the relationship? Will he in fact make good on his obligations? How long can one retain faith in the absence of action on part of the Almighty? Here, as we shall see, the length of delay was interpreted as an indicator of the measure of sin.

A version of this conundrum revisits the earliest of Christianity, in the so-called "delay of the parousia," the postponement or perceived delay in the expected return of Christ, which early Christians anticipated would occur imminently, within their lifetimes. As time passed and Jesus did not return, this delay became a significant theological issue for the early Christian community. A theodicy (an explanation or conception of suffering) had to develop that could account for the absence of God's action in fulfilling the covenant in lived space and time, by delaying or postponing fulfillment indefinitely, to a "point" outside of history; or, alternatively, our conception of God must change. It is the incredible torque around God's apparent unwillingness or inability to make good on his promises in a reasonable timeframe that Jack Miles takes up in the second volume of his "biography" of the biblical God, *Christ: A Crisis in the Life of God*.

The Iniquity of David

The terms *sin* and *iniquity* are basically homonyms, with the latter perhaps retaining the sense of wickedness and malevolence that mark a harmful act as especially egregious. A classic example of sin/iniquity is the story of King David, in 2 Samuel.

From his rooftop, David sees Bathsheba, the wife of his Hittite soldier Uriah, bathing. David lusts after her and, with Uriah away at war, he takes her to his bed. To cover the tracks of the ensuing pregnancy, David orders Uriah to return to the capital from his military campaigns, encourages Uriah to sleep with Bathsheba, and then promptly orders him back to the front, secretly instructing Uriah's superior to place Uriah directly in harm's way, whereupon he is killed. In Dante's rungs or levels of hell, the centermost circle is filled not with murderers but rather the treacherous.

In the ninth circle of hell, Dante witnesses the sufferings of Judas Iscariot, betrayer of Jesus, and Brutus and Cassius, who betrayed Caesar. Just above the treacherous are the fraudsters. David's affair with Bathsheba is a transgression of a moral code and most certainly wrong; but what makes David lecherous and a candidate for the ninth ring is his abuse of power, the deceit, duplicity, and betrayal at the core of his acts.[9]

My simple summary of the story in no way matches the subtleties of the original in conveying David's monstrousness; for example, in his return to the front, Uriah bears the sealed letter written by David with the instructions detailing how Uriah is to be killed. David's actions, thankfully, "displeased the Lord," though the Lord's response is chilling: Yahweh elects to kill the son that Bathsheba bore as punishment for David's "utter contempt of the Lord." The text is silent on how Bathsheba might have felt about that decision. Yahweh makes David witness his neighbors having sex with his other wives, and the child is stricken with a sickness and dies. David begins to pray and fast as acts of avoidance, but to no avail.

The impulse for revenge and a logic of violence for violence plagues Jewish and Christian tradition. In books such as Exodus, Numbers, and Deuteronomy, we read that Yahweh is slow to anger and forgives transgressions; on the other hand, for the guilty Yahweh makes promise to visit punishment on the sons and even generational descendants of the wrongdoer: "The Lord is slow to anger, and abounding in steadfast love, forgiving iniquity and transgression, but he will by no means clear the guilty, visiting the iniquity of fathers upon children, upon the third and upon the fourth generation" (Num 14:18). One could argue that such passages are personified casual analysis, where the gross transgression of social norms creates a wake of harm that ripples across multiple generations, as in the case, say, with the legacy of slavery in the history of the United States. Understood in such fashion, God is not a vengeful, transcendent other-than-human actor but the personification of an understanding how sin infects and persists as a power in the social body across generations. Nevertheless, critical reflection on the morality of a wrathful God visiting harm on the offspring of wrongdoers is surely behind those other Hebrew texts that repudiate attribution of the sins

---

9. Dante describes Circle nine in *Inferno*, cantos XXXI–XXXIV: "Oh you who are the lowest dregs of all, // Put in this place which it hard to speak of, // Better if here you had been sheep or goats!" (XXXII, 13–15, Oxford World Classics). Here, we find Judas, Brutus, and the giant Nimrod, among others. King David, however, rests in paradise, as one of the six lights of the eye of the eagle of divine knowledge and justice.

of the fathers to sons, which is as much to say that Yahweh undergoes changes. For example, in Deuteronomy, a book that echoes Numbers in repeatedly warning Yahweh will inflict pain on the descendants of those who transgress his law, we also find counter claims: "The fathers shall not be put to death for the children, nor shall the children be put to death for the fathers; every man shall be put to death for his own sin" (24:16). We need not contort ourselves into knots attempting to reconcile these two positions to save God's integrity and consistency.[10] God is an idea or absolute metaphor, often personified as a character, one who changes across time and place, and Scripture is an amalgam of texts, cut and pasted together, sometimes in inconsistent fashion, though not necessarily without an interpretive through line.

The remainder of the events recounted in 2 Samuel are politically complex. The short version is that David manages to prevail, and 2 Samuel closes with David's praise to the LORD for delivering him from the "hand of all his enemies." In the middle of that praise, the author of 2 Samuel (or a subsequent editor) is at pains to erase from the figure of David any contact with sin, putting these words into David's mouth:

> The LORD has dealt with me according to my righteousness;
>   according to the cleanness of my hands he has rewarded me.
> For I have kept the ways of the LORD;
>   I am not guilty of turning from my God.
> All his laws are before me;
>   I have not turned away from his decrees.
> I have been blameless before him
>   and have kept myself from sin.
> The LORD has rewarded me according to my righteousness,
>   according to my cleanness in his sight. (2 Sam 22:21–25)[11]

David, it seems, has suddenly become oblivious to the horror of his interactions with Bathsheba and Uriah.

---

10. The narrative voice in Deuteronomy is that of Moses, not God or Yahweh, with Moses reporting God's words.

11. The poem in 2 Sam 22, with minor variations, is the same as Ps 18. Likely, Ps 18 is the later text. The two books of Chronicles, which close the Hebrew Bible, consist of narrative content found in Samuel and Kings, along with details not found in the earlier Deuteronomistic history. The motive of the Chronicler seems to have been to "airbrush" the many scandalous acts of King David, and "his adultery with Bathsheba and his murder of her husband are stricken from the record" (Alter, *Hebrew Bible*, 866).

Dating biblical materials is not an easy matter, but there are some general lines of consensus. Second Samuel is part of the books comprising what are called "Deuteronomistic histories," a theoretical notion that suggest common source material informing the books of Joshua, Judges, Samuel, and Kings. It is theorized that these "historical" books were edited and collated in the context of the Babylonian exile and in keeping with the emerging theology found in the book of Deuteronomy. The period around 583 B.C.E. saw the destruction of the temple in Jerusalem, the killing of thousands of Jews, and deportation of vast numbers of them to Babylon as slaves. It is during this experience of exile that proto-Judaism undergoes significant development. What is crucial is that the picture of David presented in the praise of thanksgiving in 2 Samuel is very different from that found in certain of the psalms, more than half of which tradition takes to have been written by David himself.

Psalm 51 deals with David's reaction to his dealings with Bathsheba and Uriah; it is a plea or lament for forgiveness. Most biblical scholars agree that Ps 51 is "Davidic," meaning if not actually written by David (and this will never be known with certainty) it nevertheless dates from the Davidic era, well before the Deuteronomistic histories. The author of 2 Samuel has David describe himself as "blameless," "clean," and "righteous." In Ps 51, in stark contrast to 2 Samuel, David understands himself as anything but clean. Here is Ps 51, in its entirety:

> *To the choirmaster. A Psalm of David, when Nathan the prophet came to him, after he had gone in to Bathsheba.*
> Have mercy on me, O God,
>   according to thy steadfast love;
>   according to thy abundant mercy blot out my transgressions.
> Wash me thoroughly from my iniquity,
>   and cleanse me from my sin!
> For I know my transgressions,
>   and my sin is ever before me.
> Against thee, thee only, have I sinned,
>   and done that which is evil in thy sight,
> so that thou art justified in thy sentence
>   and blameless in thy judgment.
> Behold, I was brought forth in iniquity,
>   and in sin did my mother conceive me.
> Behold, thou desirest truth in the inward being;

> therefore teach me wisdom in my secret heart.
> Purge me with hyssop, and I shall be clean;
> > wash me, and I shall be whiter than snow.
> Fill me with joy and gladness;
> > let the bones which thou hast broken rejoice.
> Hide thy face from my sins,
> > and blot out all my iniquities.
> Create in me a clean heart, O God,
> > and put a new and right spirit within me.
> Cast me not away from thy presence,
> > and take not thy holy Spirit from me.
> Restore to me the joy of thy salvation,
> > and uphold me with a willing spirit.
> Then I will teach transgressors thy ways,
> > and sinners will return to thee.
> Deliver me from bloodguiltiness, O God,
> > thou God of my salvation,
> > and my tongue will sing aloud of thy deliverance.
> O LORD, open thou my lips,
> > and my mouth shall show forth thy praise.
> For thou hast no delight in sacrifice;
> > were I to give a burnt offering, thou wouldst not be pleased.
> The sacrifice acceptable to God is a broken spirit;
> > a broken and contrite heart, O God, thou wilt not despise.
> Do good to Zion in thy good pleasure;
> > rebuild the walls of Jerusalem,
> then wilt thou delight in right sacrifices,
> > in burnt offerings and whole burnt offerings;
> > then bulls will be offered on thy altar.

David's lament, his horror at his "bloodguilt," is a distillation of key conceptions of (and responses to) sin in the religious practices of ancient Israel, to which we now turn. Significantly, David's lament raises the question of whether and how animal sacrifice is a viable route to restore David to a state where he may experience "the joy of thy salvation," a sign that the ritual killing of animals has come under some level of critical scrutiny.

Animal Sacrifice

If sin is an act that "misses the mark," that miss creates consequences, it generates a wake of conditions and forces that, if not dealt with in some way, will perpetuate or generate more misses. Things gone awry must be set right; the twisted must be straightened; the stained cleaned; the burden lifted; the debt settled; the trespass rectified; the ransom paid; the polluted expelled. Pick your metaphor. But precisely which metaphor a culture settles on will determine how one understands sin as a general theological category subsuming specific sins such as murder or theft; the metaphor will also shape subsequent matters of forgiveness, atonement, and repentance.

Today, a common response to a transgression is to pay a fine. A company is discovered to have violated environmental or safety standards, a transgression or sin that perhaps leads to injury or death. How to atone for this act? A fine is levied. Just how much this solution owes to historical Christianity is a story we are coming to. But if we travel back to ancient Israel, we see that David's plea for mercy and acts of atonement revolve around images of cleansing. We wouldn't have the CEO of a company that violates environmental law wash themselves clean (though perhaps we should), but this is precisely how David thinks. David metaphorizes sin as a stain that must be washed and cleansed from his soul. The Hebrew word here describing forgiveness from sin is כָּפַר (kafar), an atonement achieved through a wiping away or cleansing to become "whiter than snow."

Cleansing is but one metaphor deployed by David. Importantly, at the close of the psalm, David emphasizes that a "broken and contrite heart" are required before the sacrifice of bulls at the temple of Jerusalem can once again be considered "right." In these closing words is distilled the complex history of ancient Israel's central theological-ritual system, the understanding of which is crucial for getting one's bearings on the development of Christian notions not just of sin but of repentance and atonement. Christianity's relationship to animal sacrifice is complex and it evolved over time. Most early Christians eventually repudiated the practice, yet among the ways they reflected upon and theologized the person of Jesus was in terms of ritual sacrifice. "For our paschal lamb, Christ, has been sacrificed" (1 Cor 5:7). "They are now justified by his grace as a gift, through the redemption that is in Christ Jesus, whom God put forward as a sacrifice of atonement by his blood, effective through faith" (Rom 3:22–25). "You know that you were ransomed from the futile ways inherited from your ancestors, not with perishable things like silver or gold, but with the precious blood of Christ, like that of a lamb without defect or blemish" (1 Pet 1:18–19). "Here is the lamb of God who takes away the sin of the world" (John 1:29). In Revelation, the Son of Man is portrayed as the slaughtered Lamb whose blood has ransomed for God "saints from every tribe and language and people and nation" (Rev 5:9). More than one commentator has observed a version of what Gabriele Boccaccini describes, namely, in Paul "the sacrificial dimension of the mission of Christ is emphasized to the point that almost nothing remains of the ministry and teachings of Jesus besides his death on the cross."[12] The shedding of Christ's blood is the objective, transactional "ransom" that redeems people from sin.

The term *sacrifice* has for us become generalized, as when we refer to a firefighter "sacrificing" their life to save someone from a burning a building. But the overwhelming use of the word in ancient cultures refers specifically to ritual killing, to animal sacrifice, as well as to offerings such as grain or wine. Sacrifice was pervasive in the ancient societies of the Near East, India, and Mediterranean. In 303 C.E., Diocletian, on twenty years of rule, erected a monument in Rome. Sacrificial traditions were as old to the era of the Emperor Diocletian as Diocletian is to us. Visual culture has left a plentiful record of sacrificial rites, the practice abounds in our oldest texts and literature, and it retains a presence to this day in several religious traditions. The rectangular foundations that supported the massive columns of Diocletian's monument were covered in scenes of victory and animal sacrifice, the emperor in all his glory at a smoking altar, flanked by various deities and surrounded by the animals and entourage required for the rite known as *Suovetaurilia*. The name derives from the animals sacrificed: a pig (*sus*), sheep (*ovis*), and bull (*taurus*). *Suovetaurilia* was employed on various occasions: to mark an official census, to celebrate military victories, to commemorate jubilees, to open the planting season with agricultural rites, but also to atone for either ritual errors or moral transgressions. Roman descriptions of agricultural rites tell of families purifying themselves by abstaining from sex, carefully washing, dressing in white, and adorning themselves with wreaths, before circumambulating, three times, the perimeter of fields, animals in tow. Prayers were recited before the animals were slaughtered.

---

12. Boccaccini, *Paul's Three Paths*, 161.

The entrails were examined for omens; imperfections would necessitate another animal to be sacrificed, repeatedly, until the perfect specimen was found. Entrails and bones were wrapped in fat and burned on an altar; the edible portions would be enjoyed at a banquet. The intentions here involved assuring a bountiful harvest, protecting fields through the act of encircling, and appeasing or currying the favor of gods and powers through the offering of choice animals. We can also imagine that such feasts were the occasion for a festive atmosphere and sociability. The mood of similar rites conducted for civic and political purposes were likely more austere and solemn.

To consider one other non-biblical example, one can scarcely turn a page of Homer's *Iliad* without reading of sacrifice:

> At once the men arranged to sacrifice for Apollo,
> Making the cattle ring his well-built altar,
> Then they rinsed their hands and took up barley.
> Rising among them Chryses stretched his arms to the sky
> And prayed in a high resounding voice, "Hear me, Apollo!
> God of the silver bow who strides the walls of Chryse." . . .
> And soon as the men had prayed and flung the barley,
> First they lifted back the heads of the victims,
> Slit their throats, skinned them and carved away
> The meat from the thighbones and wrapped them in fat. . . .
> The work done, the feast laid out, they ate well
> And no man's hunger lacked a share of banquet. . . .
> And all day long
> They appeased the god with song, raising a ringing hymn
> to the distant archer god who drives away the plague,
> those young Achaean warriors singing out his power,
> And Apollo listened, his great heart warmed with joy (1.534–66).

Homeric sacrifice is generally yoked to the desire to appease the gods, which is to say, to generate a communal, convivial spirit beyond enmity and strife. Appeasing the destructive violence of war, averting plagues and misfortune, is achieved through the sharing of food and spirits, returning the combatants to a gentler, sociable mood. Sacrifice also appears in Homer in the context of oath-taking.

Descriptions, codifications, and depictions of sacrificial rites are pervasive in the texts and visual art of antiquity, so pervasive that scholars such as James Frazer and René Girard have argued that the original and primary ritual form is blood sacrifice, which is generative of the "sacred." Animal sacrifice has been theorized as a replacement for human sacrifice (a practice for which there is considerable solid evidence), a historical and sociological narrative found in the Akedah, the "binding" of Isaac. "He said, 'Take your son, your only son Isaac, whom you love, and go to the land of Moriah, and offer him there as a burnt offering upon one of the mountains of which I shall tell you'" (Gen 22:2). As Girard reads this story, we have in the Hebrew Bible the origins of disentangling God from violence. Abraham's willingness to obey God's command is a supreme example of faith, but the ultimate purpose of the command is to abolish human sacrifice. The intervention of the angel at the last moment, preventing the sacrifice, serves to demonstrate that God does not desire the blood of human victims. For Girard, this narrative represents a clear break with the sacrificial traditions of other ancient religions and is a crucial step in the gradual revelation of the God of the Bible as a God opposed to violence.[13] A very close reading of this story might lead us to propose that it is Abraham himself who leads God to change course. In calming Isaac's fear when he observes there is no ritual lamb present, Abraham tells Isaac, "God will provide himself the lamb for a burnt offering, my son." And, voila, this is what God does. The tension within early Christianity around sacrificial versus non-sacrificial understandings of the cross mirrors the tension within the Hebrew Bible.[14]

In the Hebrew Bible, we find prescriptive ritual texts, detailing and codifying how to worship but also how to perform animal sacrifice, a fundamental form of liturgical worship in early Israelite society.[15] In the Hebrew Bible, there are several dozen instances of the odor of burnt sacrificial animal flesh smelling "pleasing to the LORD." The Hebrew Bible

---

13. Girard writes in *I See Satan Fall*, xv, "Human victims were probably offered long before animal victims were substituted for humans" (Abraham's near sacrifice of Isaac in Gen 22 is probably an allusion to this.) We find a similar distinction made by Crossan, who works to disentangle an authentic, non-violent biblical God from an all-too-human violent God. See his *How to Read*. One must be very careful here, as one of the tropes of medieval Christian anti-Semitism was that Jews engage in practices of child sacrifice. The scholarly consensus is that early Israelite society included child sacrifice, as did other societies. See Arbel et al., eds., *Not Sparing the Child*.

14. Girard discusses and critiques "sacrificial" Christianity in *Things Hidden*.

15. The literature about sacrifice generally, and the Hebrew and Christian Bibles specifically, is vast. As starting points, the reader may wish to consult Burkert et al., *Violent Origins*; Gilders, *Blood Ritual*; Astell and Goodhart, eds., *Sacrifice, Scripture, and Substitution*.

also contains critical reflection on the social and moral value of the very rites ordained by God. In Exodus, Yahweh provides detailed descriptions of how to perform animal sacrifice (Exod 29–30). Yet when Jeremiah describes the exodus, he has Yahweh say: "For in the day that I brought them out of the land of Egypt, I did not speak to your fathers or command them concerning burnt offerings and sacrifices. But this command I gave them, 'Obey my voice, and I will be your God, and you shall be my people; and walk in all the way that I command you, that it may be well with you'" (Jer 7:22–23). Again, let us not trouble ourselves with such inconsistencies; the Bible is a work in progress.

Apologetics at times includes the effort to harmonize such contradictions. From a historical perspective, these kinds of inconsistencies allow us to develop an understanding, even an appreciation, for how traditions change. The prophetic tradition frequently critiques empty or hypocritical animal sacrifice, especially when divorced from justice and righteousness. Though they do not call for abolishing sacrifice, the emphasis on moral integrity would in time, in both rabbinic Judaism and early Christianity, come to replace animal sacrifice as the primary means through which to serve and relate to God. In some texts (as is the case with David's lament) animal sacrifice is to be suspended until the people's hearts are again pure, so that sacrifice will be properly performed and properly efficacious. David acknowledges that sacrifice is a known route to deliver an individual or a people from "bloodguiltiness," but that, at least for the time being, God is no longer pleased with and takes no delight in acts of sacrifice. David seeks to use prayer to cultivate a broken and contrite spirit and heart, and he overwhelmingly uses the language and acts of cleansing, washing, and blotting (rather than ritual slaughter) in his prayer of deliverance. In the prophetic texts, the institution of sacrifice is so entangled with the fallen state of the people performing it, that the institution itself comes under fire.

Sacrifice in the ancient world then was an all-purpose ritual act, used in the contexts of praise, solidarity, and thanksgiving; it was used as an act of appeasement or supplication (attempting to influence the gods, usually to control their anger or curry favor); and it was used as a means of expiation, to rectify a wrongdoing. In modern legal systems, verdict and punishment are related but distinguished; in ancient Israel, sin (both as act and verdict) generates or propels negative, often disastrous, consequences as a boat generates a wake. Punishment may deal with the individual who committed the harmful act, but that is not enough to deal with the wake produced by the act; forgiveness, atonement, repentance—these are needed to control, limit, or correct the backwash churned-up in sin's wake. The common route to effect atonement was public ritual, and this entailed ritual sacrifice, itself a metaphorical substitution and sublimation. Though the meaning of animal sacrifice in ancient Israel is heavily contested, there is broad agreement that atonement was mediated through public ritual sacrifice, wherein the animal served as a ritual substitute—absorbing impurity or symbolically representing the offender—to restore or renew the covenantal relationship with God. The act was less about satisfying God's wrath through diverting punitive violence onto a surrogate than about purifying the sanctuary and community. Strict penal substitution in sacrifice is exceptionally rare in the Hebrew Bible. Still, there are texts that reflect penal logic (such as 2 Sam 21:1–9, which involves human execution, and the scapegoat rite in Lev 16:20–22, which removes sin rather than punishes it). Moreover, the Hebrew Bible frequently depicts Yahweh as a God who "smites" (*nakah*, נכה) enemies, offenders, or even Israel itself (Exod 12:29; Num 14:12; 1 Sam 6:19; 2 Sam 6:7). While these portrayals of divine wrath are not systematically tied to sacrificial atonement, they provided conceptual raw material for later Christian theology to develop notions of penal substitution. Perhaps the aim is to metaphorically kill the animal within by literally killing an animal. My reading is that the dominant trajectory in Christian thought, especially in Protestant theology, concretized and ontologized sin as an inherent "condition" plaguing humanity (rather than merely specific acts of particular agents) and reinterpreted the crucifixion of Jesus through a sacrificial lens—framing it as a cosmic resolution to sin's grip, akin to the functional logic of ancient atonement rites. While this developed into theories of "penal substitutionary atonement" (a later theological construct often anachronistically projected onto Scripture), such readings are heavily contested. As mentioned, the Hebrew Bible's sacrificial system primarily addressed ritual purification and covenantal restoration, not the satisfaction of punitive wrath. Even Anselm's *Cur Deus Homo* (eleventh century), though foundational for satisfaction theologies and theories, is distanced from strict penal substitution by emphasizing honor-restoration rather than punitive violence. Nevertheless, these later frameworks—however debated—came to dominate Western atonement theology.

Weight, Debt, and Trespass

There are three words used in the Hebrew Bible to describe forgiveness or atonement from sin: *nasa*, *salah*, and *kipper*. The verb *nasa*, by far the most frequent, means "to bear," "to lift," "to carry," as when Cain pronounces, "My punishment is more than I can bear" (Gen 4:13). Cain imagines his punishment as a weight bearing down on him, and this is how sin is typically characterized in the Hebrew Bible. The etymology of *salah* is obscure, but the term is used in the sense of forgiving or pardoning of sins. *Kipper* is seldom used, but it refers to atonement as a wiping away or cleansing of sin; the Jewish celebration of Yom Kippur (Day of Atonement) uses this language of wiping and cleansing. As Gary Anderson has discussed, a variety of metaphors are deployed throughout the Bible in thinking about sin: "What is most striking is the frequency of the idiom 'to bear [the weight of] a sin' within the Hebrew Bible; it predominates over its nearest competitor by more than six to one. For Hebrew speakers in the First Temple period, therefore, the most common means of talking about human sin was to compare it to weight."[16] Anderson dives deep into the philological weeds in his superb analysis of variations and nuances in biblical Hebrew surrounding matters of sin, offence, transgression, guilt, punishment, forgiveness, and atonement. His study is masterful and much of what follows in this section derives from my reading of Anderson's work.

The Hebrew word *nasa* is used biblically in the dual sense of both assuming and carrying a burden. Moses, for example, experiences Yahweh's directives as his placing a burden upon Moses, which when so placed must then be carried. Similarly, an act of sin is metaphorically conceptualized as accruing a heavy weight, in which case the forgiving or atoning for that sin is understood as a removal or lifting of the weight. For example, "He who blasphemes God shall bear the weight of his sin" (Lev 24:15). Forgiveness is the act of lifting the weight. "Bear away, I urge you, the burden of the sin of your brothers who treated you so harshly" (Gen 50:17). Anderson emphasizes that how one metaphorically understands sin will shape how one thinks it is dealt with. If sin is a stain, then cleansing is required. If sin is a weight, the removing the weight is needed. If sin is a debt, then payment is the route to atonement. Again, the dominant metaphor in ancient Israel is that of weight, as when Isaiah

---

16. Anderson, *Sin*, 17.

uses the phrase "people heavy laden with iniquity" in describing the sinful state of the nation (Isa 1:4).

The metaphor of lifting burdens is related to the prominent scapegoat rite, described in Leviticus. On the Day of Atonement, the rite for the removal of the sins of the Israelites involved the use of a "scapegoat," a pack animal.

> According to the Bible, the high priest puts both hands on a goat's head, confesses the sins of Israel over it, and then sends the animal into the wilderness, never to return (Lev 16:21–22). The animal has thus assumed the weight of Israel's sins and carries them to the heart of the desert—an area that was thought to be beyond the reach of God—where the sins will disappear forever. God will not be able to "view" them there. It is not enough for Israel to fast and repent; the physical material of the sin that had rested on the shoulder of every Israelite must be carted away into oblivion.[17]

Echoes of this conception and handling of sin are clearly in the New Testament, in the efforts to articulate the meaning of the death of Jesus, as in 1 Pet 2:24, where we read, "He himself bore our sins in his body on the tree, that we might die to sin and live to righteousness. By his wounds you have been healed." While this language uses substitutionary language reminiscent of Isa 53, it lacks the later Protestant and Reformed emphasis on divine wrath. Instead, it frames the cross as a transformative act—freeing believers from sin's power ("die to sin, live to righteousness") and effecting healing ("by his wounds"). This suggests an early Christian adaptation of sacrificial imagery, not yet systematized into penal substitution, but clearly providing grist for such a mill. In Origen, two centuries later, we read how the "devil and his angels and the opposing powers" seek "to burden [the soul] with sins" but "if we live rightly and carefully, we should endeavor to shake off such a burden."[18] Such an imaging of sin as weight remains a permanent part of our cultural history.

What Anderson demonstrates, however, is that in late Second Temple Judaism, around the time of Jesus, the dominant metaphor for sin had shifted from sin as *weight* to sin as *debt*, a long process whose roots Anderson locates in the era of Persian rule (538–333 B.C.E.) and the rise of Aramaic as the language of the empire. If we consider the Hebrew version of Gen 50:17, its translation into English reads, "So you

17. Anderson, *Sin*, 6.
18. Origen, *On First Principles*, 8 (Preface, 5).

shall say to Joseph, bear away ... *the burden of the sin of your brothers* who treated you so harshly." As the Persian Empire came to dominate the region, Hebrew texts were translated into Aramaic, with a distillation in the Aramaic Targum text, which is still used liturgically by Yemenite Jews. Again, translating Gen 50:17 from this Aramaic text into English, we have, "So you shall say to Joseph, 'Remit *the debt of the sin of your brothers* who treated you so harshly.'"[19] By the era of Jesus, in other words, this transition from weight to debt was largely complete. As one of many examples, from the Lord's Prayer, Jesus prays, "And forgive us our *debts* as we have also forgiven our debtors." Sin and debt had come to function as equivalent, transferable and substitutable word-concepts. Here, the forgiveness of sin is conceptualized with aid of accounting practices in the form of debt forgiveness.[20]

Should the reader come from Anglican/Episcopal, Methodist, or Catholic traditions, you may know this line from of the Lord's Prayer as "forgive us our trespasses," owing to William Tyndale's English translation of the Bible and the Book of Common Prayer, in the 1520s. Since the production of the King James Bible in 1611, English translation have generally used "debt." The shift to "trespass" in Tyndale's translation likely had to do the growing conception of private property in the early modern era, with religiously derived notions of sin intermingling with legal and criminal language. "Trespass" is a complex word. In England, it entered the language around 1250 as a synonym for "sin," but was quickly wed to legal discourse. The effect was to shift the conception of sin in Anglo-Protestant cultural and religious circles towards notions of criminality and punishment. Just as a thief breaks civil law, so humans violated divine law. The language of guilt and so-called "forensic" theologies distinguish Christianity's metaphorical center of gravity in modernity from the matrix of metaphors that dominated during its origins and medieval periods. Cleansing a stain, lifting a burden, paying a ransom, paying a debt, trespassing, and doing time for one's criminal acts—these are unique understandings, and generate corresponding sets of practices and entailments.

In traditional English Common Law, tenants (those who lived on and worked the land of their feudal lords) were allowed basic usage rights: hunting, fishing, farming, mining, milling. As landowners began

---

19. Anderson, *Sin*, 17–28.

20. Regularized forgiveness of debts was an integral part of economic practice in the ancient Near East. See Hudson, *Forgive Them Their Debts*.

enclosing this common property for their own private uses (through various legislative acts starting in the fifteenth century), tenants became the equivalent of today's migrant workers. That English sectarian movements such as the Diggers and the Levellers in seventeenth-century England opposed the enclosure movements points to a worldview that tends to align private property with sin, rather than identifying sin in terms of "trespassing."[21] Constitutive, favored metaphors always come with implications, especially economic and political ones. Today, these interconnections are easily seen with the rise and popularity of the so-called "prosperity gospel," an "American gospel of pragmatism, individualism, and upward mobility." Kate Bowler offers an in-depth history of the movement, around the core themes of "faith, wealth, health, and victory." At the risk of oversimplification, a central dimension of the prosperity gospel is that through the acts of Christ the "power of sin was broken. Clear-eyed believers henceforth possessed God's ability and authority to rule over the material world."[22] Here, sin is a force that holds one back from being wealthy, from being healthy, from being powerful, from being influential, and so on. A faith that Christ defeated sin puts one on the track to an unfolding victory over sin, evidenced by material riches and personal well-being. The correlate of this "gospel" is conceiving sickness, poverty, being in debt, being socially marginal, being a "loser" as the penalties of sin, as signs of being sinful. Given the distance between this prosperity gospel and any reasoned understanding of New Testament texts, it is little wonder that many Christian churches have denounced it as a form of idolatry and thoroughly non-scriptural. For those who wish to take a deeper dive into the prosperity gospel movement, I recommend Bowler's fair-minded study.

Let us not lose sight of the point here: an understanding of the metaphors undergirding religious thought and practice requires some sense of the broader social-cultural field from which those metaphors derive their intelligibility and power, the source domains, the on-the-ground contexts that serve-up those metaphorical images used to articulate, understand, and develop certain ideas, concepts, beliefs, dogmas, and ritual practices. The metaphors of "energy," "flow," "transmission,"

---

21. Both the Diggers and the Levellers advocated on behalf of the commons and were critical of enclosure acts and movements. The Diggers went a step further, largely rejecting conceptions and institutions of private property and ownership. See Rees, *Leveller Revolution* and Gurney, *Brave Community*.

22. Bowler, *Blessed*, 8–11.

and "magnetism" that abound in the New Thought movements of nineteenth-century Spiritualism rely on developments in thermodynamics, electricity and magnetism, and the social world of steam engines and electrical transmission lines.[23] Religious, political, economic, and legal discourses and systems of thought have always been deeply intertwined. It would be folly to try and understand the prosperity gospel without knowing something of the development of capitalism in America over the past two hundred years. So too with attempts to understand the gospel of Jesus, and the development of notions of sin and atonement in early Christianity, as these are rooted in metaphoric resources drawn from existing cultural domains. Crucially, in the era of Jesus, sin had come to be understood mainly through the metaphor of debt, and its connection to ameliorative animal sacrifice was still prominent.

Sin and Suffering in the Worlds of Empire

It is easy to overlook that monotheism is just three thousand years old, and that the conception of God that has emerged in the Abrahamic traditions since that time was unknown to earlier cultures. In the middle of the seventeenth century, James Ussher, an archbishop of in the Church England, set out to write a history of the world from creation to the year 70 C.E. He titled his book *The Annals of the World*. Reading the Bible literally, he used genealogies and other historical markers to determine the date of creation, which he reckoned at 4004 B.C.E. Modern geology has, of course, long since refuted the idea. But in a way, Ussher was right: if 4004 B.C.E. is not the age of the earth (and it isn't!), it is nevertheless an accurate dating of the emergence of a new kind of human culture—the Bronze Age. It is precisely here that we must look to find the emergence of God in the record of cultural development. Theology and metaphysics ought not to ignore or scorn materiality, the lived realities and relationships of social life. We need to close the seeming gap between wheat and the Eucharist, between God and alphabetic writing, between accounting and atonement.

The story of the concept of sin as developed in Christianity begins in the transition from Neolithic (Stone Age) to Bronze Age culture in Mesopotamia. Mesopotamia means "between the rivers," the vast fertile delta

---

23. As Bowler discusses, the emphasis in the New Thought movement on wealth, health, and prosperity had a direct influence on the development of the prosperity gospel. See Bowler, *Blessed*, 32–35.

area between the Tigris and Euphrates rivers, which flow south from the mountainous regions of Anatolia (present day Turkey) through Syria and Iraq to the Persian Gulf. Around the same time, along the Nile in Egypt, Stone Age cultures gave way to Bronze Age cities and kingdoms. These river valleys were the "cradles" of new civilizations, new forms of social-cultural systems, scattered along a great fertile crescent of land from the Persian Gulf, north along the Tigris-Euphrates rivers, back south and west along the Mediterranean coastline to Egypt, and then down the Nile and its tributaries. Sumer is the earliest known permanently settled civilization in Mesopotamia, emerging around 4500 B.C.E., close to Bishop Ussher's estimate of the creation of the world.

Technological advances in bronze smelting (a combination of tin and copper), took place around 3200 B.C.E., allowing for advances in tools and weaponry; a thousand years later would see the development of iron, and the art of producing iron spread, over a period of roughly another thousand years, through the ancient Near East, the Mediterranean, and eventually north into Europe and south and east into India and Asia. These developments in metallurgy were accompanied by a host of related changes that marked a radical break from the prior Neolithic, Stone Age cultures, and the emergence of a truly new world. Among these changes are the invention of written language; the conception and development of irrigation systems, the plough, the wheel, agriculture, and the domestication of horses; urbanization and social stratification; trade, cultural diffusion, and syncretism; the making of complex musical instruments and wheeled vehicles; the building of palaces, fortifications, and temples; the creation of myths and rituals; the emergence of priestly and monarchical classes, as well as state bureaucracies and functionaries. This was also an era marked by cycles of warfare, conquests, empire building, harsh taxation, mechanisms for relieving recurring burdensome debt, the hunt for and use of slaves, the domination, exploitation, and oppression of one group of people by another. In many respects, we still live in the cultural world birthed and nursed in these cradles of civilization. It is in this world, and this world only, that God finally arrives on the scene, having deemed the domestication of fire, the creation of the pentatonic scale, and the mastery of pottery techniques as no cause for an intervening concern. But around six millennia ago, God makes his appearance, eventually striking up a contract with a politically inconsequential wandering people and, later, assuming the form of an ordinary man who, scandalously, gets himself crucified.

Michael Mann argues for a conception of "civilization" in this era in terms of the integrated emergence of three "insulating and caging factors." Ceremonial and religious centers served to protect or ward off threats of the unknown. Writing was an insulation against time, allowing memories, knowledge, and information to be fixed and transmitted. Cities, with their walls and fortifications, were insulators against the threats of the outside—natural and human antagonists. Mann sees four examples of such civilizations emerging independently in Mesopotamia, Egypt, the Indus valley in present-day Pakistan, and along several rivers systems in North China. In Mann's analysis, civilization, social stratification, and centralized state power emerged in consort, with interactions between a dominant political center and surrounding "hinterland" as "intensified . . . overlapping networks, embodying permanent, coercive power" which was a "long, drawn out business." As Mann summarizes, around 2500 B.C.E., each of the roughly dozen important city-states for which we have considerable evidence "seem to have been led by a king with despotic intentions." The development of city-states and empires proceeded through militarism, the monopoly or control of armed force, and considerable violence, in consort with other forms of power: economic power controlled labor and material production; political power controlled the organization and operation of state institutions; ideological power controlled the production of interpretations and meaning.[24] In Mesopotamia and Egypt, city states such as Sumer, Akkad, and Thebes grew into larger geopolitical powers, constantly seeking to expand, harassing or assimilating—occasionally being defeated or stymied by—smaller entities: Babylonians, Amorites, Elamites, Hittites, Philistines, Chaldeans, Canaanites, Jebusites, Hivites, Perrizites, and Israelites—these, and more, are among the nations named in the Hebrew Bible.

By convention, the Iron Age begins around 1200 B.C.E., a useful date that marks a convergence of several factors in the ancient Near East: the widespread use of carbon steel; a widespread collapse of Bronze Age cities leading to centuries of near permanent social-political chaos; the beginning of a rather clear historical, textual record; and, for our purposes, the first mention in the textual record of Israel. Around 1200, the Egyptians were occupied with robust attacks on the Nile Delta by a people it referred to as "peoples of the sea." Lybians were harassing Egypt's western flank, while Semitic peoples from Arabia were entering Palestine. A common

---

24. Mann, *Sources of Social Power*, 1:77; 1:98.

artifact of the Iron Age in this region are stela; large carved stone tablets or pillars, made for commemorative occasions, often successful military campaigns. One such stele marks a successful campaign of the Egyptian Pharaoh Merneptah, in 1207 B.C.E. Most of the inscription deals with Merneptah's victory over the Libyans, but the last three of the twenty-eight lines shift to the territory of Canaan:

> The princes are prostrate, saying, "Peace!"
> Not one is raising his head among the Nine Bows.
> Now that Tehenu (Libya) has come to ruin,
> Hatti is pacified;
> The Canaan has been plundered into every sort of woe:
> Ashkelon has been overcome;
> Gezer has been captured;
> Yano'am is made non-existent.
> Israel is laid waste and his seed is not;
> Hurru is become a widow because of Egypt.

Though it is the only mention of Israel in the Egyptian record, it is a priceless inscription for it tells us that the Egyptians, a little before 1200 B.C.E., know of a group of people somewhere in the central highlands of Palestine—a loosely affiliated tribal confederation of some sort, called "Israelites." The Merneptah stele is one of only or four Iron Age stela references to Israel outside biblical literature. The small number of references reveals that ancient Israel was a rather minor player in the fertile crescent; but these extra-biblical records also allow for a limited amount of historical validation. One other important point about the Merneptah stele: the phrase "his seed is not" could refer to the destruction of this people's grain stores, a common-enough practice; but it is also a sexual metaphor suggesting that the people has been exterminated. Merneptah was certainly wrong: in 1200 B.C.E., Israel was beginning to emerge as a regional power in Palestine.

Kingdom and empire are forms of political authority and governance unfamiliar to most of us. The French, Haitian, and American Revolutions led to replacing kingship with democratic parliaments and emperors with elected presidents and prime ministers. Where monarchies still exist, such as in the United Kingdom, Sweden, and Belgium, they are constitutional monarchies, with royalty playing little to no role in the legislative and political affairs of state. It is difficult for us to imagine life under empire, but if we are to understand the past, imagine it we must; for several millennia empires and kingdoms ruled the roost. Ancient Israel was sandwiched between two great cultural-power centers. To the east was Mesopotamia, to the west Egypt. The emergence of Christianity is shaped to its core with the story of the rise and fall of the kingdom of ancient Israel, and with its associated religious and cultural practices, narratives, rituals, and beliefs, which develop and change in response the sociohistorical situation.

Around 1000 B.C.E., under the reign of David and Solomon, the various tribes of Israelites consolidated into a small, regional, and relatively autonomous kingdom in the region of Palestine. That kingdom was weakened at its northern border by a conquest carried out by the Assyrians over several decades, around 740 B.C.E. Tens of thousands were subject to forced migration, never to return, producing the so-called "lost ten tribes of Israel." The Assyrians besieged the southern portion of Israel, at Jerusalem, but were unable to take the city. Less than two hundred years later, the Babylonian Empire, which had by then displaced the Assyrians, conquered Jerusalem, laying waste to the city, including its temple complex, which was the heart of religious, economic, and political life. As was the norm in such conquests, thousands were exiled to a life of enforced labor—the Babylonian exile.

To round out this ridiculously short history, there are three more pivotal moments. First, the Persian Empire, centered in what is now Iran, defeated the Babylonians in 550 B.C.E., and allowed Jews living in exile to return to re-establish a presence in Jerusalem. This marks the beginning of the so-called "Second Temple Period" with a smaller temple rebuilt in Jerusalem (this is the temple Jesus would have known, though it was significantly expanded under the reign of Herod, who died in 4 C.E.) Israel managed to carve out a quasi-independence under the successive empires that would rule the region during this era. Second, with the conquests of Alexander the Great in 330 B.C.E, the ancient Near East and Mediterranean were Hellenized—that is, transformed by the deliberate spread of Greek language, political institutions, and cultural ideals, creating hybrid Greco-local syntheses across the region. Lastly, Rome arrive on the scene, in what was by then known as Judea, and began waging a series of wars, whittling away at Jewish independence, eventually sacking Jerusalem and destroying the temple in 70 C.E.

Empire is a violent business. King Assurbanipal, who ruled Assyria in the seventh century B.C.E., was clear about how to deal with those who resisted or rebelled:

> As for those men ... who plotted evil against me, I tore out their tongues and defeated them completely. The others, alive, I smashed with the same statues of protective deities with which they had smashed my own grandfather Sennacherib—now finally as a belated burial sacrifice for his soul. I fed their corpses, cut into small pieces, to the dogs, pigs, zibu-birds, vultures, the birds of the sky and to the fish of the ocean.[25]

Alexander is reputed to have crucified over two thousand people after finally taking the besieged Phoenician city of Tyre. Why Alexander is remembered as "great" is something of a mystery to me. What the Assyrians invented, and Alexander transmitted, the Romans would perfect. For some five hundred years the Roman Empire used the punishment of crucifixion before it was abolished during the reign of Constantine, in the fourth century.

The term *Judaism* appears for the first time in a text (2 Maccabees), dating from the second century B.C.E., written by a Jew living in a Greek-speaking environment, describing the military and cultural clash between the Jews of Judaea and the Hellenistic rulers of that territory. That same book also contains the earliest use of the term *Hellenism*. The political and cultural impact of Hellenization upon Jews led to numerous armed revolts, to patterns of martyrdom, and to apocalyptic narratives and the expectant hope for a *messiah* (God's "anointed one") who would lead the people back to their former glory. A revolt launched under the Maccabees consolidated the rule of the Hasmonean kingdom, which after about a century gave way the Herodians, who presided over the last days of Jewish presence and influence in the region, falling to the newly established Roman Empire. Leading towards the era of Jesus, Rome transitioned from a republic to an empire under the rule of Julius Caesar, who assumed the title of emperor in 44 B.C.E., followed by his adopted son Augustus, who reigned from 27 B.C.E. to 14 C.E., after successfully waging war against multiple opponents. Jesus grew up in a turbulent Judaea, where Roman occupation and Herodian rule stoked tensions. These tensions erupted catastrophically decades later. In 70 C.E., the Romans sacked Jerusalem. The Jewish historian Josephus estimated over one million deaths (likely exaggerated), with survivors enslaved or dispersed—marking the traumatic birth of the Jewish diaspora.

A point to be emphasized here is that the history of ancient Israel and the emergence of Christianity out of currents of Judaism takes place in a

---

25. Quoted in Mann, *Sources of Social Power*, 234.

context of cultural memories and lived realities constituted by perpetual wars of empire and conquest. This is not unusual. Even in the modern era of the liberal, democratic nation state, national consciousness and identity were formed out the violence that accompanied nation building. In the United States, for example, the Indian Wars, slavery, the Civil War, and Vietnam are constitutive of American narratives and conceptions of the nation. Secondly, this violent history in Judea at the level of war and conquest was amplified by the persistent, low-level violence of daily life. Procuring adequate food and a measure of security from bandit raids and military campaigns were a part of everyday life in the ancient Near East. A poor harvest or famine would decimate the population. Reflection on the plight of the poor, notions of social justice, awareness of the gross discrepancy between elites and the poor, and concern over the horrors of empire building and need for peace are as integral to the culture of ancient Israel as are those narratives that underwrite Israel's conquest and the killing of their enemies. Again, this is not unusual. To take America as a comparative example, abolitionists responded to slavery, a worker's movement to the ill-effects and injustices of industrial capitalism, and an anti-war movement protested America's war in Vietnam and (as President Eisenhower described the matter) the dangers posed by the nation's "military industrial complex." The God of the Hebrew Bible and New Testament is associated with both genocidal campaigns against enemies and the welcoming and caring for strangers and the poor. In the books of the Bible, we can observe its authors working through the issues, problems, and possibilities that constitute Bronze and Iron Age culture.

The Logics of Sin

The notion of a divine assembly, a gathering of the gods, is found in the literature of Mesopotamia, Egypt, and Israel. One of the earliest of this assembly genre is a Sumerian lament dating to around 2000 B.C.E. The lament was written at the fall of the city of Ur to the Elamites, and describes the goddess Ningal, speaking before an assembly of gods, weeping for her city after failing to prevent the gods An and Enlil from halting the destruction at the hands of the invading Elamites. "I verily clasped legs, laid hold of arms, truly I shed my tears before An, truly I made supplication, I myself before Enlil: 'May my city not be ravaged, I said to them, May Ur not be ravaged.'" But Ur was ravaged, as were so many cities, including Jerusalem, over and over again. "The good house of the lofty untouchable mountain, E-kic-nu-jal, was entirely devoured by large axes. The people of Cimacki and Elam, the destroyers, counted its worth as only thirty shekels. They broke up the good house with pickaxes. They reduced the city to ruin mounds."

Many of the towns and cities of the ancient Near East, including Jerusalem, were, for defensive purposes, "good houses" on "lofty, untouchable mountains," fortified elevated locations in the terrain. But they were certainly not "untouchable."

> Its people's corpses, not potsherds, littered
> the approaches.
>
> The walls were gaping; the high gates, the roads, were
> piled with dead.
>
> In the wide streets, where feasting crowds (once) gathered,
> jumbled they lay.
>
> In all the streets and roadways bodies lay.
>
> In open fields that used to fill with dancers, the people lay
> in heaps.
>
> The blood now filled its holes, like metal in a mold;
> bodies dissolved—like butter left in the sun.
>
> (Nannar, god of the Moon and spouse of Ningal, appeals
> to his father, Enlil)
>
> O my father who engendered me! What has my city done
> to you?
>
> Why have you turned away from it?
>
> O Enlil! What has my city done to you?
>
> Why have you turned away from it?
>
> The ship of first fruits no longer brings first fruits to the engendering father, no longer goes in to Enlil in Nippur with your bread and food portions!
>
> O my father who engendered me! Fold again into your arms my city from its loneliness![26]

In laments such as this, the scourge of war is often imagined as a storm or plague ravaging the city. Wars of conquest are also conceptualized and reflected upon in terms of the existing concept of sin.

---

26. The complete text of the Lament of Ur is available on the University of Oxford's The Electronic Corpus of Sumerian Literature at etcsl.orinst.ox.ac.uk.

In the Hebrew Bible, the language of sin was used to describe violations of the law, the violence of Cain, and iniquity of David, but it was also assimilated to large-scale macro sociohistorical forces, including war and conquest. Laments and related texts often plead for answers as to why disaster has struck; some, including the literature of the Hebrew Bible, imagines the disaster of war and dispossession as a kind of educative punishment from God in which, after a period of suffering, fortunes will be reversed, the people and the lofty city will be restored. The biblical Book of Lamentations is a collection of poems mourning the destruction of Jerusalem after the Babylonian conquest. Unlike the exilic perspective of texts like Ps 137 ("By the rivers of Babylon") or Ezekiel—which reflect the anguish of those deported—Lamentations voices the trauma of those left behind in the ruins. This contrast—between the cries of the displaced and the cries of the forsaken—enriches our understanding of how Jews processed catastrophe in different ways.

> How lonely sits the city
> that was full of people!
> How like a widow has she become,
>   she that was great among the nations!
> She that was a princess among the cities
>   has become a vassal.
> She weeps bitterly in the night,
>   tears on her cheeks;
> among all her lovers
>   she has none to comfort her;
> all her friends have dealt treacherously with her,
>   they have become her enemies.
> Judah has gone into exile because of affliction
>   and hard servitude;
> she dwells now among the nations,
>   but finds no resting place;
> her pursuers have all overtaken her
>   in the midst of her distress . . .
> Jerusalem sinned grievously,
>   therefore she became filthy;
> all who honored her despise her,
>   for they have seen her nakedness;
> yea, she herself groans,
>   and turns her face away.
> Her uncleanness was in her skirts;
>   she took no thought of her doom;

> therefore her fall is terrible,
>   she has no comforter.
> "O LORD, behold my affliction,
>   for the enemy has triumphed!"
> ... Zion stretches out her hands,
>   but there is none to comfort her;
> the LORD has commanded against Jacob
>   that his neighbors should be his foes;
> Jerusalem has become
>   a filthy thing among them.
> "The LORD is in the right,
>   for I have rebelled against his word." (Lam 1:1–3, 8–9, 17–18)

Once a princess, the city is now naked and filthy, with unclean skirts. The sexual imagery of prostitution and whoredom fills the Hebrew Bible; conceptions of sexual impropriety are often used to understand a less than desirable social-political situation.

Such texts introduce into the discourse of sin a causal logic, the notion of a relationship between a current social-political malaise or chaos and past behavior. "Jerusalem sinned grievously," hence its destruction by its neighbors. This, on the face of it, seems reasonable enough. The idea of reaping what one sows, of karmic returns on our behavior, seems in accord with a garden variety morality. When Malcolm X described the assassination of President John F. Kennedy as the "chickens coming home to roost," he was offering a similar analysis. A nation founded on injustice, on exploitation, on an abuse of power is sure to not simply flounder but suffer under the repercussions of past behavior. Slavery in the United States has left a "stain" that the nation still has not cleansed. If "the LORD has commanded against Jacob," is understood as a way of describing a set of action-reaction causes and effects, it may make some sense. "Our fathers sinned, and are no more; we bear their iniquities" (Lam 5:7). Whether the demands of justice can be squared with descendants suffering from the misdeeds of their ancestors is a central theme in the Hebrew Bible. In any case, we need not imagine "the LORD" here as some divine agent surveying affairs from on high and meting out intergenerational punishment with an eye to correcting behavior, but rather to talk about how forms of collective violence self-perpetuate, how sin generates sin; from such perspective, the analysis offered by the prophetic texts in the Hebrew Bible deserves our attention.

Most of the prophetic books of the Hebrew Bible were produced in the context of the two great dislocations suffered at the hands of the Assyrians and Babylonians. An overarching concern is understanding why, given the supposedly privileged covenant relationship of Israel with an all-powerful God, the nation is subject to so much suffering. We can take Amos as a representative example. The book was likely written just prior to the Assyrian onslaught, in a time of relative peace, but certainly not security. Amos describes the violent defeat of various of Israel's hostile neighbors (surely to the delight of his readers), but then turns the matter on its head, prophesying the violent defeat and destruction of Israel itself at the hands of an angry, vengeful God. Along with worry over a backsliding into the religious practices of surrounding cultures, Amos rails against the abuses of the rich and powerful, and the corresponding plight of the poor and marginalized. The leaders of his chosen people "turn justice to wormwood"; and "trample upon the poor."

> For I know how many are your transgressions,
>   and how great are your sins—
> you who afflict the righteous, who take a bribe,
>   and turn aside the needy in the gate. (Amos 5:12)

Amos imagines (or prophesies) that if the nation does not change its ways, God will subject it to the harshest of punishments. Sin is closely tied to curse, and the two feed on one another, like a snake swallowing its tail. God is to send signs, progressively worse in their effects, in the hopes the people receive the message and change their ways: drought, poor harvest, disease and pestilence, eventually foreign incursions—God sends them all, but these warnings will be ignored. The only thing capable of getting his people's attention is to afflict them with conquest and years of hardship and servitude under a foreign yoke. Only then, after a period of protracted, educative suffering, will the fortunes of the nation be restored. Sin requires a payment, and the form that payment takes is suffering.

The prophetic tradition excoriates the arrogance, decadence, and moral degeneracy of the nation's elites, sleeping as they do on beds of ivory while not just ignoring but actively turning away the poor. There is a permanent, universal social analysis in these books worthy of our deep consideration. But connecting the broad suffering of a people to a form of corrective punishment means that suffering comes from God, in the form of an unfolding plan in which the suffering is in some fashion a necessary evil, part of a plan, and hence meaningful.

Debt Slavery

Along with the emergence of Mesopotamian city-states and the larger national geopolitical entities of empire came increased social stratification. Historians typically distinguish three strata of social class: free citizens, semi-free citizens, and chattel slaves. The first class consisted of free citizens comprised of priests, state functionaries, merchants, and extended kinship families. Typically, this class owned or controlled land and other means of production. The second class was comprised of semi-free citizens who worked for the state, but with minimal control of land or other assets. The third class consisted mainly of foreign captives acquired through war and chattel slaves bought and sold in foreign and domestic markets or born into their households of their master. With the development of the economies of these new geopolitical entities, growing numbers of the middle class of free citizens became increasingly dependent on large landowners and state resources, and were often forced into debt at high rates of interest. If unable to pay their debts—say, due to a poor crop—insolvency or the threat of it would lead people to sell themselves or family members into debt-slavery, using their physical labor for the holder of their bonds as a form of debt payment. The system often meant that land controlled by a small kinship group would be forfeited to larger, wealthier landowners, leading to a new and large class of landless poor, who served in households or the lived marginal lives as tenants and sharecroppers of larger estates. Social mobility in this new economic world was generally downward. By some estimates, the ruling elites of these agrarian-based monarchies comprised roughly 2 percent of the population, who controlled more than half of the goods and services.[27]

This system of debt-slavery upon which the economy was built was understood at the time to be a social, moral, and religious problem of some magnitude, as evidenced by the laws and edicts devised to curb its rise and soften its ill effects. Though it was rarely the case with chattel slaves, there were process of manumission for debt or bond-slaves. One of the great achievements of the Hebrew Bible was to recognize the poor

---

27. For a comprehensive discussion of the institutions of debt-slavery, see Chirichigno, *Debt Slavery in Israel*.

and the class of debt-slaves as people worthy of consideration and care. There are laws, for example, against charging the poor interest. We may know something of the Ten Commandments, but do we know that "if you lend money to my people, to the poor among you, you shall not deal with them as a creditor; you shall not exact interest from them" (Exod 22:25). The Hebrew Bible often sides with the victim, and endeavors to elevate the poor in the minds of the literate well-to-do, while setting down practical measures to lessen the burdens of debt slavery.

The psalmists and the prophets consistently upbraid religious, political, and economic elites for their treatment of the *anawim*—the poor, the vulnerable, the marginalized, those of lowly status without earthly power. The meek, not the well-to-do, are perceived as closest to God's concern, and the rich are painted as moral degenerates in their treatment of the poor. A few representative passages from Isaiah make matters clear:

> The knaveries of the knave are evil;
>   he devises wicked devices
> to ruin the poor with lying words,
>   even when the plea of the needy is right. (Isa 32:7)

> When the poor and needy seek water,
>   and there is none,
>   and their tongue is parched with thirst,
> I the LORD will answer them,
>   I the God of Israel will not forsake them.
> I will open rivers on the bare heights,
>   and fountains in the midst of the valleys;
> I will make the wilderness a pool of water,
>   and the dry land springs of water. (Isa 41:17–18)

> O my people, your leaders mislead you,
>   and confuse the course of your paths.
> The LORD has taken his place to contend,
>   he stands to judge his people.
> The LORD enters into judgment
>   with the elders and princes of his people:
> "It is you who have devoured the vineyard,
>   the spoil of the poor is in your houses.
> What do you mean by crushing my people,

by grinding the face of the poor?" says the Lord GOD of hosts.
(Isa 3:12–15)

> Woe to those who decree iniquitous decrees,
> and the writers who keep writing oppression,
> to turn aside the needy from justice
> and to rob the poor of my people of their right,
> that widows may be their spoil,
> and that they may make the fatherless their prey! (Isa 10:1–2)

In this vein, the laws of the Hebrew Bible are devised to ease the plight and debts the poor. According to sabbath laws found in Deuteronomy and Leviticus, each seventh year was to be a land sabbath, which meant tenant farmers were freed from laboring for their bond holders, and free to gather from the land it what they could, for their own use. Debts incurred by the poor were annulled every seventh year. After seven cycles of such, that is, every forty-nine years, there was to be a Jubilee Year, in which all families that sold their land to pay slave-debts would have that land returned to them. For all these efforts to limit its harm, at the base of the debt-slavery model is the idea that a suffering body can be a substitute for the payment of a debt. In the absence of money or goods to cover a debt, one could offer up one's body.[28]

We have then at the beginning of the Christian era a constellation of factors providing the metaphorical vocabulary that will variously be applied to the redemptive work of Christ in the texts of the New Testament. Sin had been reconfigured from the metaphorical language of weight to that of debt. Mechanisms to deal with debt, particularly the debt-slavery mechanism, were correspondingly mapped onto a conception of sin. The notion of sin had been extended from Cain's impulse to violence and transgressive personal acts, such the iniquity to David, to describe macro-level societal trajectories—the sin of an entire nation or people. Israel's post-exilic reflection on the experience of dispossession and enslavement at the hands of the Babylonian Empire was interpreted

---

28. "Physical punishments, severity towards the body, therefore, came to be thought of as a means of paying for one's crime, transgressions, sins. This idea comes directly from the experience of debt-slavery, which had a long legal precedent throughout the ancient Near East. In this tradition, anyone unable to repay a loan could work as a debt-slave for the creditor until the loan was paid off. . . . Although the punishments remained physical, the metaphors for sin became distinctly economic, having been influenced by the linguistic, legal, and historical specificities of that era." Anderson, *Sin*, 8.

as a corrective outcome of collective sin, and narrativized as a punishment or hard service comparable to a period of debt slavery. Hence, Isaiah writes, "Comfort, comfort my people, says your God. Speak tenderly to Jerusalem, and cry to her that her penal service is ended, that her sin has been paid off, that she has received from the LORD's hand double for all her sins" (40:1–2). These are the background metaphors shaping early Christian attempts to understand the redemption said have been instituted by the cross.

There existed in the Mediterranean and ancient Near East a pervasive institutional form for dealing with transgressions, with sins: public confession and expiation through animal sacrifice. Herod's Temple in Jerusalem was a center for animal sacrifice, with pilgrims constantly journeying there for the purpose of partaking in sacrificial rites, for various purposes, including praise, fidelity, and expiation. Sin was fully incorporated into a logic of exchange and the language of economy; sin and debt were, in effect, synonymous. If a debt was incurred, and it could not be paid in cash or in goods, it could be paid with one's body, through hard labor in the system of debt slavery. The suffering, enslaved body became a form of currency in the alleviation of debt. Suffering was thereby linked to the alleviation of sin, since debt and sin are, in effect, the same thing. Running this logic in reverse, if one is suffering, one must have sinned or be in a state of sin. Covenant traditions seem to have started with a forward-looking logic: if you obey these laws and are steadfast in your faith, then you will be blessed; if you fall short, then there will be trouble. But it was a relatively simple matter to reverse this logic: if things are good, the people are obviously in a state of righteousness; if things are bad, the people must have done something that merits their plight.

While there might be something to this way of thinking, it can clearly become heartless and callous; it can descend into a form of victim blaming, even if the victim is yourself or your people. The book of Job, one of the greatest books in world literature, is a direct refutation of such a logic, but it seems a difficult piece of reasoning to emancipate oneself from. Just as Job's friends are certain that Job's sufferings must be the outcome of a prior sin, so too do early Christian writers begin seeing in the suffering of Christ a prior original sin. The crucifixion was embraced by early Christians as a redemptive act, but the theological explanation of how this death accomplished salvation developed in stages, each reflecting its historical context and drawing upon root metaphors. Initially, second- and third-century theologians like Origen articulated a ransom theory, envisioning Christ's death as payment to Satan to free humanity from bondage. This reflected late antique conceptions of cosmic warfare and property rights. By the eleventh century, Anselm of Canterbury—writing in a feudal honor culture—radically reinterpreted this framework in *Cur Deus Homo*, arguing that human sin had offended God's honor rather than Satan's claims, requiring Christ's sacrificial death as satisfaction. Finally, Reformation theologians transformed this satisfaction model into penal substitution, where Christ bears God's wrath in place of sinners—a distinctly early modern legal formulation, yet connected to the legalistic metaphors which abound in biblical texts.

What unites these diverse atonement theologies is their shared substitutionary logic: Christ stands in humanity's place to resolve an impossible dilemma. Yet they differ profoundly in their underlying assumptions: about whether the debt is owed to Satan or God, whether the primary issue is bondage, honor, or justice, and what kind of payment could suffice. Early ransom theories posited Satan as humanity's illegitimate owner, requiring Christ's death as payment for our release—making God paradoxically complicit in a transaction with Satan. Anselm's satisfaction theory rejected this demonic accounting, yet still framed salvation through an economy of honor, where God both demands and provides the payment. The Reformation's penal substitution would later intensify this paradox by having God simultaneously impose and endure the penalty. These developments reveal a deeper, unsettling logic underlying all satisfaction models: they imagine the divine economy as requiring payment through suffering, whether conceptualized as ransom, honor-restoration, or penal justice. A key tension between these frameworks—is the debt owed to Satan or God?—exposes their shared assumption: that salvation requires divinely-sanctioned violence to balance some cosmic account.

The theological threads that would later inform Christian atonement theories emerged amidst tensions around sacrifice within Hebrew Scripture and later Second Temple Jewish thought, though they manifested in radically different ways. While later Christian developments like Anselm's satisfaction theory or Calvin's penal substitution were foreign to Jewish categories, the fertile ground of Hebrew Scripture contained its own complex wrestling with sacrifice, divine justice, and redemption. In the era of Jesus, the Jerusalem temple's sacrificial system remained institutionally central yet existed in creative tension with prophetic traditions that had long challenged mere ritual observance. Texts like Isaiah's "What to me is the multitude of your sacrifices?" (Isa 1:11) and Amos's rejection of festivals (Amos 5:21) were not so much calls to abolish the cult as pleas for ethical transformation. But the prophetic critique of sacrifice, while never rejecting the institution outright, created an intellectual and spiritual tension that would contribute to its abandonment in both rabbinic Judaism and early Christianity. When Isaiah thunders, "I have had enough of burnt offerings" (Isa 1:11), or when Jeremiah questions whether sacrifices were ever God's primary desire (Jer 7:22), they were indeed responding to specific cultic abuses—the hypocritical show of temple observance as a mask placed over corruption and moral backsliding. Yet the cumulative effect of these polemics, preserved in scripture and continually reinterpreted, established a powerful counter-tradition that privileged moral transformation over the mechanism of sacrificial atonement. Hosea delivers one of the Hebrew Bible's most potent challenges to sacrificial rites: "For I desire steadfast love and not sacrifice, the knowledge of God rather than burnt offerings" (Hos 6:6). Where other prophetic critiques condemn hypocritical worship, this declaration goes further in positing love, knowledge, and covenantal loyalty as a replacement for sacrificial systems. Centuries later, Jesus would invoke this very text (see Matt 9:13; 12:7), not merely to critique legalism but to announce the arrival of a covenant no longer bound to sacrificial rites.

Surrounding the practice of sacrifice is worry about whether an Absolute Being capable of calling on a father to kill his son—and animal sacrifices are haunted by the substitution of animals for people—should even exist in the first place. This worry was exacerbated when the Almighty, after sparing Isaac, "abandoned his own Son to the sweat and dread of Gesthsemane."[29] A tension had formed within Jewish culture around what kind of God could be hoped for, mostly revolving around matters of violence.

Psalm 137 ends with a rather shocking image of retribution:

> O daughter of Babylon, you devastator!
> Happy shall he be who requites you
>   with what you have done to us!
> Happy shall he be who takes your little ones
>   and dashes them against the rock!

---

29. Blumenberg, *St. Matthew Passion*, 88.

In the book of Revelation, Christ returns on a warhorse charging through knee-deep rivers of blood in meeting-out God's justice. Is God a God of retributive violence? Is God a God of redemptive violence, entangled in the smashing of a child's head or casting unbelievers into a furnace of fire? Is God involved with using suffering as corrective punishment, as a kind of currency to pay off incurred sin/debt, even should this require the brutalizing, torture, and killing of his own Son? Are forgiveness and atonement transactional in nature, a kind of economic exchange, purchasable with violence? The prophets preached social justice, but they also threaten violence, imagining Israel's years of servitude and hardship as a divinely imposed sanction. Messianic hope for an agent of God, a figure of grandeur and power, perhaps a great leader like King David, one who would, through violent means, restore justice to God's people, fueled the speculative imagination of Second Temple Judaism. Is violence ever sacred or only merely human? Is God a God of love, mercy, and forgiveness? Does God want retributive or distributive justice? Is there a way to reconcile and combine these visions? Or are they mutually exclusive?

Are we but "sinners in the hands of an angry God"?[30]

---

30. The phrase is the title of sermon preached by Jonathan Edwards, in Enfield, July 8, 1741, during the Great Awakenings, a series of revivals in American Protestant Christianity.

Chapter 6

Christianity and Redemptive Violence

> Then I looked, and lo, a white cloud, and seated on the cloud one like a son of man, with a golden crown on his head, and a sharp sickle in his hand.
>
> And another angel came out of the temple, calling with a loud voice to him who sat upon the cloud, "Put in your sickle, and reap, for the hour to reap has come, for the harvest of the earth is fully ripe."
>
> So he who sat upon the cloud swung his sickle on the earth, and the earth was reaped.
>
> And another angel came out of the temple in heaven, and he too had a sharp sickle.
>
> Then another angel came out from the altar, the angel who has power over fire, and he called with a loud voice to him who had the sharp sickle, "Put in your sickle, and gather the clusters of the vine of the earth, for its grapes are ripe."
>
> So the angel swung his sickle on the earth and gathered the vintage of the earth, and threw it into the great wine press of the wrath of God; and the wine press was trodden outside the city, and blood flowed from the wine press, as high as a horse's bridle, for one thousand six hundred stadia.
>
> —Revelation 14:14–20

ON THE LINTEL ABOVE the entrance to his home, C. G. Jung had inscribed the Latin phrase, "*Vocatus atque non vocatus deus aderit*" (Called or not called, God will be there.) But which God? Which God will be there? God answers Moses's call to name himself with an object lesson in transcendence: "I AM WHO I AM" (Exod 3:14). But no theism can "afford to contradict human needs, to renounce everything in favor of the absolute purity of the concept . . . to deny itself concessions to identification with a nation, to the aesthetic optics and acoustics of the cult, to images, to desires that souls should be taken care of."[1] Ideas need embodiment. On one hand, to ask which God will be there is indebted to an idolatrous conception of God, for it imagines God as simply an object amongst other objects. This is the reason for apophatic mysticism: God is not this, God is not that. On the other hand, mind and body abhor a vacuum, and something must be said of the nature, character, and desire of God.

The problem I wrestle with in this chapter is Christianity's commitment to a narrative of redemptive violence, developed in violently apocalyptic renderings of Jesus's eschatological message and sacrificial renderings of the passion in theologies of expiatory, substitutionary atonement. Can we, should we, hope for the God who will smash the heads of the children of our enemies? Can we, should we, hope for the God who requires the sacrifice of animals to erase transgressions? Can we, should we, hope for the God who correctively employs punishments and requires the death of his Son for the rectification of his honor (as Anselm argued)? Can we, should we, hope for a sickle-wielding Christ, agent of a God of wrath, who pours blood upon the earth? Or can we, should we, hope for the God who out of love divests himself of power to struggle, suffer, and die alongside us, as an executed political prisoner? If not a God of force, with its incumbent propensity to judgment and sanction, at least a God of love and solidarity?

Christianity's entanglement with a violent God is partly the result of becoming, in the fourth century, the official state religion of the Roman Empire. The subsequent centrality of the Christian church within the political life of empires, kingdoms, and nations has meant the church has had to live and function in the world, and the world is violent. In this regard, Christian violence is no different than secular violence. Christian thought and culture have no monopoly on being instrumentalized for nefarious purposes. Nevertheless, Christianity's relationship to violence runs deep. The struggle to articulate "true" Christianity is age-old. One could say that Christianity has far too often been distracted from its true mission of promoting well-being and peace through an occasional instrumentalizing of minority elements suitable to the aims of racists, oppressors, and conquerors. But violence

---

1. Blumenberg, *Work on Myth*, 229.

is more integral to Christian thought than this position allows, partly due to the metaphorical logics of sin discussed in the previous chapter, and how this logic came to be applied in formulating the question to which "redemption" through Christ was the received answer.

The Meaning of the Death

The language of redemption is spontaneously present in the earliest of Christian texts, and takes a variety of forms: redemption, reconciliation, liberation, sanctification, justification, atonement, freedom. Redemptive language emerges out of the event of Christ—the complex of passion-crucifixion-resurrection is experienced and received as a redemptive or salvific event: in this death is new life. The meaning of the death of Christ as a redemptive death came to have the status of a fundamental answer—redemption is the heart of Christianity. Yet this raises a problem. Aside from the problem of how what appears to be ignoble defeat is actually a victory of sorts, if it is an act of redemption, from *what* is that we are redeemed? "For freedom Christ has set us free; stand fast therefore, and do not submit again to a yoke of slavery" (Gal 5:1). But Paul uses "slavery" here metaphorically, with notions from antiquity of property relations mapped onto human relationships to "powers." The slavery-freedom metaphor drives the question, to what or whom are we enslaved such that redemption through "Christ crucified" is required? That God became man, was crucified, and ascended is the core of the creed (the answer or position adopted in early dogmatic statements of the faith). But why did he do this? To what end? Questions do not always precede answers. And "neither in the New Testament nor in subsequent patristic theology is there any uniform theory of the cross or the death of Jesus."[2]

The search for a suitable answer goes through several iterations, before a final settlement, at least in the western church, was crafted by Augustine, for whom original sin is generative of the need for redemption. As Blumenberg describes the trajectory of early Christian thought, "Dogma's late discovery of Original Sin crystallized out, as the question that had been absorbed in it, what it actually was that redemption had to redeem people from."[3] The full implications of this settlement are only worked out centuries later, in Anselm's effort to formulate the question

---

2. Küng, *On Being a Christian*, 420.
3. Blumenberg, *Work on Myth*, 183.

laying behind another central truth-answer that is present in the earliest of Christian thought and culture, the incarnation. Though there may not be a single uniform theory of the need for or meaning of the crucified Christ, there has certainly been, for nearly a millennium, a center of gravity in the theology of the Latin West, namely, expiatory sacrifice. Original sin and substitutionary atonement became the cornerstones for medieval theology, later modified by Luther; the result, given the metaphorical logics informing the conception of and response to sin is that violence is embedded within, not extracted from, divinity. In thingifying (ontologizing) sin, that is, in removing it from its metaphorical and mythical backgrounds in service of dogmatic formulations, Christian thought, especially in the Catholic and Protestant traditions, folds divinity into the violence embedded in the juridical, cultic, and economic source domains that were drawn upon in formulating the concept of sin.

The first attempts to articulate the background question that the redemptive act of the cross answered were so-called "ransom" theologies and the "Christus Victor" paradigm. The Christus Victor model is rooted in the early church's understanding of atonement, evident in the writings of various church fathers. It was not formalized as a distinct theory until the work of the Lutheran theologian Gustaf Aulén, in a book published in 1930. In this Christ-as-victor theology, atonement is primarily seen in terms of a favorable outcome in a cosmic battle between good and evil. Christ's death and resurrection are viewed as the decisive victory in this battle (this is something of paradox, since death and crucifixion seem to signal inglorious defeat). Various New Testament passages depict Christ's work as a victory over hostile powers. For example, in Col 2:15, we read that Christ "disarmed the rulers and authorities and put them to open shame, by triumphing over them in him." By willingly dying and then rising from the dead, Christ defeats the powers of sin, death, and the devil, liberating humanity from their bondage. Aulén, a theologian, didn't merely describe this theological paradigm; he embraced it as a superior alternative to legalistic satisfaction theologies. This mythological theology emphasizes the triumph of God's power over evil. It portrays Jesus not as a sacrificial victim but as a triumphant warrior who conquers the "principalities and powers" that are the ultimate enemies of humanity.[4] This approach, however, leads to the crucifixion being doubly

---

4. René Girard's theory of sacrificial violence can be understood as a variety of this Christus Victor paradigm, with the crucifixion of Christ laying bare the social-political mechanisms of scapegoating. The defeat of the cross is actually the victory

haunted. A victory through defeat is a move that will always be subject to a Nietzschean kind of doubt whether one is simply fooling oneself. If the crucifixion is framed in the shape of a game, contest, or battle, the claim that the "loser" is really the "winner" is open to the charge of self-deception. The model may also leave us feeling rather powerless, subject to the interactions of forces and powers beyond our control.

For Odo Marquard, at the core of Blumenberg's thought is the "idea of an unburdening from the absolute. Humans cannot bear the absolute. They must, in various forms, gain distance from it."[5] If redemption was won in a cosmic battle in which we do not and cannot participate, and if, as is typically the case, defeated powers regroup to fight another day, redemption will be haunted by a potential threat. Can evil ever be finally vanquished? From this perspective, the Christus Victor model falls short. In the very effort to ease the burden of the absolute by conquering the extra-human absolutist powers holding us in their grip, we ontologize those powers as substantive. It isn't obvious that a defeat is a victory; what is wanted is a "real" victory, and so it is not surprising that a "second coming" and armed battle against the reorganized opponents of Christ was quickly postulated. The problem with this approach to understanding redemption is that there will never be a "war to end all wars." Such thinking leads only to the next great war; it is hard to keep faith with failure.

Also popular in early Christian thought was the ransom model, based on the idea that Christ's death was a ransom paid to free humanity from bondage. This theology is rooted in the interpretation of numerous biblical passages and was a prevalent theory in the early church. One key passage is in Matthew, where Jesus says, "The Son of Man came not to be served but to serve, and to give his life as a ransom for many" (Matt 20:28). Another is in 1 Timothy, a reference to Christ Jesus who "gave himself as a ransom for all" (1 Tim 2:5–6). The ransom theory was articulated by early church fathers such as Origen, Gregory of Nyssa, and Augustine. The ransom paradigm does distance, reduce, or limit the absolute nature of powers to which we are subject. Evil powers in the world can be, if not defeated, at least reasoned and reckoned with through exchange

---

of knowledge. Quite literally, Christ's persecutors "do not know what they are doing" (Luke 23:34)—but the reader of these texts knows.

5. Marquard, "Unburdening from the Absolute," 228. Marquard goes on to note that Blumenberg, in a conversation, confirmed that "everything more or less comes down to that idea."

mechanisms: we are not permanently "captive" to them. But this fundamental myth also has problems. Ransom begs the question by whom we were held captive, and Satan is the obvious answer. The ransom model thereby puts the Almighty in the awkward position of making deals and exchange with Satan, and, evil being what it is, one can never be sure that another kidnapping won't occur. The whole affair casts God in an indecent light where deals with the devil are necessary. Oddly, having a God who must stoop to property-like deals with the devil doesn't ease the burden of the absolute; a weaker all-powerful (good) God simply doubles down on the real power of a (malevolent) absolute; that these two powers will, from time to time, do deals (as in the case of the story of Job) doesn't exactly ease our concern. Blumenberg sums-up the problem:

> In all of this, the question remains why this powerful being, who could create an entire world with his "outstretched arm" and the power of his word, would let himself be dragged into negotiations that belie his majesty. The basic thought that "everything has its price" could hardly belong to the most powerful being, even if he still lacked the attribute of omnipotence that was bestowed on him later.[6]

Over time, both the Christus Victor and the ransom models gave way to that of substitutionary atonement, which mobilized the full range of judicial, economic, and cultic metaphors at work in the concept of sin, a move that, in effect, replaced the great accuser Satan with humanity's congenital sin.

Physical, Systemic, and Rhetorical Violence

Historical Christianity's affinity for actual physical violence is well known, and it ought to be excavated and laid bare for all to see and judge. Ideological or theological violence—the violence of discourse, imagery, metaphor, myth—is often trickier to root out, and its influence more difficult to assess. I am not a proponent of the view that religion is uniquely and inherently violent. Such a view is a matter of definition (often informed by polemics) not empirical evidence.[7] There is a thread

---

6. Blumenberg, *St. Matthew Passion*, 37.

7. Phillips and Axelrod, eds., *Encyclopedia of War*, documents the history of recorded warfare. The authors list 1,763 wars and conclude that only 121 can be said to be religious in origin, which is less than 7 percent of all wars and less than 2 percent of all people killed in wars. They estimate the Christian crusaders killed somewhere

of thought in modernity, emerging during the Enlightenment and heavily promoted in last couple decades by atheistic secularists, that drops all violence inside a box labelled "religion." I reject such polemics. But there is also an apologetic camp that wants to save the phenomenon by creating another religion box, inside of which one only finds niceties, love, and kindness. Far from a mere byproduct of a life lived in what Augustine terms the "city of man" or the "earthly city," a significant part of Christian thought, rhetoric, and imagery is thoroughly intertwined with violence. This must be the case, since Christianity is among the religions of the Book. The biblical God is portrayed both violently and non-violently, and this double-faced nature extends to the figure of Christ.

In the wake of the golden-calf episode, Moses, channeling "the Lord God of Israel," asks and commands,

> "Who is on the Lord's side? Come to me." And all the sons of Levi gathered themselves together to him. And he said to them, "Thus says the Lord God of Israel, 'Put every man his sword on his side, and go to and fro from gate to gate throughout the camp, and slay every man his brother, and every man his companion, and every man his neighbor.'" And the sons of Levi did according to the word of Moses; and there fell of the people that day about three thousand men. And Moses said, "Today you have ordained yourselves for the service of the Lord, each one at the cost of his son and of his brother, that he may bestow a blessing upon you this day." (Exod 32:26–29)

Shockingly, this scene is not one of an imagined divine violence directed against "the enemy" in the context of an imperial campaign (which is awful enough to contemplate),[8] but internally at the "enemy within," an intra-genocidal act. Christianity too has its method of singularizing

---

between one and three million people, and the Catholic Inquisition in which perhaps three thousand people were killed. More than thirty million soldiers and civilians died during the course of the First World War, the principle cause of which was embittered relations between nation states over tariffs and trade. I cite this study not as definitive evidence of religion's relative lack of involvement in war, but to highlight the polemical, rather than the empirical nature of the claim "religion causes violence."

8. There are of course numerous examples of such in the literature of antiquity, including the Bible. "When the Lord your God brings you into the land which you are entering to take possession of it, and clears away many nations before you, the Hittites, the Gir'gashites, the Amorites, the Canaanites, the Per'izzites, the Hivites, and the Jeb'usites, seven nations greater and mightier than yourselves, and when the Lord your God gives them over to you, and you defeat them; then you must utterly destroy them; you shall make no covenant with them, and show no mercy to them" (Deut 7:1–2).

group identity by casting out the deviant internal other via violent images and rhetoric.

To my mind, one of the more disturbing features of the character of Jesus, who is otherwise in many respects admirable, is the indifference to his conviction that the mass of humanity will suffer eternal torment in hell. "And if any one will not receive you or listen to your words, shake off the dust from your feet as you leave that house or town. Truly, I say to you, it shall be more tolerable on the day of judgment for the land of Sodom and Gomor'rah than for that town" (Matt 10:14–15). Abraham, at least, raised his voice against God, chiding him for his willingness to kill the just men and women of Sodom and Gomor'rah alongside the wicked (Gen 18). In the book of Revelation (or Apocalypse), the final book of the New Testament, traditionally ascribed to St. John, we find, as C. G. Jung describes the matter,

> a terrifying picture that blatantly contradicts all ideas of Christian humility, tolerance, love of your neighbor and you enemies and makes nonsense of a loving father in heaven and rescuer of mankind. A veritable orgy of hatred, wrath, vindictiveness, and blind destructive fury that revels in fantastic images of terror. . . . Blood and fire overwhelms a world in which Christ had just endeavored to restore to the original state of innocence and loving communion with God.[9]

Jung is too much the liberal Protestant here, for Revelation makes explicit what is latent in the spine-chilling division between "wheat" and "chaff" found throughout the Gospels. Forever wanting to have our cake and eat it too, Jung sees "love" as inherently Christian while "wrath" contradicts Christianity.

> As the people were in expectation, and all men questioned in their hearts concerning John, whether perhaps he were the Christ, John answered them all, "I baptize you with water; but he who is mightier than I is coming, the thong of whose sandals I am not worthy to untie; he will baptize you with the Holy Spirit and with fire. His winnowing fork is in his hand, to clear his threshing floor, and to gather the wheat into his granary, but the chaff he will burn with unquenchable fire." So, with many other exhortations, he preached good news to the people. (Luke 3:15–18)

---

9. Jung, *Answer to Job*, CW 11, par. 708.

The threshing floor is a common trope for the battlefield. Christ the avenging warrior is as much the "good news" of the New Testament as is Christ the minister to the sick and unwanted, or the crucified Christ of redemption, atoner of all sins.

It simply won't do, *pace* Jung, to call the orgiastic violence of Revelation "un-Christian," leaving for authentic Christianity the abode of peace and compassion, humility and love. Christianity is the stepping in front of a mob about to stone a woman to death; but it is also the conviction (even, in some cases, gleeful conviction) that there will be a great cosmic stoning. In Luke's Gospel, Jesus is rather matter of fact about the fate of many:

> And some one said to him, "Lord, will those who are saved be few?" And he said to them, "Strive to enter by the narrow door; for many, I tell you, will seek to enter and will not be able. When once the householder has risen up and shut the door, you will begin to stand outside and to knock at the door, saying, 'Lord, open to us.' He will answer you, 'I do not know where you come from.' Then you will begin to say, 'We ate and drank in your presence, and you taught in our streets.' But he will say, 'I tell you, I do not know where you come from; depart from me, all you workers of iniquity!' There you will weep and gnash your teeth, when you see Abraham and Isaac and Jacob and all the prophets in the kingdom of God and you yourselves thrust out." (Luke 13: 23–28)

And the reason the door is shut? As the coda to Mark's Gospel has it, "He who believes and is baptized will be saved; but he who does not believe will be condemned."[10] Belief, not a morally exemplary life, is the key to heaven. The Gospels reflect a discernible shift in the mechanism of salvation—from ritual sacrifice to personal faith and sacramental participation. While Hebrew Bible traditions emphasized atonement through sacrificial offerings, the New Testament presents belief—expressed through baptism, Communion, or personal trust—as the new threshold of grace. Where Levitical sacrifice required animals, Christian participation requires confession of belief in Christ. John's Gospel, though less explicit about institutional rites than the Synoptics, develops this logic metaphorically: to "eat the flesh of the Son of Man" (John 6:53) or to

---

10. To be fair to the author of Mark, this verse is a latter addition, the earliest manuscripts ending at verse 8: "And they went out and fled from the tomb; for trembling and astonishment had come upon them; and they said nothing to any one, for they were afraid."

receive foot-washing (John 13:8) are signs of receiving or surrendering to divine grace. Moral transformation remains an expected fruit of such participation but not its prerequisite. The tension between ritual efficacy and ethical living persists. As John writes,

> He who believes in him is not condemned; he who does not believe is condemned already, because he has not believed in the name of the only Son of God. (John 3:18)

> So Jesus said to them, "Truly, truly, I say to you, unless you eat the flesh of the Son of man and drink his blood, you have no life in you; he who eats my flesh and drinks my blood has eternal life, and I will raise him up at the last day. For my flesh is food indeed, and my blood is drink indeed. He who eats my flesh and drinks my blood abides in me, and I in him." (John 6:53–56)

For the author of John's gospel, Jews and pagans who refused to see the figure of Jesus in a certain light (as the only Son of God), or who had not been baptized, or who did not partake in Communion—for such a one, "the wrath of God abides on him" (John 3:36). Not moral shortcomings or atrocious acts, but a failure of belief is the source of eternal damnation. That Jews refused to receive Jesus as God's messiah is a faith position that would come to have horrific consequences.

The examples above are of narrative, rhetorical, and symbolic violence in the Bible. The exodus, as the best historical and archeological evidence indicates, was not an actual event, but part of the national mythology through which a people was formed as a cohesive unit. The "primal scene of anti-miscegenation policy," as Peter Sloterdijk describes the butchery that follows the dancing around the golden calf is "largely literary fiction, written in the mode of *a posteriori* prophecy. . . . The true location of all these events [described in Exodus] is purely in the stories themselves."[11] It is precisely the lack of history that makes the symbolic nature of these stories even more worthy of our attention. Ethnogenesis has generally proceeded through a violent casting out (actual, mythological, or both) of the other. History is important, but fabrication is too, and the later also has actual effects. Symbols, not just bulldozers, move mountains.

No doubt there are descriptions or accounts of actual violence in the Bible—the attempted stoning of the adulterous woman and the crucifixion of Jesus come to mind, since stoning and crucifixion were both

---

11. Sloterdijk, *Shadow of Mount Sinai*, 25–27.

juridical punishments. But I don't imagine there is coming a literal day of reckoning, judgment, and retributive violence delivered at the hands of a righteous God. Nor is there a fire in the corner of the universe somewhere in which condemned souls are burning. No Christ with a double-edged sword protruding from his mouth will appear to pour out the blood of armies in the vicinity of Megiddo. Tertullian, the second-century silver-tongued theologian, is not, at this moment, lounging in heaven, still triumphantly anticipating what he so longed for while walking this earth:

> But what a spectacle is already at hand, the return of the Lord, now no object of doubt, now exalted, now triumphant! What exultation will that be of the angels, what glory that of the saints as they rise again! . . . What sight shall wake my wonder, what my laughter, my joy and exultation? as I see all those kings, those great kings, welcomed (we were told) in heaven, along with Jove, along with those who told of their ascent, groaning in the depths of darkness. And the magistrates who persecuted the name of Jesus, liquefying in fiercer flames than they kindled in their rage against the Christians! those sages, too, the philosophers blushing before their disciples as they blaze together, the disciples whom they taught that God was concerned with nothing, that men have no souls at all, or that what souls they have shall never return to their former bodies! And, then, the poets trembling before the judgement-seat . . . of Christ whom they never looked to see! And then there will be the tragic actors to be heard, more vocal in their own tragedy; and the players to be seen, lither of limb by far in the fire; and then the charioteer to watch, red all over in the wheel of flame; and, next, the athletes to be gazed upon, not in their gymnasiums but hurled in the fire. . . . Such sights, such exultation, . . . all these, in some sort, are ours, pictured through faith in the imagination of the spirit.[12]

When Nietzsche condemns Christianity as a sickly religion of sin, guilt, and revenge, he has precisely texts such this in mind.[13] *Schadenfreude* is no stranger to Christian culture, and no doubt many true believers

---

12. Tertullian, *De Spectaculis*, 297–300.

13. In the *Genealogy of Morals* (I, 15) Nietzsche quotes this passage from Tertullian's *De Spectaculis* as an example of a Christian "phantasmagoria of anticipated future bliss" constituted by an eternal revelling in the sufferings of the masses of humanity. Lest we write off Tertullian (far from a marginal figure in patristics) as momentarily becoming unhinged, Nietzsche also quotes in this section of the *Genealogy* the thought of Dante and Thomas Aquinas, the latter holding, in the (Christian?) spirit of Tertullian, that the bliss of those in heaven is made "more delightful" through their ability to behold the suffering of the damned.

take delight imagining (if only in secret or in the unconscious) the future sufferings of unwashed souls.[14] Heaping imagined suffering on the evil is one thing, but on dancers, gymnasts, and the writers of tragedy? Apparently, the "joy" that awaits in watching "poets trembling before the judgment-seat of Christ" is one of the boons of faith.

We need to distinguish between actual, physical violence (war, murder, rape, plunder, destruction), systemic institutional violence (racist laws, inequities in access to basic services such as education and health care), and discourses of violence (bigoted language, calls for revenge, depictions and representations of torture). Just how these three forms of violence are related is not always an easy matter to determine. Violent discourse is not necessarily a direct cause of actual violence; much depends on context. Playing *Assassins Creed* or watching Quentin Tarantino films are unlikely sources of actual violence. If they are, likely they are not the only or primary cause. One might argue that some representations of violence serve to mitigate actual violence, by sensitizing us to the sufferings of others, or allowing a fictionalized outlet for pent-up aggression. Still, it seems a safe assumption that the higher levels of actual and systemic violence in a society are built upon a broad base of violence within everyday institutional operations and cultural discourses—in exclusionary laws, in hiring practices, in wage inequities, but also in stories, rituals, myths, and visual culture. The expulsion of Jews from Spain, a Christian state, in 1492, must be conditioned (legitimated, underwritten, justified, if not directly caused) by the hostile, inflammatory, and bigoted description of Jews in John's Gospel. The genocidal massacre carried out by the Levites on the slopes of Mt. Sinai is likely fiction, but it must relate in some fashion to the willingness of the Maccabees to murder Jews who were willing to assimilate to Hellenistic culture.[15]

Rhetorical or ideological violence, in so far as it is a causal factor in forms of physical violence, ought to be condemned on ethical grounds. "Blood," speaks Nietzsche's Zarathustra, "is the worst witness of truth; blood poisons even the purest doctrine and turns it into delusion and

---

14. Though, it must be said, also among the true believers are many who wrestle with this most "unChristian" notion laying at the heart of the Christianity. Still others solve the problem by ignoring its presence.

15. The Maccabean Revolt, while primarily a rebellion against the Seleucid Empire's imposition of Hellenistic practices, also had a significant internal dimension where the Maccabees targeted Jews who had embraced Hellenism.

hatred of the heart."¹⁶ But even where a tight connection between discourse and overt practice is difficult to make, much violent discourse can still be condemned on aesthetic grounds. Narratives of redemptive (and retributive) violence are, simply put, ugly. They appeal to our lesser natures. There is something not simply immoral about Tertullian's glee in watching the damned suffer—it is also obscenely grotesque.

In mobilizing an existing set of images and metaphors in making sense of the person of Jesus, aspects of early Christian thought laid down the basis on which rhetorical, systemic, and actual violence would be justified across the centuries. In the mythological imagination of the New Testament, violent death by crucifixion is not simply how Jesus dies, or how he might expect to die, should he run afoul of Roman authority in his mission to improve the plight of the disenfranchised, but precisely how he *must* die, for soteriological reasons. As the Letter to Hebrews puts it, "Without the shedding of blood there is no forgiveness of sins" (9:22). To be reconciled to God, there must be, there will be, blood, an oddly idolatrous notion, since it makes even God subject to some system of exchange or balance. Jesus is the one who must suffer, bleed, and die, a mythic notion that implicates God in redemptive violence, which is to say good violence, just violence. As St. Jerome imagines, the blood of Christ has a kind of alchemical potency in mediating exchanges between earthy and heavenly realms. As "we are redeemed by the blood of Christ, the only fitting return that we can make to Him is to give blood for blood," and so "the blood of the martyrs served as repayment for the blood of Christ," a variation on the metaphor of the scales of justice, only in this case volumes of blood are used to reckon balance.[17] As Biale observes, Jerome's model fits "into the way historians of religion have characterized some sacrifices as forms of rendering to the gods compensation for their beneficence."[18] This paradigm has also, historically, driven a perverse imitation of Jesus through "self-flagellation or cult of miracles and stigmatization . . . in order to demonstrate discipleship." But "Jesus," writes Hans Küng, "did not seek suffering; it was forced on him. Nor do I believe that human beings are nearest to God when they suffer.

---

16. Nietzsche, *Portable Nietzsche*, 205. Nietzsche quotes this passage in *The Anti-Christ*, in his rebuttal of the "seductive" idea that behind martyrdom must rest deep truths. For a fascinating read on the symbolic role of blood, see Biale, *Blood and Belief*.

17. Quoted in Biale, *Blood and Belief*, 74.

18. Biale, *Blood and Belief*, 74.

That would make heaven hell."[19] Jesus is neither a masochistic martyr nor a tired suicide: he was brutally executed by the state.

C. S. Lewis's fantasy series The Chronicles of Narnia is Christian allegory. Lewis imagines children playing their roles in a great cosmic battle against evil, guided and aided by the creaturely world. Written during the 1940s, violent conflict was clearly and rightly on Lewis's mind, and we should perhaps not be too hasty to fault Lewis for understanding the fight against Nazism in cosmically religious terms. And yet, and yet . . . Lewis has the lion-king Aslan, the book's Christ figure, instruct the young Peter, king in the making, "You have forgotten to clean your sword, . . . whatever happens, never forget to clean your sword." In the Gospels, Jesus instructs Peter to put his "sword back in its place, for all who take the sword will perish by the sword" (Matt 26:52). John Dominic Crossan invokes Lewis as example of how the Jesus of Revelation (in contrast to the non-violent Jesus of the Gospels that Crossan emphasizes) has informed popular Christian literature. Crossan knows that the typically Christian solution of distinguishing a violent Old Testament Yahweh from a loving New Testament Father is pure apologetics. In Revelation, Jesus unleashes the four horsemen who proceed to produce "human horror and divine terror."[20] Even in Crossan's counter-example to Lewis's Aslan, in the words of Jesus at his arrest, where he tells Peter to sheath his sword, we still find the shadow of violence, for Jesus proceeds to tell Peter, "Do you think that I cannot appeal to my Father, and he will at once send me more than twelve legions of angels?" (Matt 26:53–54). That Jesus holds the legions back is, as he goes on to explain, because "scripture has to be fulfilled"—that is, Matthew's Jesus seems to think his death is not merely imminent, but necessary, which is to say that God thinks it is necessary, since Jesus, it turns out, is God. In this scenario, even God is bound to follow lockstep the logic of using the suffering body to deal with sin.

End Times

"Eschatology" means, literally, the study (*logos*) of the end (*eschatos*). By the time Rome came to power in Judea, many people throughout the Mediterranean world believed they were living in an "end time" or "last days."

19. Küng, *What I Believe*, 157.
20. Crossan, *How to Read*, 10–15.

Following Alexander's death in 323 B.C.E., the region was buffeted by the forces of successive empires, as Hellenization continued to whittle away at past traditions. This political and cultural undermining of order and identity came to a head during the reign of Antiochus IV, who sought to impose imperial culture in Judea. From that point on, Jews would live in a near constant state of war. It is in this context that there emerged messianic expectations and apocalyptic narratives, cosmological in scope and political in nature, such as we find in book of Daniel. Where earlier traditions had largely resisted apocalyptic speculation along the lines of Egyptian notions of resurrection, the crisis produced visions like Daniel's—texts that wielded cosmic imagery to interpret historical trauma.

On the one hand, apocalyptic narratives express a hope for radical change; on the other, they may be viewed as an expression of resignation, as one's sights begin to shift to visions of another world. Whereas earlier forms of Judaism had rejected interest in matters of apocalypse, immorality, and resurrection (such as found in neighboring Egypt), in the era of Hellenization there developed a growing dissatisfaction with this world and, along with it, speculations about another world, a better world, located on the other side of life and history, accompanied by a sense of impending transformation.

The historical Jesus was born into a world that had, for some time, been in extensive disarray. The violence of war and the domination and exploitation of Rome had filled the land with healers, prophets, messiahs, mystery cults, and hopes of a supernatural salvation. Jesus knew nothing of Hellas, but emerging Christianity would weave together elements of the eschatological-apocalyptic spirit within both Jewish and Greek culture. Jesus lived among the rural fishing and artisan communities in the region of Galilee. He was a "Mediterranean Jewish Peasant." What was his world like? The life of a peasant was hard, a life lived at the level of subsistence, constantly teetering on the line between poverty and destitution. This life was made harder by heavy Roman taxation and the commercialization of the fishing industry. Herod Antipas, the Jewish client king of Rome, reigned in the region. The evidence indicates Herod Antipas imposed aggressively extractive measures and taxation on fishing communities which, coupled with his extravagant spending on regal projects, only served to increase levels of poverty and debt slavery. Jesus, if not himself a fisherman, would have known the plight of those living in Galilee's fishing villages. He would have been familiar with Jewish Zealot movements that sought to meet the violence of empire with violence. The Zealots yearned for political independence from Rome and fostered messianic expectations, the coming of an agent of God who would, through righteous violence, right past injustices, defeat the enemies of God's people, and institute a new order.[21]

Rome's eventual response to the Jewish rebellion that lasted from 66 to 135 C.E. was genocidal. Prior to the doomed uprising of the first century, the Jews of the Roman Empire had remained a highly organized, unified, populous and prosperous nation. It was for these reasons that their revolt against Rome had the potential for success, and Rome reacted with extreme violence. In the conflict, the temple in Jerusalem that Jesus would have known was destroyed, perhaps a Roman attempt to erase all sense of a distinctive national, cultural, and religious way of life for Jews. Crucifixion was an extreme though not atypical form of punishment used by the Romans for political prisoners and runaway slaves. Jews during this period were crucified in the thousands or tens of thousands. Josephus, in his history of these wars, states that during the siege of Jerusalem in 70 C.E., more than five hundred Jews were crucified in single day.

There are various responses to the imposition of empire by a foreign imperial power: collaboration, flight and escape, armed or nonviolent resistance, travail and hope for a return to better times. All of these were at work when Jesus arrived on the scene. Among the religious responses to the hardships of imperial rule, the eventual destruction of the Jewish temple in Jerusalem, and the wars raged and lost against Rome was a proliferation of apocalyptic literature (such as the book of Ezra and the Apocalypse of Abraham), drawing on connections between sin, evil, life after death, and salvation that had emerged in the era of late Hellenism. It is in this world that the writers of the Gospels told their varied versions of the story of a crucified and resurrected savoir.

The sense of living through the last days was as true of pagans as it was of the Jews of Palestine. As Jews were suffering under the yoke of Roman domination, Roman citizens were suffering a political and existential crisis, in the form of a protracted civil war as Rome transitioned from republic to empire, a period of crisis in which Caesar Augustus, the adopted son of Julius Caesar, would emerge as the first emperor of Rome. Augustus brought an end to the crisis with his decisive defeats of Sextus Pompeius and Anthony and Cleopatra, in the 30s B.C.E. The *Pax Romana* (peace of Rome) was peace through victory, peace and

---

21. See Crossan, *Historical Jesus*.

stability by the sword. Augustus was quickly apotheosized as the "savior of the world," the "redeemer," and the "son of God." Jesus was born in the midst of this widespread clamoring for salvation, heightened eschatological expectation, and a vigorous consolidation and expansion of imperial power, sometime around 6 B.C.E.

The classicist E. R. Dodds argues that the Imperial Age of Alexander and Hellenism (following on the heels of the Classical Age of Greek tragedy, Plato, and Aristotle) witnessed the decline of reason and humanism and a turn to astrology, magic, and cultic mystery religions promising salvation of the soul. The intellectual climate of the Mediterranean world was changing. The affirmation of the material cosmos and sense of its unity with transcendent principles was giving way to "a feeling that the physical world . . . is under the sway of evil powers, and that what the soul needs is not unity with it but escape from it." Cultural forms increasingly focused on

> techniques of individual salvation, sometimes some relying on holy books allegedly discovered in Eastern temples or dictated by the voice of God to some inspired prophet, others seeking a personal revelation by oracle, dream, or waking vision; others again looking for security in ritual, whether by initiation in one or more of the now numerous "mysteria" or by employing the services of a private magician. There was a growing demand for occultism, which is essentially an attempt to capture the Kingdom of Heaven by material means. . . . Philosophy followed a parallel path on a higher level. Most of the schools had long since ceased to value the truth for its own sake, but in the Imperial Age they abandon, with certain exceptions, any pretense of disinterested curiosity and present themselves frankly as dealers in salvation.[22]

Just why the late Hellenistic era exhibits a marked change in spiritual temperament is a difficult question to answer. No doubt several factors were involved, including a loss of political freedoms, the impact of war, and economic insecurity. Dodds further speculates that the sense of personal freedom injected into culture by Greeks rationalism and humanism—to which we could add the moral demands of the Hebrew prophetic tradition—generated kickback. It is difficult to embrace personal freedom and moral responsibility, and the irrationalism and the emphasis on a nebulous salvation and flight to another world that characterized the era

22. Dodds, *Greeks and the Irrational*, 248.

represents "the unconscious flight from the heavy burden of individual choice which an open society lays upon its members."[23] This is an idea to which we return, for one way to understand Christianity's historical influence is that it injected a rather dizzying freedom into the world, to which it had to respond by implementing dogmas and practices to render salvation to relieve individuals of the burden of freedom.[24]

Echoing Dodds, Eric Voegelin argues that in both Israel and Greece there had emerged in the respective forms of prophetic and wisdom traditions a break with the cosmological orders of earlier imperial societies in Mesopotamia and Egypt. Jewish prophetic writings and Greek philosophical schools introduced a transcendent element that called for society to be ordered and grounded not only or merely in power, but in truth. "For I am the LORD who brought you up out of the land of Egypt, to be your God; you shall therefore be holy, for I am holy," we read (Lev 20: 45). Socrates, addressing his accusers in court, rejected acquittal in exchange for his silence because of his "greater obedience to God than to you, and so long as I draw breath and have my faculties, I shall never stop practicing philosophy and exhorting you and elucidating the truth for everyone I meet" (*Apology*, 29d). This vertical dimension to culture was shaped by the prophets, who chastised imperial elites for their neglect of the word of God, and by the philosophers, who responded to factionalism and despotism with a public order based on the rule of reason and noetic consciousness. With the coming of Alexander, however, the "empires closed in again on the clearing they had left in history for Israel and Hellas to flower. The attempts at ordering society by the truth of existence, be it the revealed word of God or the philosopher's love of wisdom, appeared to have come to their end."[25] Other methods and paradigms were courted, including apocalyptic eschatology, what Crossan terms the "great cleanup of the world."

There is much debate and confusion over the meanings of the terms "apocalyptic" and "eschatology." Our present-day social imaginary may well lead us astray when we encounter apocalyptic discourse in ancient texts. Apocalypse today suggests matters of space and time, of cosmology, and the literal end of life: the demise of the human being via genetic engineering, the collapse of the biosphere due to climate change,

23. Dodds, *Greeks and the Irrational*, 252.

24. This is of course the charge laid at the feet of Christ by the Grand Inquisitor in Dostoevsky's *Brothers Karamazov*.

25. Voegelin, *Ecumenic Age*, 115.

extinction by meteorite. But cosmic imagery in Jewish discourse describing a "coming new age ... cannot be read in a crassly literalistic way without doing it great violence." When in the Hellenistic world someone thought in apocalyptic or eschatological terms, it wasn't necessarily the literal end of the world they imagined but matters of justice and restoration; eschatology plumbed the "theological significance of cataclysmic sociopolitical events."[26] The idea developed in ancient eschatological texts is that the present world order (not the world/cosmos itself) is ending, and a new era arriving. To be sure, this renewed world was often understood as the work of a transcendent power, of God or his agent, but when we read the words of Jesus (replying to Pilate's interest in whether Jesus thinks himself a king)—"my kingdom is not of this world"—we are not obliged to take this literally, as though the kingdom is located in some other quadrant of space, or beyond material space altogether. "Not this world," can mean, simply, not this world of emperors, domination, oppression, rich and poor, slavery and violence.

Crossan's way of distinguishing the *eschatological* from the *apocalyptic* is helpful. Eschatology, as Crossan uses the term, is the more general one; it is a radical, profound, explicit "No!" to the world as we experience it. "It is a basic and unusual world-negation or rejection as opposed to an equally basic but more usual world-affirmation or acceptance."[27] The Jewish historian and philosopher Philo, who died roughly twenty years after Jesus, describes a sectarian monastic community of Jews and pagans who lived outside the city of Alexandria, whom he names the "therapeutics." "They possess an art of medicine," we read,

> more excellent than that in general use in cities, for that only heals bodies, but the other heals souls which are under the mastery of terrible and almost incurable diseases, which pleasures and appetites, fears and griefs, and covetousness, and follies, and injustice, and all the rest of the innumerable multitude of other passions and vices, have inflicted upon them. . . . [They

---

26. Wright, *New Testament*, 283–84. As an example of a potential eschatological event, we can point to George Floyd's brutal killing at the hands of police officers on May 25, 2020. The incident was captured by multiple bystanders and witnesses, who used their cell phones to film the slow death of Floyd as one officer, Derek Chauvin, pinned the helpless Floyd to the ground for some eight minutes. The situation can be understood as an eschatological moment. For weeks thousands of people filled the streets of America and other countries; a very few rioted, but most gathered in solidarity and in peaceful protest, calling for justice and transformative change.

27. Crossan, *Birth of Christianity*, 259.

hold] that injustice is bred by anxious thought for the means of life and for money-making, justice by holding and following the opposite creed. The first entails inequality, the second equality, the principle by which nature's wealth is regulated and so stands superior to the wealth of vain opinion. So when they have divested themselves of their possessions and have no longer aught to ensnare them they flee without a backward glance and leave their brothers, their children, their wives, their parents, the wide circle of their kinsfolk, the groups of friends around them, the fatherlands in which they were born and reared, since strong is the attraction of familiarity and very great its power to ensnare. And they do not migrate into another city like the unfortunate or worthless slaves who demand to be sold by their owners and so procure a change of masters but not freedom. For every city, even the best governed, is full of turmoils and disturbances innumerable which no one could endure who has ever been even once under the guidance of wisdom. Instead of this they pass their days outside the walls pursuing solitude in gardens or lonely bits of country, not from any acquired habit of misanthropical bitterness but because they know how unprofitable and mischievous are associations with persons of dissimilar character. . . . They do not have slaves to wait upon them as they consider that the ownership of servants is entirely against nature. For nature has borne all men to be free, but the wrongful and covetous acts of some who pursued that source of evil, inequality, have imposed their yoke and invested the stronger with power over the weaker. In this sacred banquet there is as I have said no slave, but the services are rendered by free men who perform their tasks as attendants not under compulsion nor yet waiting for orders, but with deliberate goodwill anticipating eagerly and zealously the demands that may be made.[28]

The therapeutics rejected the existing ordering of the world; their dissatisfaction with the day-to-day practices and beliefs of late Hellenistic culture—no to folly, no to money, no to slavery, no to injustice, no to inequality—makes them exemplary of the eschatological outlook. Their eschatology was of a certain kind, an ascetical and contemplative practice lived with like-minded people who had rejected, renounced, turned their backs on what the world had to offer.

The culture of the therapeutics was quite different from the eschatological atmosphere of, say, the community of Essenes located at Qumran

28. Philo, *On the Contemplative Life*, 115, 123, 157.

on the shores of the Dead Sea. Each were in turn different from early Jesus movements, within and across which there was also considerable variety. The Jesus movement of the Gospels was not, as was the case with the therapeutics, comprised of relatively well-to-do renunciates, but of the peasantry who possessed nothing to begin with. Making a virtue out of social necessity, they were not "invited to give up everything but to accept their loss of everything as judging not them but the system that had done it to them."[29] Eschatology, notes Crossan, can take varied forms: prophetic, ascetic, political, militant, utopian, anarchistic, future oriented, realized in community, and apocalyptic. The later form, apocalyptic eschatology, is characterized by a perspective that views the world as so disordered, so "irrevocably beyond human remedy that only immediate divine intervention can rectify it." Such apocalyptic eschatology is further marked by a violence executed by a discerning divine judgment through which "we" are liberated, exalted, saved, redeemed, while "they" are variously punished, converted, or annihilated.[30] Liberation and justice, revenge and divine vengeance—these walk hand in hand.

Part of the debate within historical Jesus scholarship is to what extent, if at all, Jesus preached an apocalyptic eschatology. Certainly, the authors of many early Christian texts claim he did: "The Son of man will send his angels, and they will gather out of his kingdom all causes of sin and all evildoers, and throw them into the furnace of fire; there men will weep and gnash their teeth. Then the righteous will shine like the sun in the kingdom of their Father. He who has ears, let him hear" (Matt 13:41–43). On the other hand, the Gospel of Thomas, which must be reckoned as an early, independent gospel tradition, imputes no apocalyptic sensibilities or prophecies of a coming divine judgment to the figure of Jesus. Crossan argues the message of the historical Jesus was not so much an apocalyptic but an ethical eschatology, defined by its "nonviolent resistance to structural evil."[31] "All too often," writes Crossan, "apocalypticism is perceived as a divine ethnic cleansing whose genocidal heart presumes a violent God of revenge rather than a loving God of justice."[32] If Crossan's conclusions are to be believed (his argument is convincing), the memory of the eschatological preaching of Jesus was very quickly assimilated to violent apocalyptic sensibilities and narratives.

29. Crossan, *Birth of Christianity*, 281.
30. Crosson, *Jesus*, 53.
31. Crossan, *Birth of Christianity*, 287.
32. Crossan, *Birth of Christianity*, 283.

Most historians acknowledge that the earliest Christian sects, emerging out of their Jewish background and in dialogue with a syncretic Hellenistic culture, were characterized by expectant hope and the experience of or need for salvation in the "last days" before God implemented a new order. Jesus was a preacher and healer. He ministered to those in need, calling on the traditions of social justice and love of God and neighbor inherent to Jewish tradition. He didn't offer a political program, as such, but he did console the poor and the marginalized, and he preached, in the form of parables, a message of salvation and the imminent coming of the kingdom of God. Again, such preaching was perfectly in keeping with spirit of the times: not many needed convincing that salvation should be an utmost concern.

Jesus preached to the *anawim*, to those on the margins of society, the forgotten, the destitute, the powerless, the scorned, the poor. His message was consoling, perhaps even invigorating. Take no thought of tomorrow; worry not; think not on what you will wear or what you will eat. Things are about to be radically different. The rich and powerful will be overturned, poverty will end, suffering will end, war will end—the meek will inherit the earth. On one hand, Jesus proposes a response to the social-political circumstances of his day, the fulfillment of the Torah. In Mark, Matthew, and Luke (the so-called "Triple Tradition" of Synoptic Gospels) Jesus is asked variants of the same question: What must I do to be saved? His answer is: keep the commandments, love God, love neighbor. But then Jesus takes a step further, counselling perfection via dispossessing oneself of wealth, an act that will "lay up treasures in heaven," and allow for an inheriting of "eternal life."

There is some indication that the level of violence associated with Jesus's eschatology was amped-up in the years following his death. In Mark, for example, Jesus sends out his disciples to preach and heal in surrounding villages. He instructs them, should anyone not receive them warmly, that "when you leave, shake off the dust that is on your feet for a testimony against them" (Mark 6:11). Jesus means here something along the lines of "forget about them" or "wash your hands of them." A negative judgment is passed on these unwelcoming communities—their refusal is a testimony against them—but the image is not particularly violent. In historical research, this is an important passage in Mark, for in the earliest manuscripts of Mark's Gospel, the passage ends here. But at some point in the historical transmission of the text it must have seemed to someone that Jesus's counsel here was not strong enough, and so a line was added: "Verily I say unto you, it shall be more tolerable for Sodom and Gomorrah in the day of judgment, than for that city." The reasonable conclusion is that this line was added by a copyist who had in mind the quite similar passage found in Matthew. Luke's Gospel agrees with the earliest Markan manuscripts. The general consensus is that Matthew and Luke wrote their gospels with a copy of Mark in hand. Matthew added the line about Sodom and Gomorrah, which was then later copied into the text of Mark.

This kind of manuscript detective work is important for historical research, as it reveals that the person writing or copying a text infuses the memory of Jesus with concerns, theological, practical, ethical, and otherwise—concerns that may not have been shared by or central to the historical Jesus. Perhaps the message of the historical Jesus was less violent, less apocalyptic than a simple reading of the Gospels suggests. Such a conclusion is not meant to "save" Jesus from being violent, but to highlight the way notions of divine violence shape an understanding of events.

Are political oppression and economic destitution problems to be solved or things that will be utterly done away with in a cleansing, eschatological transformation ushered in from on high, through violent or other means? It is impossible to find a definitive historical Jesus within the fecund mixture of imagery and ideas generated in the four canonical Gospels, to say nothing of the non-canonical writings. We have the Gospels according to Mark, Matthew, Luke and John, but the gospel of Jesus is a slippery elixir that cannot be fully distilled. There is, however, quite a broad consensus that the thinking of Jesus "was wholly and entirely dominated by the prospect of the better future. . . . He expected an imminent radical change in the situation. . . . Like many devout people of his time, he believed in the advent in the near future of God's rule over the world, which would bring with it the eschatological and final summation of the world."[33] Jesus offered the hope, the promise, of redemption, of salvation. But salvation and redemption *from what*? This is not exactly clear. Suffering, illness, poverty—yes, these are positive evils for Jesus, and he seeks to overcome them. But there is more. As Hans Küng notes, his message is meant to generate not just hope but joy, a "message of forgiveness, justice, freedom, brotherliness and the love."[34] A change

---

33. Küng, *On Being a Christian*, 181–82.
34. Küng, *On Being a Christian*, 182.

of heart. Again, Jesus is not a philosopher or theologian or politician trying to provide answers and solutions to pressing questions. He is endeavoring to provide comfort to the afflicted. He is not trying to answer questions but offer hope and love. To say as much is not to slight Jesus. One dying of cancer is not in need of a treatise on the growth of cancer cells, but our presence, our care, and our love. Religion as consolation is only denigrated by those who have either suffered little or have little sympathy for those who suffer. Nor do I question the sincerity of Jesus. In all likelihood, he believed—urgently believed—in the coming of the kingdom and wanted to save people so they could experience it—but we must conclude his sense of timing was off, and this presented emerging Christian communities with a problem.

In Hebrew texts, the "day of the Lord" refers to the saving action of God in history, variously understood as a time of blessings but also of wrath and punishment. "The sun shall be turned to darkness, and the moon to blood, before the great and terrible day of the Lord comes. And it shall come to pass that all who call upon the name of the Lord shall be delivered" (Joel 2:31–32). In early Christian theologizing, this day of the Lord was evoked through the Greek word *parousia*. The word can mean both *arrival*, as when someone enters a room, but also *presence*, connoting the manifestation and charisma of the spirit of the gods in a ceremony: George is present; George has a presence of authority about him.

The historical Jesus was fixated on the immediacy of the salvation and transformation about to be affected by God. Albert Schweitzer, whose thought I am following here, has convincingly argued that as time rolled on following the crucifixion the "distant view" of the kingdom replaced the "near view" of its imminent arrival, and there began a long, elaborate reshaping of the faith, one that had to come to terms with the significance and meaning of the life, death, and resurrection of Jesus. For Schweitzer, Jesus is not simply a moral reformer; he is also an eschatological prophet: the end is nigh; the world is about to turn on its axis; a new kingdom is forthcoming. We ought to love our neighbor, because it is the right thing to do. But Jesus also links such moral behavior to promises of salvation, introducing an otherworldly motive into his call to obey the law. "It is hard," Schweitzer writes, "for us to bring ourselves to the point of admitting that Jesus, who is uniquely endowed with the Spirit of God, and is for us the supreme revealer of religious and spiritual truth, does not stand above his age in the way that might seem to be demanded by the significance which he has for all ages." In other words, "all attempts to avoid the admission that Jesus held a view of the Kingdom of God and its coming which was not fulfilled and cannot be adopted by us involve the shirking of the truth."[35]

In the New Testament Gospels, we find evidence that the early Christian community wrestled with making sense out of the eschatological preaching of Jesus; they had to wrestle with it because a straightforward acceptance of the message became increasingly difficult as the years continued to pass. In Luke's Gospel, we read that "when you see these things taking place, you know that the kingdom of God is near. Truly, I say to you, this generation will not pass away till all has taken place" (Luke 21:32). On the other hand, we can also read in the same gospel that "the end will not be at once" (Luke 21:9). This tension has come to be known as the problem of the "delay of the parousia." The disjunction between what Jesus preached was about to happen and the continuation of the world as usual no doubt had the potential to generate a cognitive and spiritual catastrophe for the nascent Christian community.

The absence of the arrival of the kingdom did not bring an end to Christianity, but it did necessitate changes. For Paul, writing within a generation of Jesus, the crucifixion-resurrection of Jesus means the kingdom had come and so must, in relatively short order, manifestly flourish, but the problem of delay is apparent and the march of time made this view increasingly difficult to hold; by the second generation the kingdom is displaced to a future time; eventually, its arrival becomes both infinitely far away and expected any minute. Schweitzer shows how Christianity ceased to be "faith in the kingdom of God and became the religion of faith in the resurrection and the remission of sins."[36] Given that violent imagery accompanied conceptions of the in-breaking of the kingdom, it is not unexpected that Christianity's shift to distributing remission from sin would absorb and transmit this violence. As mentioned, it is no simple matter to determine just how violently apocalyptic was the eschatological teaching and worldview of the historical Jesus. But in the Sermon on the Mount, blessings and curses reverberate. The logic is dualistic, and, at times, chilling: do this, receive your reward; don't do this, receive hell fire. God is about to reorder the world; things will be transformed in the wink of an eye; the world will be redeemed; get on board or experience a "wailing and gnashing of teeth" (Matt 13:42). The coming transformation, we

---

35. Schweitzer, "Conception of the Kingdom," 112, 115.
36. Schweitzer, "Conception of the Kingdom," 92.

are led to conclude, will be affected through violent means. According to John the Baptist, the Messiah will baptize with "Spirit and fire," wielding a "winnowing fork," the instrument used on the "threshing floor" to separate wheat from "chaff," the latter, we are told, to be consigned to burning in an "eternal fire" (Luke 3:15–17).

The myth of redemptive violence still holds us captive. It is the idea that violence can be a means to achieve justice, order, or salvation—that by using overt, physical force, the world can be set right. This myth presents violence not just as a necessary evil but as a righteous force that reorders a disordered world; often this reordering is ascribed to the actions of a heroic figure or divine power who confronts and defeats chaos or evil. The myth has been explored and critiqued by various scholars, with Walter Wink being one of the most prominent voices. In his influential work, *The Powers That Be* (1998), Wink delves into how this myth operates within society, particularly in Western culture, where it permeates media, politics, and even Christian theology. He argues that the myth of redemptive violence perpetuates a cycle of violence by continually legitimizing violent responses to conflicts and challenges.[37]

The reception of the New Testament has been crucial in shaping and perpetuating this myth. Over the centuries, certain interpretations, especially those focusing on the violent imagery in the book of Revelation or the concept of Jesus's death as a sacrificial atonement, have reinforced the idea that violence is not only inevitable but also divinely sanctioned as a tool for redemption. Theories of expiatory atonement have played a significant role in this regard. However, there are alternative readings of the New Testament that challenge this myth. These interpretations emphasize the nonviolent teachings of Jesus, particularly as seen in large sections of the Gospels. In this way, the myth of redemptive violence has been both reinforced and challenged through the centuries. While some interpretations of Christian theology have perpetuated this myth, others have offered a powerful critique, calling for a return to the nonviolent core of Jesus's message. As thinkers like Walter Wink and René Girard have shown, the true challenge lies in recognizing the destructive power of this myth and seeking to dismantle it in favor of a more life-affirming and peaceful vision of redemption.

---

37. See Girard, *Violence and the Sacred*; Brock and Parker, *Saving Paradise*; Slotkin, *Regeneration Through Violence*; Myers, *Binding the Strong Man*; Pahl, *Empire of Sacrifice*.

Anselm or Abelard?

Anselm of Canterbury's *Cur deus homo* (Why God Became Man) appeared in 1098; it is paradigmatic of medieval Latin Christianity. The theory of atonement worked out in this text became central for Western Christian theology; in many respects, it remains so. As Rowan Williams has observed, the liturgy of the Eucharist first emerged as a "memorial of an event which increasingly gathered to itself sacrificial metaphors."[38] In the work of Anselm, conceptions of the expiatory and substitutionary efficacy of violent suffering comes to fruition. Anselm considered the ransom theologies and discourses of a cosmic battle overly dramatic and mythical. The idea of God tricking or tripping up Satan with the lure of the cross seemed ridiculous.

Often overlooked in the ransom paradigm is that the legal-juridical metaphorical source domain informing the concept suggests the interaction of three parties—God, the devil, and humanity—each with its respective claims. Within this framework, enslavement is not itself an injustice, but part a legally grounded matter of property rights. As such, even the devil has a role to play in the saga of redemption; without serving a period of enslavement that is considered what humanity was due (owing to its primal sin), there can be no redemption. In the twelfth century, the influential Hugh of St. Victor developed an updated theology of atonement grounded in the ransom metaphor, in which he considers the devil as though he has rights over humanity. When Peter Abelard was brought before the Council of Sens in 1140 on charges of heresy, among the claims made against him was his denial that Christ was incarnated "in order to liberate us from the yoke of the devil."[39] The ransom theory was already thoroughly critiqued a few decades earlier by Anselm, though it had a remarkable staying power.

What was needed, in Anslem's view, in the context of a Christendom that had come to permeate the fabric of society, was a rational accounting of the need for atonement and the mechanism by which Christ's passion did its redemptive work. Anselm refused the fundamental myths of a cosmic battle (Christus Victor), the notion of a property exchange found in ransom theologies, and the gnostic view of a world created by a demiurge. But his reformulation of the concept of atonement was just as metaphorically rooted as the earlier efforts that relied on contexts of

---

38. Williams, *Eucharistic Sacrifice*, 31.
39. Mews, "Lists of Heresies," 108.

expiation. "The nub of the question," writes Anselm in the form of a dialogue between himself and a student named Boso, "was why God became man."[40] His answer: the restoration of human nature. What often goes unnoticed in discussions of Anselm is the centrality of a second question, intimately related to the first: Why did God create humans? With the logic of the syllogism and by transferring the emphasis in feudal society on honor to the realm of human-divine relations, Anselm introduced a new and most spectacular fundamental myth.

Following an idea from Augustine, Anselm proposed that God created humans to replenish the ranks of the heavenly choirs that had been diminished by Lucifer's rebellion. God, as the Sovereign, had his honor offended by his vassals, Adam and Eve. When they sinned, they failed to uphold the righteousness of will that was their sole and complete obligation to God. Instead of overcoming the devil through obedience, they succumbed to his temptations and placed themselves under his influence, acting against God's will and honor. Moreover, through their fall, Adam and Eve disrupted God's plan for the future of humankind, leading to the corruption of all human nature. The human being, created to prove worthy of angelic promotion, miserably fails the appointed task; they are not fit for taking their place in the eternal choir of jubilation, according to God's original plan. Our rejection of the offer of angelic status is received by God as an insult and injurious to his honor (the common social exchange in medieval Europe entailed the feudal Lord offering his subjects safety and protection, and the subjects give their Lord the honor, respect, and tribute they deserve). Refusing their role in restoring the choir of angels, humans dishonor God—this dishonoring of God is man's sin (here, we have come a long way from the original biblical sin, namely, Cain's murder of his brother). Given that no one can make satisfaction except God, and no one ought to make it except man, it is necessary that one who is a God-man should make it. So runs Anslem's logic.

In Blumenberg's reading of Anselm, this narrative reflects the medieval mindset, which often accepted such narrative ideas without questioning their broader implications, like why God, omnipotent as he is, couldn't simply create new angels instead of using humans as replacements. Blumenberg notes that this acceptance signals a transition from myth towards dogma, where stories come to serve as answers to unasked questions while (unlike myth) simultaneously discouraging further

40. Anselm, *Cur Deus Homo*, 2.6.

inquiry. Anselm's theory, Blumenberg suggests, reveals a tension within medieval scholasticism: the attempt to reconcile faith with reason and the need to justify God's actions within a framework that doesn't diminish his omnipotence. Anselm cautiously addresses the idea that humans were created as a solution to a problem—replacing the fallen angels—while still allowing for a meaningful human prehistory, though also writing us out of having an active role to play in the unfolding of history.

Blumenberg points out that Anselm's approach demonstrates the medieval tendency to ask and answer more questions than found in the foundational Christian texts. Anselm's argument eventually replaces the gnostic idea of Christ purchasing humanity's freedom from the world's ruler with a new myth: the infinite atonement made to God the Father by the Son. This shift, according to Blumenberg, introduced into theology a kind of necessary logic, where God's plan for salvation could only be fulfilled by Christ's passion and death, ensuring that theological explanations adhered to a rigorous equivalence between sin and atonement: crucifixion as a necessary death. In Anselm's work, myth and reason coexist, but the focus shifts towards the necessity and inevitability of God's plan for salvation, culminating in the incarnation-crucifixion. Blumenberg argues that this narrative was plausible in the medieval context because it aligned with the view that God's ultimate goal was his own glorification. The idea that God created the world, and humanity, for his own glory, rather than, say, for our benefit and enjoyment, reflects a shift towards a rationalized theological rigor that marginalized the humanistic elements of Christian tradition. The more medieval theology emphasized original sin and divine grace, the more it distanced humanity from the world's inherent goodness, portraying nature as something hostile to humans in their fallen state. If redemption has been accomplished, there is little for us to do other than assent (or not) to this extravagant story; active participation in redemptive action is not required.

As theology progressed, the world was no longer seen as created for the benefit of all humanity but only for the elect—those predestined for salvation. If only a select number of humans were to be elevated to the divine choir, what is the fate of all the others? Here is the origin of a suspicion "that there might be an accidental surplus [of people], which would inevitably lead to the *massa damnata* and would make the divinity's will to salvation fail to be credible for mankind as a whole, because it would be without a function."[41] This theological perspective made the world's meaning inaccessible to us, as it became purely a demonstration of God's omnipotence and will, rendering irrelevant any philosophical or rational inquiry into the world's purpose or functioning. Blumenberg highlights that this development culminated in a significant consequence: the division between theology and philosophy. Ultimately, this transition contributed to the autonomy of philosophy by challenging the idea that the omnipotent God and the God of salvation could be rationally understood as one. This shift paved the way for the modern age, where philosophy began to operate independently of theological assumptions, especially those concerning the teleological purpose of the world for humanity.[42] Blumenberg discerns in Anselm's theory of atonement a leave-taking of the incarnation as solidarity—with the biblical-anthropological God's interest in history and concern for humanity—in favor of a "theocentric: God of "transcendence, sovereignty, hiddenness, [and] fearsomeness."[43]

Anselm asks his readers "whether it is fitting for God to forgive a sin out of mercy alone, without any restitution of what is owed to him."[44] It is not. If there is no punishment, "no satisfaction is given, the way to regulate sin correctly is none other than to punish it."[45] Here, punishment is understood as corrective, necessary, and just. It seems even God is subject to some form of cosmic balance. Within this paradigm of what Blumenberg terms "theological absolutism," what can humanity do to demonstrate gratitude for access (for some) to an unmerited grace? Anselm's answer appears to be, we can imitate the sacrifice of Christ, who died for the sake of justice.

> There can, moreover, be nothing that a man may suffer—voluntarily and without owing repayment of a debt—more painful

---

41. Blumenberg, *Work on Myth*, 250. According to Augustine, all of humanity is born into a state of sin and is thus deserving of damnation. However, God, in his mercy, elects some individuals for salvation while the rest remain part of the mass of the damned (*massa damnata*).

42. Blumenberg offers several dense pages of reflection on Anselm's *Cur Deus Homo*. See his *Work on Myth*, 248–52 and *Legitimacy*, 170–75.

43. Blumenberg, *Legitimacy*, 484. "Fearsomeness" comes to be a central feature of medieval Christian culture, a history discussed in some detail by Brock and Parker, in *Saving Paradise*, a book whose subtitle condenses the history of the shift from patristic to medieval Christendom: *How Christianity Traded Love of This World for Crucifixion and Empire*.

44. Anselm, "Why God Became Man," 263.

45. Anselm, "Why God Became Man," 284.

or more difficult than death. And there is no act of self-giving whereby a man may give himself to God greater than when he hands himself over to death for God's glory.[46]

The purpose of incarnation is death, and our purpose, to the extent we have any, is to die for God. Anselm seems to be some distance from Christ's view of his own impending death, which is that "Greater love has no man than this, that a man lay down his life for his friends" (John 13:15). Anselm emphasizes incarnation, not as an act of the divine's solidarity, concern, and commitment to us—the *kenosis* (self-emptying) of Christ—but part of a sacrificial mechanism for dealing with sin. Anselm's theory of atonement is from beginning to end wrapped in consideration of God's glory, God's honor, and the need for balanced rectification.

An obvious problem with substitutionary atonement as devised by Anselm is that it implicates Divinity in retributive violence, in a system of exchange that requires violence as a solution to a problem. Both the notion of an "original sin" that is "inherited" (regardless of one's moral acts) and the idea that a sacrificial ceremony whereby Jesus of Nazareth is brutally executed as the means to dealing with this fundamental sin are morally suspect. Alongside the considerable (largely negative) implications of assimilating Augustine's theology in this new paradigm of substitutionary atonement is that it embeds violence into the Divinity, violence is the mechanism used by God to rectify problems. Augustine is a master at evoking the sense of God's love, but no amount of rhetorical beauty can get one around the ugliness of the father who tells his son, while loosening his belt, that the impending beating "will hurt me more than it hurts you." In this paradigm, redemption is conceived with the aid of those juridical and cultic conceptions and practices (discussed above) whereby the suffering body is an instrument of exchange, an in-kind cash payment used to erase debts/sins.

While the New Testament frequently employs sacrificial metaphors for Jesus's death (e.g., Rom 3:25; 1 Pet 1:19), their theological functions remain contested. As Hans Küng observes, "Only in the comparatively late letter to the Hebrews, by an unknown Hellenistic author, partly utilizing Pauline motifs, is the theme of sacrifice broadly developed in cultic terminology."[47] Earlier texts like 1 Cor 5:7 ("Christ our Passover") or

---

46. Anselm, "Why God Became Man," 331.

47 Küng, *On Being a Christian*, 424. A reading of the New Testament in terms of expiatory sacrifice is rejected by many scholars, including Girard. Paul Tillich, in his effort to turn the tide on substitutionary atonement, suggests doing away altogether with language of atonement and justification. As these are "biblical" terms, they can't be entirely exorcised, but they "should be replaced in the practice of teaching and preaching

Mark 10:45 ("a ransom for many") deploy sacrificial imagery primarily to signify liberation or covenant renewal—not the expiation as articulated in Hebrews, where Christ's blood is said to "purify your conscience" (Heb 9:14). By Anselm's era, this imagery had evolved into a satisfaction theory wherein Christ's death—as an act of infinite worth—honors God in a way humanity cannot. Though feudal rather than penal (God demands no punishment, only owed honor), this framework retains sacrificial logic's risky implication: that divine justice or honor requires suffering. Later Reformers would radicalize this further, imposing a forensic, penal-substitutionary reading onto texts originally more participatory than transactional.

Anselm's is also a theology well-suited to underwriting both the practice of holy war and submission to draconian authority. Paradoxically, Anselm can hold that "no one [should] take vengeance, except . . . him who is Lord of all," and yet "when earthly powers take action . . . in accordance with right, it is the Lord himself, by whom they have been appointed for the task, who is acting."[48] As has often been noted, "If God delivers His Son to a violent death in order to satisfy His justice, it seems natural that, guided by the same idea of justice, human society would approve the death penalty or just war."[49] Elsewhere, Anselm imagines God as "that than which nothing greater can be conceived"; but here, in *Cur Deus Homo*, there seems something greater than God, namely, God's apparent subordination to some form of debt repayment in the form of a corrective violence that bridges the divide between injury and reparation, between guilt and atonement, between dishonor and honor. Anslem's focus on debt repayment is not yet the punitive violence of Reformed theology, but it establishes a template wherein divine reconciliation requires suffering as a form of currency. Even God, it seems, is rent between infinite freedom and a sacrificial economy that God ostensibly transcends yet perpetuates.[50]

Blumenberg does not integrate minority reports into his analysis of forms of theological absolutism and the way it lay the groundwork

---

by the term 'acceptance.'" Similarly, the language of "forgiveness of sins" is a "religious symbolic expression taken from such human relations as that between debtor and the one to whom he is in debt. . . . As in every symbol, the analogy is limited" Tillich, *Systematic Theology*, 3:224–25.

48. Anselm, "Why God Became Man," 285.

49. Koryakin, "Abandoning Penal Substitution," 785.

50. For a concise (and, to my mind, a devastating) critique of Anselm's theology of atonement and sacrificial interpretations of Christ's death, see Küng, *On Being a Christian*, 421–27.

for the response that came to be called modernity. And there are many representatives of such a minority position, a moment in history where what would become the status quo is but one among various options. Hildegard of Bingen, for example, develops a very different theology than that of Anselm. For Hildegard, "Christ's incarnation [is] the sign that the Spirit of God had penetrated all human flesh and sanctified earthly life with incandescent beauty." Jesus is "the most beautiful of human beings, the very image and essence of beauty."[51] Similarly, Peter Abelard's theory of atonement is strikingly different than that of Anselm (and of his contemporary, Hugh of St. Victor). Abelard's view is that a theology of redemption needs to disentangle itself from matters of justice, law, and honor, as he details in his *Commentary on St. Paul's Epistle to the Romans*. Redemption is not about the propitiation of God, systems of exchange, or the expiation of sin, but about love.

Abelard's rejection of substitutionary, sacrificial logic sounds strikingly modern. He refuses to bind God's freedom to the grim necessity of a propitiatory sacrifice on the cross. Theories such as Anselm's are both logically and ethically flawed:

> How very cruel and unjust it seems that someone should require the blood of an innocent person as a ransom, or that in any way it might please him that an innocent person be slain, still less that God should have so accepted the death of his Son that through it he was reconciled to the whole world.[52]

Reflections such as these, writes Abelard, "inspire a not insignificant question, namely, concerning our redemption and justification through the death of our Lord Jesus Christ."[53] Abelard's answer in his commentary is clear and concise:

> Redemption is that supreme love in us through the Passion of Christ, which not only frees us from slavery to sin, but gains for us the true liberty of the sons of God, so that we may complete all things by his love rather than by fear. He showed us such great grace, than which a greater cannot be found, by his own word: "No one," he says, "has greater love than this: that he lays down his life for his friends."[54]

---

51. Quoted in Brock and Parker, 290.
52. Abelard, *Commentary*, 167.
53. Abelard, *Commentary*, 167.
54. Abelard, *Commentary*, 168.

The incarnation, the "God-man" is not required for atonement but is rather a manifestation of divine love, of the reality of love. Forgiveness of sin (release from slavery) is not found through an objective transaction between foreign powers but in the knowing and practice of love. Abelard's theory of redemption emphasized regeneration and sanctification, not satisfaction and justification. Abelard rejects not only the image of the Father requiring or demanding the blood of his Son; he further rejects the idea of there being a price for the release from captivity or slavery that is sin. The devil, in other words, never acquired any actual rights over us; we do not "belong" to him but to God. And God cannot, logically, demand a payment from himself.

Abelard's theology of redemption is often referred to as "exemplarism," which holds to the view that Christ's death primarily serves as an example of obedience to God's will, which embodies divine love; the cross is not an alchemy of blood but rather inspires a response in the human heart—specifically, a love for God. This theory is also known as "subjective" redemption because it focuses on the individual's personal response. In contrast, the "objective" model assumes that Christ's death itself secured salvation for humanity (or a portion thereof), independent of any human response.

"Perfect charity," writes Abelard (quoting Paul), "casts out fear," and such love is given to us, through an act of grace, in the passion.[55] The passion accomplishes reconciliation with God through its effect on the human heart. Whether this position is worthy of the charge of Pelagianism—deemed one of the great heresies of church history—is an open question; a further question is whether, if the charge is true, there is anything so terribly heretical about it.[56] Whether one naturally or supernaturally is brought to love is perhaps a moot point, and a good example of the empiricism and pragmatism of William James:

> In other words, not its origin, but the way in which it works on the whole, is . . . [the] final test of a belief. This is our own empiricist criterion; and this criterion the stoutest insisters on supernatural origin have also been forced to use in the end. . . . By their fruits ye shall know them, not by their roots. . . . The roots of a man's virtue are inaccessible to us. No appearances whatever are infallible proofs of grace. Our practice is the only sure evidence, even to ourselves, that we are genuinely Christians.[57]

---

55. Abelard, *Commentary*, 77.

56. For a deeper dive into the matter of Abelard's supposed Pelagianism, see Williams, "Sin, Grace, and Redemption."

57. James, *Variety of Religious Experience*, 37.

Chapter 7

God

> God is the reason why there is something rather than nothing, the condition of possibility of any entity whatsoever. Not being any sort of entity himself, however, he is not to be reckoned up alongside these things, any more than my envy and my left foot constitute a pair of objects. God and the universe do not make two. In an act of Judaic iconoclasm, we are forbidden to make graven images of this nonentity because the only image of him is human beings.
>
> —Terry Eagleton, *Reason, Faith, and Revolution*

THE ANTHROPOLOGIST ROY RAPPAPORT takes as foundational that "it is plausible . . . that religion's origins are, if not one with the origins of humanity, closely connected to them." Examining the ethnological record, we observe that "no society known to anthropology or history is devoid of what reasonable observers would agree is religion."[1] Without delving into the details of cognitive psychology and paleoanthropology, it is a plausible assumption that, just as humans generically and genetically have the capacity for language, we also have the competence and drive for transcendence—for the sacred, the holy, the divine . . . in a word, for God. The difficult methodological and theoretical problem is, as Regis Debray writes, to try and distinguish between "the innate

---

1. Rappaport, *Ritual and Religion*, 1. One feature of religion is the drive to transcendence, though certain kinds of materialism, physicalism, and cognitivism deny there is anything transcendent to observable, physical reality, and hence the term is, in effect, meaningless. This is not my view, as discussed earlier.

and the acquired, what persists and what changes, the scenario of the genome and the hidden design of the centuries."[2] Debray observes that while we may well possess the genetic and cultural capacity for God, the biblical God is characterized by a relatively unique set of narratives, images, conceptions, and metaphors, which arrived, in evolutionary terms, very late on the scene.

Historians debate whether significant changes in worldviews occur rapidly, marking clear breaks from the past, or gradually as part of a continuous process. Proponents of rapid, transformative shifts cite examples like the rise of settled agriculture with the invention of the plow, the emergence of Renaissance humanism, and the technical advances of the Industrial Revolution, suggesting these periods quickly ushered in pervasive, fundamental changes. Critics emphasize that such shifts are often the culmination of longer, incremental developments that build on existing ideas and practices. Despite these debates, sociocultural change is a real phenomenon, and this includes changes in how different cultures conceive of and relate to God. An even more difficult question is whether these changes are headed anywhere, whether the changes that transpire in religion, politics, economics, and other domains are in service of truth, beauty, and goodness. Martin Luther King Jr. famously claimed, in the context of the civil rights movement, that "I am convinced that we shall overcome because the arc of the moral universe is long, but it bends toward justice." A name for this arc, or that toward which the arc bends, if it bends, is God. To hold to the existence of such a "bend" was King's faith position, one that allowed him to "hew out of the mountain of despair the stone of hope."[3] It is trite to dismiss such a faith as merely an example of wishful thinking; beside, even if it is wish, or, in King's language, a "dream," this does nothing to discount its truth.

The conception of a male, singular, creator-covenant God is roughly four thousand years old, appearing in the ancient Near East in the mid-Bronze Age, during which time the transition from small-scale hunting and gathering to intensive plow- and irrigation-based agriculture along the great river systems of the Tigris, Euphrates, and Nile was largely complete. Prior to the invention of plow-based agriculture, God imagery in the ancient Near East was overwhelmingly female, leading anthropologists to suggest that where women work gardens with a hoe, God is

---

2. Debray, *God*, 17–19. Just why this is the case is a fascinating question but one beyond the scope of this book.

3. King, *Testament of Hope*, 277.

a Woman; where men work fields with a plow, God is a Man.[4] That conceptions of God in the monotheistic religions bear the imprint of a turn to patriarchy and male-oriented and male-privileged social organization does not mean that God is male or masculine, and fortunately there are other metaphors in biblical texts; still, metaphors have both sources and consequences, and feminist critiques of patriarchal God-talk remain in high demand. Fast forwarding a few millennia, early Christians began advancing ideas about God that, in Paul's words, the Greeks deemed "foolish" and the Jews a "stumbling block" (1 Cor 1:18–25). There are now many studies examining changing conceptions of God amongst Jews and Christians.[5] The Bible itself, as we have noted, tracks these changes. For example, at one point in the books of law, God instructs how to practice ritual sacrifice but later in the prophetic books he condemns it, if not in principle at least in its current form of practice.[6] In brief, conceptions of God change, and the task in this chapter is to detail a core of these changes around which early Christianity organized and consolidated itself—the incarnation. But we first must address the question of whether we can even beg the use of the word God, which Martin Buber described as the "most heavy-laden of all human words."[7]

A Sphere in the Woods

The philosopher Richard Taylor describes a thought experiment involving your coming across a large, smooth sphere while out for a walk in the woods. Your immediate reaction may well be to wonder about the origin and nature of the sphere. Questions would naturally arise: How did it get here? What is it made of? Who or what put it here? Taylor's aim

---

4. See Chafetz, *Sex and Advantage*; Sanday, *Female Power*; Sanday and Goodenough, eds., *Beyond the Second Sex*. Ken Wilber develops this line of thinking in his *Sex, Ecology, Spirituality*. Wilber, drawing on anthropological research, points out that the invention of the plow pushed women out of food production, as operating a plow beyond the first trimester greatly increases the likelihood of miscarriage.

5. Minimally, a multidisciplinary dive into this literature might include, Assman, *Price of Monotheism*; Miles, *God: A Biography* and *Christ*; Debray, *God*; Wright, *Evolution of God*.

6. By "later" here is meant later in the ordering of the books of the Hebrew Bible. Dating these books historically is not easy, and it may be that the prophetic books were closed prior to the completion or even writing of the Torah. Isaiah, in other words, likely never read Genesis.

7. Buber, *Eclipse of God*, 6.

is to illustrate our propensity to seek explanations for things that appear out of the ordinary or that stand out as anomalies in our environment. Taylor concocts the sphere scenario to introduce *the principle of sufficient reason*, which holds that everything must have a reason or cause. We are often moved to ask "whence" questions and not only of mysterious spheres but of everyday things, like trees, rocks, and people—even the universe as such.

"If one thinks about [the principle of sufficient reason]," writes Taylor, "he is apt to find that he presupposes it in his thinking about reality."[8] Even though it cannot be proven to be true, the principle is a reasonable position that we often presuppose to be the case. We tend to reason that everything comes from somewhere, has something behind it or informing it, depends on other things for its existence. Another word for this dependency is *contingency*. Taylor uses the sphere thought experiment to argue that our natural inclination to seek explanations is fundamental to metaphysical inquiry. It underlines the philosophical pursuit of understanding the existence and nature of the universe.

The unexplained presence of the sphere in the woods is not unlike our experience of the universe. We find ourselves in a world that we did not create, and we quite naturally seek to understand its origin, purpose, and meaning. It is as perfectly reasonable to be as shocked or puzzled by the fact of existence as by the fact of a strange, out of place sphere: "Why this sphere in the woods?" and "Why anything at all?" are related questions. Perhaps the oldest philosophical or existential question is, as Leibniz posed it, "Why is there something rather than nothing?"[9] In my view, this question can receive no definitive answer. But everyone answers it in one form or another, explicitly or tacitly, consciously or unconsciously, and the range of answers runs from nihilistic faith—we (along with the universe) are here for no reason at all—to religious faith—we are created in the image of God and are here to love God. A feature of modernity is its tendency to nihilism, to hold there is no formative reason behind or within existence, no "arc" that is "bending," just random chaos. But nihilism is a position, not a conclusion; it is stance one takes, not an outcome

---

8. Taylor, *Metaphysics*, 100–101.

9. The formulation is found in his essay, "Principles of Nature," a popular account of philosophy of nature and metaphysics. Here, Leibniz observes that a "sufficient reason for the existence of the universe can't be found in the series of contingent things—that is, in bodies and the representations of them in souls." See Leibniz, "Principles of Nature."

of scientific thinking. In fact, the nihilistic position may be less reasonable than that of faith.

A Tale Told by an Idiot?

Nietzsche, in announcing the reality of the "death of God," expressed the truth that the modern era is awash in nihilism; far from promoting nihilism, as many believe, Nietzsche sought a way out of it. As Michael Allen Gillespie has argued, the nihilism that Nietzsche observed was centuries in the making, with roots in medieval nominalism. Nominalism introduced a new understanding of God and reality, one that emphasized the absolute power of God's will over his connection to reason, eternal truths, and love. When we ask of the medieval era, which God was it medieval people thought they could have? The answer is the omnipotent, abstract, distant God described by nominalism, "a God whose absolutistic qualities eventually led to self-dissolution."[10] The nominalists, as described by Gillespie, Blumenberg, and others, laid the groundwork for a worldview where traditional metaphysical and moral orders were questioned to the point of complete erasure, which is also a feature and danger of currents of contemporary postmodernism.[11] Modern nihilism arose from this longer historical transformation in the conception of God, with its concomitant changes in human self-perception and values, expressed, for example, in the self-assertion of human will (which Blumenberg argues is the characteristic feature of modernity).[12] This is not the place to pursue the merits of Nietzsche's solution to nihilism (one that pushes human self-assertion to its limits), but to point out that there is another route to resolve the problem Nietzsche and other modernists faced, namely, to reject not God as such but the nominalist picture of God. This is the argument a young Hans Blumenberg made in an essay (from 1954) on Kant's conception of God, where he observes that concepts that seem fixed and secure were at one point in history merely possibilities. If we

---

10. Rasmussen, *Memory of God*, 187.

11. See Eagleton, *Illusions of Postmodernism*.

12. Gillespie, *Nihilism Before Nietzsche*, xxii, writes, "My argument also resembles the argument presented by Hans Blumenberg in *The Legitimacy of the Modern Age*. I agree with Blumenberg's general thesis that modernity developed in response to the intractable questions that arose out of late medieval thought, but I argue, contrary to Blumenberg, that the modern notion of will, or what Blumenberg calls self-assertion, is not a new construct that reoccupies an intellectual position that skepticism opened up, but the secularization of the idea of divine omnipotence."

can wind our way back to these transitional moments, we can better see the possibilities that were annulled by the victory of an ascendant point of view. The nominalist conception of God, in Blumenberg's analysis, only served to exacerbate the problem of the absolutism of reality. And so Blumenberg wonders "whether [today] the return of God is among these [refused] possibilities" of the past.[13]

Modern thought, argues Blumenberg, was born out of the need to deal with problems generated by medieval nominalism; but perhaps we need not reinvent the wheel, perhaps we can retrieve and recover views of God that were displaced by nominalism. To fine-tune Blumenberg: Is the return of a certain kind of God a possibility for us?[14] Blumenberg does not simply negate or reject the absolutist God but rather illuminates its paradoxes to make space for an alternative conception.[15] Again, we must cite Blumenberg's basic openness to retrieval; in studying the formative metaphors of religious concepts (indeed, of all concepts), we take "metaphors [as] fossils that indicate an archaic stratum of the trail of theoretical curiosity—a stratum that is not rendered anachronistic just because there is no way back to the fullness of its stimulations and expectations of truth."[16]

The universe may be a tale told by an idiot, full of sound and fury and signifying nothing; it may be pure accident and randomness; it may be the outcome of efficient causes running their course according to the fixed, mathematical laws of nature; but it may be, to evoke another account of existence, that there is an uncaused, uncreated, infinite source of all that is, a source that is perfectly *transcendent* to all things, which means that it is also fundamentally *immanent* to all things, and that towards which we are drawn. Paul Tillich wrote of authentic symbols as participating in the reality to which they point, but we tend not to think this way anymore, for we imagine no reality on the other side of our endless chains of signification: there is nothing to approach. For Hans-Georg Gadamer, the task of modern philosophy is to mediate between the assumptions and consequences of science, which he acknowledges as modernity's "unassailable and anonymous authority" and the "totality of our experience of life," with an eye to reconnecting "the objective world of technology" to

13. Blumenberg, "Kant und die Frage," 554.
14. This question is pursued by Rasmussen in *Memory of God*. I've learned a great deal from Rasmussen.
15. Rasmussen, *Memory of God*, 187–88.
16. Blumenberg, *Shipwreck with Spectator*, 82.

"those fundamental orders of our being that are neither arbitrary nor manipulable by us, but rather simply demand our respect."[17] But, again, many of us no longer believe in such non-arbitrary, unmanipulable orders of being. Infinite malleability, infinite manipulability—these are the hallmarks of an oppressive totalism in which "man" disappears.

Here it must be admitted that there is ultimately no way of deciding between, say, the "world-as-accident" and the "world-as-God's-creation." These are not two different propositions that one can empirically test to see which is correct—they are positions one assumes, perspectives that one takes up and holds as a matter of faith. We tend to think that our metaphysical and ontological commitments simply align with the way things are. In modernity, the general tendency has been to assume the world is, in the end, absurd and meaningless, a refusal of King's bending arc, a position of despair and nihilism that Shakespeare magnificently describes in the character of Macbeth. But, again, this is a faith position, which is not to say there is nothing to be said for it; the slings and arrows that accompany most lives can leave one grasping for meaning and purpose: indeed, it may even be correct view of things: there may be no arc. But in the absence of knowing for sure (and no one can be certain, since, to follow Shakespeare a little further, death is "an undiscovered country from which no traveller returns"), we can but take-up reasonable positions, and see how they work. As William James put the matter, judge a faith or worldview by its fruits, not its roots.[18] We simply don't know the answers to ultimate questions, though we seem to need to pose the questions and settle on answers of some sort.

Erik Erikson, a developmental psychologist and psychoanalyst, proposed a theory of psychosocial development comprising eight stages that span from infancy to adulthood. Each stage presents a central conflict that must be resolved for healthy psychological development. Erikson

---

17. Gadamer, *Philosophical Hermeneutics*, 3–4.

18. This perspective is a cornerstone of James's pragmatic philosophy, extensively discussed in his seminal work, *Varieties of Religious Experience*. James asserts that the true measure of religious experience and faith lies in their "fruits"—the tangible benefits and moral outcomes they produce—rather than their "roots"—the metaphysical or historical origins. He believes that religious experiences are valid if they contribute positively to an individual's life and well-being, fostering virtues such as charity, patience, and courage. He suggests that the authenticity and value of religious experiences are best judged by their ability to bring about positive change and moral improvement in individuals, since definitive final answers to ultimate questions are, in the end, beyond our capacities.

believed that each stage builds on the outcomes of previous stages.[19] The first, foundational stage is known as "Trust vs. Mistrust," during which an infant acquires (or fails to acquire) a basic sense that the world is a loving, trustworthy place to be. The infant's development of trust in their caregiver, along with taking comfort and pleasure in their surroundings, can be seen as a specific instance of a more general existential trust in the existence of a benevolent, sustaining power, what Tillich termed the "ground of being." This comparison need not be interpreted in terms of theories of "projection," where religious images and concepts are seen as the product of psycho-social needs. Rather, Erikson's theory is the result of a discovery of a basic structure or pattern at work in the world. If there were no such pattern, why would one wish a child to develop a basic sense of trust in the first place? Is trust merely a relative social construct? In Genesis, we read that God deems his acts of creation "good" and "very good." The fittingness of creation, our belonging in it and to it, is an experience one has, a position one assumes, a faith one embodies, despite the sufferings to which we are each variously subjected. Faith includes the dimensions of doubt precisely due to the fact it is often difficult to affirm a foundational goodness to the world.

The question of the existence of God is often posed within what Terry Eagleton calls the "yeti-theory of religion," according to which God is conceived of as a being among other beings. But "God and the universe do not make two." Faith is an existential and ontological matter, not an empirical one. God is not an object or being that could, for example, be photographed (as could, in principle, the Yeti or Loch Ness monster) but rather, as Eagleton writes, "the reason why there is something rather than nothing, the condition of possibility of any entity whatsoever. Not being any sort of entity himself, however, he is not to be reckoned up alongside these things, any more than my envy and my left foot constitute a pair of objects."[20] Now, one may of course hold there is no reason there is something rather than nothing, but this is an assumed posture, a "fundamental ontology" that imagines it has refused metaphysics. Moreover, if the principle of sufficient reason has weight, nihilism may be the extreme expression of unreason.

---

19. Erikson, *Childhood and Society*.
20. Eagleton, *Reason, Faith, and Revolution*, 7–8.

The Argument from Contingency

It isn't possible to reason oneself to a position of faith (or, to use Erikson's language, "basic trust"). Faith, like love, is experiential and performative not empirical and propositional. "I have faith in God" is closer to "I believe in democracy" or "I love my partner," than it is to "I believe aliens exist." Performative statements do not merely describe a situation but perform intentional acts (such as trusting, promising, committing, desiring) in and through the very act of being spoken. They bring about a certain state of affairs, certain kinds of relationships ("I will pick you up at 8, no worries"). Once assumed, faith can, in the classic formulation, "seek understanding" and give reasons for itself[21] ("He's never failed to pick me up, so I'm certain he'll be there"). Faith without reason, a position known as *fideism*, has long received criticism and even condemnation in church history ("Even though he's never picked me up when he said he would, he will be there tonight").

One reasonable argument for the existence of God, the reality of a "ground of being," is the argument from contingency. In his discussion of the principle of sufficient reason Taylor draws the distinction between *contingent* and *necessary* truths. It is quite common today to think that all things are contingent—everything depends on something else. But if one holds that all things are contingent, it logically follows, according to the principles of modal logic and metaphysical argument, that there must be some-thing that is not contingent.[22] This non-contingent entity would be necessary, thereby providing the ultimate explanation for the existence of all contingent things and beings. Without such a necessary entity (or matrix or foundation), the existence of contingent beings and things would lack a sufficient reason, leading to an infinite regress, which many philosophers and not a few theologians argue is not a satisfactory explanation for the existence of the world. The traditional word for this necessary "entity" is God. Should you ask at this

---

21. The phrase "faith seeking understanding" derives from Anselm's work *Proslogion*, where he presents the ontological argument for the existence of God. In this work, Anselm explores the relationship between faith and reason, arguing that faith is the foundation upon which reason builds to seek greater understanding.

22. The language of "thing" can lead us astray, for it implies a concrete, observable, physical-material object, one that could, in principle, be measured, weighed, photographed. To be a materialist of a certain kind is to hold that only matter exists, and so this argument from contingency leads the materialist to conceive of God as a thing, an object in the universe alongside other objects. But a conception of God as an object, as a thing, is, in Judeo-Christian tradition, an example of idolatry.

point "But where does God come from?" you've missed the boat, since God is not a thing among other things but the *reason* there is something rather than nothing. This is what it means to think ontologically. Another way to put this is to distinguish essential causation from accidental causation. Though Aristotle distinguished four different kinds of causation—material, formal, efficient, and final—in the wake of the scientific revolution and positivism, we are left with only efficient causation. In modernity, people tend to no longer think that things or beings are "ordered to a given end," that "they have a goal or proper purpose."[23] But one certainly can think this, and not without good reason.[24]

"Which God Did We Think We Could Hope For?"

> People are not yet finished; therefore, neither is their past, which continues to affect us under a different sign, in the drive of its questions, in the experiment of its answers; we are all in the same boat. The dead return transformed.
>
> —Ernst Bloch, *Subjekt-Objekt*

Hegel famously observed that there was no true philosophy prior to Kant. Before Kant philosophy lacked a critical foundation and systematic method capable of comprehensively addressing the nature of knowledge and reality. In Hegel's view, earlier philosophies were characterized by a form of dogmatism whereby philosophical systems were based on assumed principles without critically examining their foundations. Kant's critical philosophy, especially as outlined in his *Critique of Pure Reason*, introduced the idea that the mind actively shapes our experience of reality through categories and concepts. This marked a departure from the traditional "copy theory of knowledge," which understood knowledge as merely a passive reception of information from the external world. In the *Critique of Pure Reason*, Kant posed four fundamental questions that he believed encapsulated the core of philosophical inquiry: "What can we know?" "What should we do?" "What may we hope?" and "What is the human being?" The fourth is perhaps the linchpin of the set; this

---

23. Illich, *Rivers North*, 72.

24. Thomas Aquinas develops this line of argument in his *Summa Theologiae*. See, for example, his discussion of possibility and necessity: "Therefore we cannot but postulate the existence of some being having of itself its own necessity, and not receiving it from another, but rather causing in others their necessity. This all men speak of as God" (Q2, a3, reply 1).

was certainly Kant's own view, as he reasoned that an answer to the basic question of what it means to be human is fundamental to answering questions about knowledge, morality, and hope. But Kant's anthropology isn't very robust and is limited to largely moral and pragmatic aspects without a comprehensive integration of cultural and historical dimensions. He did, however, lay the groundwork for what would become philosophical anthropology. As discussed earlier, Blumenberg's philosophical anthropology endeavors to make philosophical sense of the basic discoveries of modern anthropology.

Blumenberg proposes a subtle change to Kant's formulation. Rather than ask "What can we know?," Blumenberg puts the matter this way: "What was it that we wanted to know?" Similarly, "What may we hope?" becomes "What might we have hoped for?"[25] This historicizing of philosophical (and religious) concepts is what makes Blumenberg a historian of ideas and not merely a philosopher. The answer Blumenberg proposes to Kant's fourth question is that the human is the creature that must deal with the experience of the absolutism of reality. His speculative philosophical anthropology emphasizes the inherent complexities of the human situation, which includes the need for orientation, myth-making, and symbolic frameworks to cope with reality. Blumenberg sees no great tension between *mythos* and *logos*, both being means at our disposal to deal with what life throws at us. Blumenberg is critical of teleological narratives that claim to predict or dictate the direction of human history, emphasizing instead the importance of understanding history as a series of contingent and context-dependent developments.

In the context of the Scientific Revolution, we speak of the rise of the Newtonian worldview. But in the moment of its emergence, it is but one among a set of possibilities. As empirical, quantitative, mathematical science in the spirit of Galileo and Newton was taking deep root in European society, Johann Goethe took issue with the dominance of Newtonian science (which he thought too reductive and mathematized) and produced an alternative to Newton's theory of light. In the strict sense of quantitative science, Newton's theories about light and color are correct and form the basis for our understanding of optics. But Goethe's theories, while not scientifically accurate in the same way, offer significant insights into the perceptual and psychological aspects of color and vision, which are important in different contexts, especially in the arts

---

25. Blumenberg, *Readability of the World*, 1–2.

and humanities. We can revisit Goethe's analysis, and when we do, we see it as a possibility that was, in large measure, rejected or ignored, but nevertheless one still available to us. This is precisely the route taken by Walter Kaufmann, who argues that, when it comes to understanding the life of the mind, Goethe's holistic science is more suitable than Newton's reductive and mathematical approach.[26]

As Blumenberg surveys the history of religious, philosophical, and scientific thought in the West, he asks two kinds of questions. First, he examines the extent to which and in what ways a new idea allows us to navigate two fundamental anthropological problems: the experience of the absolutism of reality and the need to create meaningful "worlds" in which to live. This work he terms "metaphorology," which aims to uncover and analyze the deep metaphors and symbolic structures that underpin human thought and culture. Metaphor is more than figure of speech, more than mere rhetorical flourish—thought is premised on "absolute metaphors," which defy straightforward expression, and they cannot be fully explained or replaced by literal description. These metaphors serve as the bedrock for entire systems of thought, influencing how we perceive and interpret various aspects of reality. Examples analyzed by Blumenberg include "truth as light," "life as a sea voyage," "history as a story," and the "universe as a book." That "these metaphors are called 'absolute' means only that they prove resistant to terminological claims and cannot be dissolved into conceptuality." To say anything at all about truth, life, history, or the universe we necessarily rely on metaphor—we cannot resolve "life" into the real, into logicality, into literal speech. Importantly, though absolute metaphors resist literalness, it is "not that one metaphor could not be replaced or represented by another, or corrected through a more precise one. Even absolute metaphors therefore have a history."[27] This is the also the case for conceptions of God, the absolute metaphor of absolute metaphors. God is a metaphor for reality as such, which means it incorporates other absolute metaphors (truth,

---

26. Kaufmann, *Goethe, Kant, and Hegel*, 35, writes: "Goethe's opposition to Newton has not been appreciated sufficiently. Although Goethe himself considered his scientific work as important as anything he had done, his admirers are for the most part embarrassed by his polemics against Newton and either ignore them altogether or concede quickly that Newton was right about colors, and then change the subject. But even if we grant that Newton was right about colors—for our purposes it does not matter who was right—Goethe's refusal to equate science with Newtonian science represents his fourth major contribution to the discovery of the mind."

27. Blumenberg, *Paradigms for a Metaphorology*, 5.

life, history, freedom, and universe, for instance) and this metaphor, like all absolute metaphors, has a history.

The second kind of question Blumenberg draws our attention to involves those transitional, liminal moments in history that are inherently open and unstable. Blumenberg would have us reflect on two things: the fact that answers often precede their questions and how both questions and answers can be viewed in terms of a deeper question, namely, "whether our world is the world we wanted," a question that "belongs in the realm of political rhetoric."

> Such rhetoric must give rise to the justified impression that there are (or were) different worlds to choose from; perhaps the wrong one was chosen, in which case corrections will be both necessary and legitimate. Yet what thus flows into the imperious gesture of setting the world to rights can in fact be asked of any historical epoch: Which was the world we believed ourselves capable of having?[28]

We can ask this question of early Christianity and indeed of each of the transitional moments in the history of Christianity.[29] To say moments of historical transition are liminal is to say they are rife with options. Early Christianity flirted with Gnosticism, for example. History becomes the story of the victorious paradigm. But these "lost" options are still there in the historical-cultural record, and hence open for consideration, even retrieval. As Ulrik Rasmussen has argued, Blumenberg's engagement with religion and theology can be understood as Blumenberg's tracking, across the centuries, the question "Which God did we think we could hope for?"[30] Which was the world early Christians thought they could live in, hoped to live in, desired to live in? To answer such questions is to produce a metaphorology of God.

"In Him We Live and Move and Have Our Being"

We can count Paul as a thinker who held that there is an order to things, including a proper goal or purpose. This is a basic perspective in ancient

---

28. Blumenberg, *Readability of the World*, 1–2.

29. Küng, in his *Christianity*, identifies six different "paradigms" in the history of Christianity. Pelikan, in his *Jesus Through the Centuries*, identifies eighteen different dominant figures of Jesus in history.

30. Rasmussen, *Memory of God*, 109.

thought, and one that Paul took in trying to make headway with the Athenians, arguing (or preaching) that within Greek philosophical tradition we find the idea of an uncaused cause, a source of all things, which in Jewish and Christian tradition is articulated in the language of creation. Greek metaphysics put an end to anthropomorphic conceptions of God: not God *as a being* but God *as Being*. Paul proclaims the reality of "God who made the world [cosmos] and everything in it"— the logically necessary entity/being/source/power that "stands behind" all contingent things and beings. God, says Paul,

> does not live in shrines made by man, nor is he served by human hands, as though he needed anything, since he himself gives to all men life and breath and everything.... Yet he is not far from each one of us, for "In him we live and move and have our being"; as even some of your poets have said, "For we are indeed his offspring." Being then God's offspring, we ought not to think that the Deity is like gold, or silver, or stone, a representation by the art and imagination of man. (Acts 17:24–29)[31]

There are two observations to be made of this extraordinary scene.

First, Paul, in appealing to Greek literary tradition, demonstrates that there is no pure discourse that can extricate itself from its historical situatedness. The great dream of analytic philosophy and positivism is that the precision and abstract nature of mathematics can serve as a model for the right and proper use of language. These schools of thought miss the fact that language, as discussed earlier, is thoroughly metaphorical in nature and embedded in sociocultural contexts (as we observed, even mathematics is grounded in metaphor). In attempting to describe, affirm, or connect with the "God who made the world and everything in it" our speech and our concepts will always move in the realms of analogy, metaphor, and symbol, drawing upon the lingua franca of one's place and time; this is not a shortcoming but simply the nature of human cognition and language. When Paul says we "move" "in him," we may well imagine swimming in a lake or running along a trail, but God is clearly not a body of water or a path in the woods. The "premise, common to all classical theistic philosophies, [is] that the words we use about God, to the extent that we use them correctly, have meanings only remotely analogous to what those same words mean

---

31. Paul quotes here from Greek literary and philosophical tradition, likely from the work of Epimenides of Crete and Aratus of Cilicia.

when we use them of created things."[32] Analogy is not the best we can do—it is how we express ourselves or formulate an idea.[33]

The second point to observe in Paul's persuasive efforts with the Athenians is that through his acknowledgement that Greek culture formulated the notion of an uncaused cause, a prime mover or first principle, Paul is setting his audience up for the further step of articulating the nature and character of the "unknown God." Philosophical analysis of contingency and necessity may lead to an awareness of a ground of being in which we live, but it says nothing about the nature, qualities, or character of that ground. Christian thought affirms the reality of a ground to being, but also seeks to describe it and our relationship to it. With respect to a conception and experience of God, Christian thought aimed to overcome the rigid dualism of Plato, in which the world of materiality was but a shifting and poor copy of the perfectly real thing, as well as Aristotle's conception of a rather cold and distant unmovable, unchangeable, and ahistorical God. For early Christianity, as for the Judaism out of which it developed, God is in this world and this world in God, who is a living, active, involved force or power.

In the effort to articulate a conception of God, Christian theologians are operating not unlike mathematicians. The language of mathematics has been employed to describe the nature and character of the uncaused cause. This tradition dates to the ancient Pythagoreans, who believed that reality was fundamentally composed of and capable of description with numbers and mathematical relationships. Plato and the Neoplatonists later extended this idea, suggesting that the ultimate reality or the ground of being could be understood through abstract mathematical forms and principles. In modern times, thinkers like Gottfried Wilhelm Leibniz proposed that the universe operates according to rational principles that can be mathematically described, portraying God as the ultimate mathematician. This was largely the perspective of Deism as well, which imagined the universe in mechanical terms as a great clock, and God as the grand watchmaker. In the realm of modern physics and cosmology, the mathematical descriptions of the universe, such as the laws of physics,

---

32. Hart, *Experience of God*, 125. I am indebted to Hart's discussion of the argument from contingency and encourage those wishing a deeper dive to take-up his book.

33. Of course, not all would agree with this, e.g., Karl Barth, for example, whose "dialectical theology" begins with the premise that God's revelation in and through the Bible is unique and self-authenticating, not dependent on human language or concepts, including metaphors.

are seen as reflecting the rationality and order of the ground of being. Figures like Paul Davies and Roger Penrose have explored the idea that the mathematical order of the cosmos points to a deeper rationality, possibly divine, underlying existence. Kurt Gödel, the renowned mathematician and logician, developed a formal ontological argument for the existence of God using modal logic, demonstrating how mathematics can be applied to metaphysical concepts. Mathematical metaphors such as infinity, symmetry, and order have become powerful tools for articulating a conception of the boundless, harmonious, and rational nature of ultimate reality. Nicolas of Cusa deployed the concept of infinity in developing his Christology. Through these metaphors, mathematics provides a bridge between empirical observation, philosophical inquiry, and theological reflection, offering a framework to explore metaphysics and ontology.

Christian theologians have worked in a similar fashion, though the root metaphors take their shape not from the language of mathematics but *through the language of persons and their interactions and relationships*. Of course there are many religious traditions, many schools of thought, each with their own unique perspectives and contributions. The Lakota understand the "Great Spirit" (*Wankan Tanka*) with reference to language of circularity, earth and sky, trees and buffalo; Daoists use the imagery of mountains and rivers to describe the eternal "Dao"; Mahayana Buddhists speak of emptiness and interdependence in describing ultimate reality; and so on. Islamic theology and mysticism are like Christianity in using deeply personal metaphors, as when Sufis speak of the human–divine relationship in terms of lover and the beloved. But Christianity and Islam also part ways in so far as Christian tradition proposes the incarnation of the uncaused cause, the Word made flesh. Just as life and death are used as metaphors for describing one's internal existential state—"I'm full of life today"—Christian thought uses the language of persons and personal relationships to articulate an understanding of God. In Trinitarian thought as developed at the council of Nicaea, God is one nature (how could God not be?) in three persons: the Father, the Son, and the Holy Spirit. Beyond the metaphysical sophistication and subtleties of this formulation, is the fact that Trinitarian thinking places relationships at the center, and relationships premised on care and love.

In his hymn to love in 1 Corinthians, Paul elevates love above knowledge, prophecy, and asceticism, just as he places love above faith and hope. The day of knowledge will come; we will see ultimate reality not as through a mirror but "face to face," partial knowledge will become "full."

Until then, "faith, hope, love abide . . . but the greatest of these is love." Blumenberg suggests that the emphasis on love in Christian thought and culture means that Christian love "deeply needs a face; it despairs before the 'physiognomically' incomprehensible, before that which is too 'pure' to take shape, to 'become flesh.'"[34] The abstract purity of mathematics is not enough to describe ultimate reality. Love drives the incarnation, just as incarnation is an expression of love. The step Paul desired the Athenians to take was to move from a conception of the reality of the ground of being to the nature of that reality, which Christian traditions holds is best expressed in the relational language of persons and love. The Christian dogmas of the incarnation and the Trinity are the end-product of this commitment to understand God in terms of the language of persons.

Incarnation: Logos Enfleshed

Following the death of Jesus the Christian community was spirit-filled and had received the vocation of being witness to the saving power of Christ.[35] Paul preached "Christ crucified." Christ didn't simply die; he was killed in a very specific fashion. He was not murdered in a back alley by thugs; he did not fall on the battlefield. He was executed by Roman authority (perhaps with the assent and backing of Jerusalem's priestly authorities) in a very public humiliation and execution reserved for runaway slaves and political opponents. The felt presence of the Holy Spirit was the lifeblood of early Christianity, and this was intimately linked to an experience of the conjunction of crucifixion and resurrection. In the simplest of terms: "You (the state and religious-civil authorities) killed him, and yet he lives." The "distinctively Christian reality is and remains the cross."[36] "In Christianity the cross is the test of everything which deserves to be called Christian."[37]

The experience of salvation in and through faith in the resurrected Christ is a perfect example of the common historical occurrence described by Blumenberg: answers often precede questions. The proclamation of salvation through fidelity to the event of crucifixion-resurrection led to the question "Saved from what?" In time, in the

---

34. Blumenberg, "Kant und die Frage," 570.
35. See Wilkens, *Spirit of Early Christian*.
36. Küng, *On Being a Christian*, 437.
37. Moltmann, *Crucified God*, 7.

Latin West, a certain answer emerged, consolidated in the thought of Augustine, moving towards a specific kind of sacrificial interpretation of the death whereby, as a sacrifice, Christ's broken body brings salvation from original sin, as a form of ransom, payment, or expiation, a move that would generate more problems than it solved, as discussed in the previous chapter. Thankfully, many can no longer conceive of such a theology, and for two very good reasons. First, despite the contractual nature of modern capitalism, where workers rent themselves out to employers, we tend to reject notions of property relations as the basis for interpersonal interactions. The crucified Christ can be understood as a form of payment only if it is possible to think of people being owned by some entity, as in the notion of being "in bondage" to Satan, from whom release is granted through a cash or in-kind payment. Secondly, though the connections between guilt and suffering are no doubt complex, we generally no longer see suffering as a sign of guilt. We've learned to not blame the victim, one form of which is charging one who is suffering as deserving of that suffering. If René Girard is correct, the Christian Gospels have played a central role in extricating us from such a faulty logic. We tend away from interpreting a person's or a group's plight and hardship as the natural outcome of past actions: suffering is understood as being socially determined, not the result of God withdrawing protection or meeting out punishment as a corrective means to restore a kind of cosmic balance of justice. As Blumenberg notes, "One does not have to be the person for whom Jesus suffers and dies in order to be shaken by the violence of this suffering and this dying."[38]

If the Christian gospel is about anything, it is about caring for one another, loving one another—a love not reserved for one's family, friends, tribe, or nation, but everyone simply because they are human. In Matthew, the Son of Man, transposed into the figure of a king, refers to his experience of nakedness, hunger, and imprisonment. A confused if earnest listener, one of the "righteous," we are told, asks, "Lord, when did we see thee hungry and feed thee, or thirsty and give thee drink? . . . When did we see thee sick or in prison and visit thee?" The king responds, "Truly, I say to you, as you did it to one of the least of these my brethren, you did it to me" (Matt 25:37–40). This is a radically participatory message of care. In Luke, Jesus advises,

---

38. Blumenberg, *St. Matthew's Passion*, 169.

> When you give a dinner or a banquet, do not invite your friends or your brothers or your kinsmen or rich neighbors, lest they also invite you in return, and you be repaid. But when you give a feast, invite the poor, the maimed, the lame, the blind, and you will be blessed, because they cannot repay you. You will be repaid at the resurrection of the just. (Luke 14:12–14)

Granted, doing such is perhaps even more estimable minus the promise of reward, but this still a reckless and risky kind of love. For Herbert McCabe, the core of Christianity is the knowledge that "if you do not love you will not be alive; if you do love effectively you will be killed." Resurrection is God's act of vindicating Jesus, the man who "set up a community of love in Galilee [and] was a threat to the colonialist and clericalist establishment and so he was killed."[39] The Father "rebels against [the] injustice [of crucifixion], angrily defying the powers of this world by raising up his murdered child." The cross is not a "legalistic placating of a vengeful patriarch," a "warped theology" in which "God is a terrorist who demands the blood of his own son as the price for having been immortally offended."[40] The cross is, per Abelard, an expression of God's love.

Already in the New Testament we find various attempts to articulate the meaning, significance, and status of Jesus. This is done through the metaphoric mapping of titles of station, status, role, or function. Though several of the titles point in the direction of divinity, Jesus was always understood to have been a real, historical person, as emphasized in the Apostles Creed.[41] For Jürgen Moltmann, the "name" of Jesus derives from and points to history, to the earthly, temporal, and material situatedness of Jesus and the disciples. The "basis and justification of Christology" are to be found in the "person and history of Jesus."[42] The "titles" variously assigned to Jesus—Son of Man, Son of God, God, Logos, Lord, shepherd—these titles state not *who* Jesus is but *what* he is; that is, they point

---

39. McCabe, *God Still Matters*, 68.

40. Eagleton, *Holy Terrors*, 40.

41. The "mythicist" claim—that Jesus of Nazareth never existed as a historical figure—is decisively refuted by rigorous historical-textual analysis. Scholars like Bart Ehrman demonstrate that mythicists misunderstand both the nature of ancient sources and the criteria of historical inquiry. While Ehrman's conclusions may unsettle some traditional believers, he dismantles mythicist assertions as poorly researched and methodologically flawed. This is distinct from recognizing the mythic and metaphorical dimensions of Jesus's significance and presentation in early Christian texts, dimensions that coexist with historical realities. See Ehrman, *Did Jesus Exist?*

42. Moltmann, *Crucified God*, 84.

to matters of meaning, significance, and consequence, to the "eternal, universal and eschatological side." The titles are metaphors, and they knit together the person Jesus with his dignity and function. And "these titles changed as the faith came to be expressed in new languages and in new historical situations." For example, "Son of Man" means something different in the era of late Second Temple Judaism than in Hellenistic contexts. The former use referred to the apocalyptic tradition of Daniel, the latter to questions of ontological essence. The name, emphasizes Moltmann, will not change: "Jesus" refers to Jesus of Nazareth. The titles (the metaphors), however, may change, in fact, will need to change, since "historical and social changes do in fact cause old world-views and religious conceptions to become outdated, and lead to the construction of new ones."[43]

A significant strand of modern biblical scholarship—represented by figures like E. P. Sanders, Bart Ehrman, and Marcus Borg—argues that the historical Jesus likely did not claim titles like "Messiah," "Son of David," or "Son of God" in the ways later ascribed to him. These scholars contend that such designations emerged primarily in post-Paschal communities as they reinterpreted Jesus's life and death. However, this view is not universal. Others, including N. T. Wright and Richard Bauckham, maintain that at least some titles plausibly originated with Jesus himself, albeit with meanings distinct from later theological elaborations. He did, however, likely use the apocalyptic title "Son of Man," which appears for the first time in the book of Daniel. But it seems the historical Jesus was not so much concerned with titles; in fact, one might go further and suggest that none of the circulating honorific titles of the day were compatible with his own understanding of his life, his mission, or even the mystery of his nature, which is frequently hinted at in the Gospels.[44] This certainly does not mean these various titles are meaningless—on the contrary, the life-death-resurrection of Jesus was experienced as so meaningful, so significant, that it demanded interpretation, clarification, understanding.

As the apostles and the Christian message moved into the Hellenic world and the name of Jesus began to be linked with certain metaphorical titles, the challenge of understanding the basis of Christian faith presented

---

43. Moltmann, *Crucified God*, 85–86. We should keep in mind that in the New Testament, dozens of titles and names are given to Jesus.

44. This is the conclusion of Hans Küng in summarizing the literature on the historical Jesus. Küng writes, "Apparently none of the familiar concepts, none of the usual ideas, none of the traditional offices, none of the current titles were appropriate to express his claim, to define his person and mission, to reveal the mystery of his nature" (*On Being a Christian*, 290).

itself through the encounter with Greek philosophy. Was Jesus mortal or divine? What was the nature of God? What was the relationship between the nature of the world, God, Jesus, and the nature of the human being? The Christians had to answer these questions, and they had to answer them in terms of Hellenic Greek philosophy. Whether we are still bound by the answers to these foundational ways of expressing Christian faith is a matter of debate and personal choice. In some measure, the terminology of tradition must be embraced, for it has been hallowed by the centuries; but as the meaning of terms change and new terms emerge, new ways of expressing the truth may be required.

For Paul, God is the uncreated *theos,* and Christ is Lord (*kyrios*). "For although there may be so-called gods in heaven or on earth—as indeed there are many 'gods' and many 'lords'—yet for us there is one God [*theos*], the Father, from whom are all things and for whom we exist, and one Lord [*kyrios*], Jesus Christ, through whom are all things and through whom we exist" (1 Cor 8:5–6). God as "Father," the central metaphor of the New Testament, is creator of all that is, while Jesus as the Son is the Lord in and through whom creation proceeds. Paul never refers to Christ as *theos*; it would remain for the development of tradition to reach for the Greek concept of *logos* to describe the nature of Christ. John's Gospel, if not the earliest to develop incarnational motifs, was certainly the most influential, with Christ identified with the "Word" (*logos*).[45]

Though there is plenty of debate and argument, there is good reason for calling Paul's thought "adoptionist," since he identifies the resurrection as the moment whereby the person of Jesus is divinized as God's "Son" ("designated Son of God in power according to the Spirit of holiness by his resurrection from the dead"; Rom 1:4).[46] One can detect in the Gospels a chronological trajectory informing claims of Christ's divinity or relationship to divinity, with each step pushing further back in time.

---

45. There are early-Pauline and Deutero-Pauline creeds or hymns that allude to the incarnation of God's Son. For example, Phil 2:5–12 has Christ existing "in the form of God" and Gal 4:4–5, which reads, "But when the time had fully come, God sent forth his Son, born of woman, born under the law, to redeem those who were under the law, so that we might receive adoption as sons." But in Acts and Romans, Christ's "sonship" is achieved in and through the resurrection, which "designated [Jesus Christ our Lord] Son of God in power according to the Spirit of holiness by his resurrection from the dead" (Rom 1:4). Support for an adoptionist reading of Paul is, in my view, strong, though these matters are hotly debated.

46. "Election" or "adoption" or "assumption" of an individual by those in high status and power roles to the status of a son was common in the political culture of Rome: witness Caesar's elevation of Octavius.

Paul identifies the resurrection as the moment of "adoption," of being raised up, vindicated by God. For Mark, baptism by John identifies Jesus as the Messiah. For Matthew and Luke, divinity is associated with conception. For John, Christ is the eternal logos. All this thinking about the nature of Christ will, over centuries, lead to the Chalcedonian formula of 451 C.E., whereby Christ is understood as one person with two distinct but united natures, fully human and fully divine. Ultimately, Chalcedon points to the mystery of Jesus, the oddness of the claim that Jesus is, in some unique way, both human and divine. This may seem paradoxical, but it is not illogical. The Chalcedonian formula only becomes illogical if we imagine God as a finite being among other beings, in which case the incarnational claim would be akin to holding a particular shape is both a circle and a square, or a particular animal both a lion and a sheep. But Jesus and God are not two of the same thing in the same way that a circle and a square are two shapes. Again, we are to think ontologically about God: God is not *a* being. As Herbert McCabe points out, the doctrine of the incarnation is not illogical or contradictory. It "does not mean that we actually understand what it means to say that Jesus is man and God. ... The doctrine of the incarnation ... is not conveying information, it is pointing a mystery in Jesus."[47] There may well be ways other than Chalcedon to try and convey this mystery, but the mystery remains.

Although Paul has little to say of the life of Jesus, adoptionist Christologies nevertheless tend to emphasize his exemplary life, which includes going to the cross as a sign of love, as the basis for God's "raising up" of Jesus—an objective or ontological status change—as well as providing a compelling demonstration of a God capable and willing to radically identify with suffering. This is also sometimes referred to as "exultation Christology," where status or identity starts from "below," in the life of the historical Jesus, and moves (via baptism, adoption, birth, exaltation, and other means) "upwards" to the heavens. The Roman centurion at the foot of the cross announcing "Truly this man was the Son of God" (Mark 14:39) entails a perceptual shift, a changing human judgment (in Luke, the centurion merely observes the "righteousness" of Jesus). Alternatively, a "high" Christology inverts this movement, using the language, imagery, and metaphor of descent or emanation, the prime example being the prologue to John's Gospel. Other than in John, Jesus is seldom referred to as "God," but this changed with the

---

47. McCabe, *God Matters*, 58.

encounter with Greek philosophy. Jesus as God's advocate, representative, or "Son," which implies matters of duty and obedience, comes to be supplemented and often replaced with concern to articulate matters of essence and nature. This latter move was accomplished through metaphors of personhood, understood ontically, not psychologically or subjectively.[48] In some respects this is where problems begin for Christian theology; in linking Jesus to conceptions of the Godhead, questions were bound to emerge: Why would the all-powerful, eternal God require the circuitous means of incarnating and suffering to set matters right? Perhaps even more disturbing: Can God suffer and die?

The most important idea of Greek philosophy for Christian thought did not come from Plato or Aristotle but from the Stoics, who developed the idea of the *logos*. Logos (which means, literally, "word") suggests a universal divine power and law of reality. Logos is natural and moral law, but also our "ability to recognize reality."[49] If we know to feed rather than tickle starving children, we know this because of the logos. Creation here is understood as a theophany, a spreading out, a filling, a sustaining of the universe that is the logos of God. The logos is the mediating power between ultimate reality and human understanding of that reality. Our capacity to know, for intelligibility, is but a specific example of the more general intelligibility of the universe. God's logos is not a distinct power among powers, but the unified, complete, sustaining quality of the cosmos that allows us, as William Blake puts it, "to see a World in a Grain of Sand // And a Heaven in a Wild Flower."

Early Christian thinkers such as Justin Martyr, Irenaeus, and Origen interpreted the event of Jesus through the concept of logos; but they went further, picking up on Paul's failed attempt to convert the Athenians, by claiming that Christianity is the completion of the truth to which Greek philosophy was pointing yet not able to fully grasp. According to the Justin Martyr and other apologists, the logos, as God's self-manifestation, has been ever present. As Augustine writes, in clarifying a passage from his earlier *On the True Religion*,

---

48. When we say that the use of the language of personhood in Greek metaphysics is an ontological approach, we mean that it is focused on the fundamental reality or existence of Christ as a single person with two natures. This contrasts with modern notions of personhood, which often emphasize psychological and subjective aspects of personal identity.

49. Tillich, *History of Christian Thought*, 8.

When I said: "In our times, this is the Christian religion which to know and follow is most secure and most certain salvation," I did so with reference to the name only, not to the thing itself of which this is only the name. That which is known as the Christian religion existed among the ancients, and never did not exist; from the beginning of the human race until the time when Christ came in the flesh, at which time the true religion, which already existed, began to be called Christianity.[50]

In other words, what is true it true.

The logos gave the Jews their law and the Greeks their philosophy. But now was the *kairos*, the right time for the logos to become fully present. What the apologists wanted to do was to show that not only was the life, death, and resurrection of Jesus understandable in terms of the logos doctrine, but that Jesus as Christ was an articulation of what Greek philosophy had but dimly perceived. "And the Word became flesh and dwelt among us, full of grace and truth; we have beheld his glory, glory as of the only Son from the Father," as John puts it (1:14). What emerged in Christian thought were two not always easily reconcilable trajectories: soteriology looked to the question of salvation from sin; incarnational theology looked to matters of participatory, embodied ontology. Holding these two positions together has not always proven easy.

Mythological tales of gods coming to earth, assuming human form, interacting with people, and then returning to the heavenly realm were relatively commonplace in Greek culture. Hellenic gods readily take the form of a person, as a cunning means to interact with heroes, but personhood "remains foreign to their authentic reality."[51] Not so with the incarnation. A story of a god's "descent" into the world remains a story if not seen in connection to the cross and resurrection. Christ is understood not merely as a god in disguise but, in some fashion, God himself; the logos had not merely taken on flesh but had *become* flesh: not an adopted persona but an enfleshed life (one gnostic image pictured God flowing through the person of Jesus like water through a pipe). Commitment to working out

---

50. Augustine, *Retractions*, 52. Similarly, for Eusebius, Christ is "the Logos of God, pre-existent, having his being before all ages.... So no one [should] think of our Saviour and Lord, Jesus Christ, as a novelty because of the date of his ministry in the flesh. ... Even if we [Christians] are clearly new ... nevertheless our life and method of conduct, in accordance with the precepts of religion, has not been recently invented by us, but from the first creation of man, so to speak, has been upheld by the natural concepts of the men of old who were fiends of God" (Eusebius, *Ecclesiastical History* I.4.39–41).

51. Blumenberg, *Work on Myth*, 137.

a theology that could hold together ascent and descent, soteriology and ontology, Son of Man as advocate and Son of God as essence—it was this unity that forged new conceptions of what constitutes our true humanity as well as the radically new idea that God himself had a capacity to suffer alongside us, cutting through conceptions of divinity found in Platonic dualism, Aristotelian immovability, and gnostic myths of the world under the sway of a false God. Key here was that the Christian conception of incarnation had to remain closely linked to the cross, which points to crucifixion as a form of self-emptying on the part of God, precisely to the point of humiliation and death. This is not to fetishize the cross. The New Testament makes it quite clear, in the agonizing scene in the garden of Gesthsemane, that Jesus does not wish to die; he is, however, willing to go to the end, if need be. He doesn't seek suffering but rather bears it, and, indeed, his life and death are a struggle against suffering.

The logos doctrine could easily lose sight of the "primary event of salvation" in the "cross of the risen Jesus" by focusing on the "appearance of a divine being in human form." Hans Küng argues that theology is haunted by a tendency to supplant the cross with an overly spiritualized incarnation and resurrection; the consequence is that "the divine life often supplants the earthly, the deification of man supplants his humanization, the calling back of the world to God replaces the transformation of the world and society."[52]

Jürgen Moltmann makes a case like that advanced by Küng, when he observes that

> if one considers the event on the cross between Jesus and his God in the framework of the doctrine of two natures, then the Platonic axiom of the essential *apatheia* of God sets up an intellectual barrier against the recognition of the suffering of Christ, for God who is subject to suffering like all other

---

52. Küng, *One Being a Christian*, 442. Küng also observes that the church's starting point of a "high Christology" can easily be put in service of power rather than of truth. He observes, for example, how Joseph Ratzinger's *Introduction to Christianity* ignores, even belittles, historical Jesus research, favoring a starting point for faith in assent to the traditional form of the creed, I believe "in Jesus Christ, the only begotten Son of God." But as Küng points out, the disciples started from the person of Jesus, "the real human being, from his historical appearance and message, his life and his fate, his historical reality and influence." Historical biblical criticism has shown that it isn't so clear that, as the church has it, both Jesus and the first disciples were declaring Jesus to be, as the first christological thesis has it, the "natural Son of God and true God." In Mark, a man refers to Jesus as "Good Teacher," and is quickly rebuffed: "And Jesus said to him, 'Why do you call me good? No one is good but God alone'" (10:18).

creatures cannot be "God." Therefore the God-man Christ can only have suffered "according to the flesh" and "in the flesh," that is, in his human nature.[53]

Moltmann considers early traditional Christology as "coming very near to Docetism," because this theology tends to a "philosophical concept of God, according to which God's being is incorruptible, unchangeable, indivisible, incapable of suffering and immortal." Cyril, for example, argues for a Christology of unity, which means he ought to have referred the cry of dereliction to the "divine nature itself," but "Cyril cannot manage that." Instead, Cyril has God suffering in Christ in his humanity but not in his divinity. Moltman develops the notion of divine "passibility," insisting the cross reveals a God who suffers with creation. For Moltman, "a God incapable of suffering . . . would also be incapable of love."[54] Aristotle's "unmoved mover" embodies *apatheia*. The Christian God is different. Not only do we, in Paul's imagery, live and move and breath in God, God in some sense also lives and moves and breathes. Of course, this is not to suggest God is a finite being, but rather that absolute reality is not cold, distant, fixed, and immovable, but rather invests in us, relates to us—in short, cares for us.

Nor are we to imagine that God hangs on the cross. The cross is an "event between Jesus and his God," and the title of Moltmann's book (*The Crucified God*) runs the risk of obscuring that fact. Jesus cries out to his Father from the cross, "My God, my God, why hast thou forsaken me? (Mark 15:34). Does it helps us to interpret this as God forsaking himself? In so far as the Father hurts from the crucifixion of his Son we may say that God suffers; he is not indifferent. But the point of the cross is not suffering on the part of God. Though Jesus is two natures in one person he is not God, not *ho theos* but *kyrios*. His nature includes the divine, he is one with God, but not God. The equation Jesus=God was never part of orthodox Christianity; both Nicaea and Chalcedon using the language of "consubstantiality" not identity: Jesus is "consubstantial with the Father" and "consubstantial with us men."

It is the prerogative of the church to require of its members a "high Christology," with all that implies, including assenting to the idea that Jesus considered himself the "natural Son of God and true God." But

---

53. Moltmann, *Crucified God*, 228. The concept of *apatheia* referred to here means freedom or release from emotion or excitement.

54 Moltmann, *Crucified God*, 228–30.

this runs the risk of clashing with the results of reasoned research into the early Christian community; it would also be a needless clash. "The doctrine of the two natures is an interpretation in Hellenistic language and concepts of what Jesus Christ really means. The importance of this teaching should not be belittled.... On the other hand, no one should get the impression that Christ's message today could or should be stated only with the aid of these Greek categories."[55]

From the Speculative Good Friday to Care

Why is this high Christological development significant? From Blumenberg's perspective, it is an advance in matters of care and unburdening from the absolute. Blumenberg's reflections on incarnation are in some respects in keeping with the speculative trend within German Idealism, which tends to interpret incarnational theology, from the perspective of God, as a change or development in the nature, character, and tenor of God. Hegel's interpretation of the incarnation and crucifixion is rooted in his dialectical philosophy. For Hegel, the cross represents a moment of "absolute negativity," a point where God experiences self-alienation through the figure of Christ. In Hegel's reading, quoting a well-known Lutheran hymn, "God has died, God is dead—this is the most fearful thought." Hegel, beginning from the perspective of a high Christology, sees in the incarnation the Absolute descending into limitation, whereby the experience of the "human, finite, frail, weak, and negative" become part of the divine.[56] Negativity comes to be experienced and incorporated by and into God. Hegel referred to this dialectical, philosophical analysis of the crucifixion as a "Speculative Good Friday" whereby crucifixion is not just as a tragic event but as an essential part of the process by which Spirit realizes itself, a grand dialectical process that eventually leads to the reconciliation of God with himself, which Hegel terms "the death of death." In Hegel's view, through the crucifixion, Absolute Spirit becomes fully immersed in the finite and suffering world, ultimately transforming and realizing itself. Post Hegel, it is difficult, though certainly not impossible, to imagine a God untouched by change and history. God is a "living God," which

---

55. Küng, *On Being a Christian*, 131. That this is also the position of, say, Jürgen Moltmann and Herbert McCabe, goes some distance to demonstrating its reasonableness. McCabe writes, "Chalcedon points to the mystery of Jesus. Let me repeat: we may well find other ways of articulating this mystery" (*God Matters*, 57).

56. Hegel, *Lectures*, 3:326.

means an active and involved God. This, it seems, is the God hoped for in the theological speculations of German idealism—a God who does not sit comfortably in a detached, unchanging heaven "above" the world but rather immersed in the world's processes.

Blumenberg is far from a Hegelian, but he does advance the Hegelian-like notion that shortcomings in God's knowledge become apparent following his act of creation, most notably God's inability to understand death. For Blumenberg, God's question to Cain—"Where is Abel your brother?" (Gen 4:9)—is not to elicit a confession, the traditional interpretation; rather, the question speaks to God's innocence in such matters, his inability to comprehend the potential upon which Cain will act; this is quickly followed by God's having to reckon with the fact that the creatures made in his image are capable of murder. As an "absolute being" God is the "sheer opposite of a deficient being," but the trajectory of biblical Christianity places demands on God, since humans are most certainly beings in need of care and attention. Not "even an absolute being [can] know *a priori* what care actually is; that requires the experience of being condemned to death, stigmatized by pain, betrayed by one's community." For Blumenberg, early Christian texts are anchored in a largely hidden contradiction between an omnipotent God and what (unexpectedly for this God) is an independent, often wayward creation that generates a painful and open-ended theodrama, culminating in God's sacrificing his Son to achieve not merely reconciliation but self-understanding. Clearly, in Blumenberg we encounter a highly speculative reading. John's Gospel (unlike the Synoptics) begins from the perspective of an intention on the part of the Absolute, namely, to incarnate, to become human. But this incarnation is driven not merely or even mainly by God's love of humanity as by God's need to understand himself. "Out of love for himself he has to seek the fulfillment of his intentions," which he only comes to fully understand in the course of events. "Without descent into the death-bound limitations of life, he could not have realized the intentions of a reciprocal and rectifying creation in his own likeness. . . . He could not bear not understanding what it meant that those created in his image and likeliness have to live in the face of death, have to experience their finitude."[57] Driving such speculations is what Blumenberg sees as the core of the Christian Gospels, namely, Christ's experience of abandonment.

---

57. Blumenberg, *St. Matthew Passion*, 92–93.

The origin of the incarnation then is in the mythic background of the story of God's creation. It is not as a response to sin that the logos descends but, and here Blumenberg follows Nicholas of Cusa, to complete creation. The theologically underdeveloped biblical motif was always, suggests Blumenberg, that we are made in the image of God. From the outset there was a special relationship between the human and the divine; anthropology and Christology belong together, which was the crucial insight of Cusa, who saw in "the proposition that man was created in God's image something like the motive for the Incarnation."[58]

In medieval scholasticism we find "avoidance of the premise that God had irrevocably obliged Himself to the only creature He made in His own image, that He had committed Himself to satisfying man's need for happiness," and this refusal of the "motivational connection between the Creation and the Incarnation"[59] reintroduced a form of gnostic dualism, which Blumenberg terms "theological absolutism": God in his world, and we in ours—this move left humanity without a privileged status in creation. While this may appeal to critics of "anthropocentrism," the way forward is not to refuse this privileged status but to recognize, embody, and act on our relatedness to God, whose image we are. Moltmann warns that rejecting God leads not to liberation but to a dangerous self-deification. Blumenberg, reflecting on the "death of God," even asks whether a "return of God" remains among the possibilities still open to us—a question that compels us to re-examine our historical origins. Blumenberg isn't suggesting religious revival but that the logic of modernity, grounded in "self-assertion," leads to new forms of absolutism that leave us longing for the very transcendence we dismantled. This possibility, writes Blumenberg, "is one of the pressing questions that moves us to illuminate our historical origins." Nietzsche's legacy, writes Blumenberg, has been both "fertile" (*ein fruchtbares Erbe*) and "fearful" (*ein furchtbares Erbe*)—fertile, in that it affirms our drive for self-affirmation; fearful, "as the experience with a power leaning toward omnipotence soon taught. The contemporary human is no longer legitimized for the carefree funeral of God: the subhuman, who emerged from the depths, has darkened the view of the rise of the Übermensch."[60]

For medieval nominalism, God is not required to be or do anything, which would be a limitation on his Absolute power. But in making us "in

58. Blumenberg, *Legitimacy*, 174.
59. Blumenberg, *Legitimacy*, 174.
60. Blumenberg, *Kant und die Frage*, 554.

his image" God is, as it were, stuck with us, and neither theology nor a metaphorology of God can abandon the covenantal aspect of the relatedness between humans and God, which is another way of saying a Christology from above must be balanced by one from below. As Blumenberg reads history, the incarnation is more than just a divine act of restoring humanity after the fall; instead, it represents the completion of creation through Christ. This idea, especially as it relates to Nicholas of Cusa, reflects a significant shift away from late medieval emphasis on God's absolute freedom. According to Blumenberg, Cusa develops a fundamental symmetry between man and God in the incarnation. The Christian motif of "man becoming God and God becoming man" has its systematic foundation here, suggesting that the incarnation was not merely a reaction to sin but rather a necessary fulfillment of humanity's potential, embedded within creation itself. Cusa's speculative theology integrates human self-assertion with divine creativity, and in so doing offers a more dynamic and relational understanding of God, humanity, and the cosmos.[61]

Blumenberg's starting point in the high Christology of John's prologue is subject to the criticism offered above, but perhaps what is most central is where Blumenberg winds up, rather than where he begins. Regardless of the original inspiration for an incarnational Christology via the Greek concept of the logos, the "idea of the Incarnation ... was an infinite fortification of human self-respect. Because of it, the form that God adopts ceased to be arbitrary and provisional, since this form

---

61. Cusa achieves this wedding of anthropology and creation via a new conception of infinity, a complex discussion that takes up most of the final section of Blumenberg's *Legitimacy*. In brief, my cursory understanding of Blumenberg's argument is as follows: Cusa introduces the idea of *coincidentia oppositorum*, (coincidence of opposites) to describe God's nature. In this framework, God is the ultimate infinite being, where all opposites, such as the finite and the infinite, are unified. God's infinity is not just an endless stretch of space or time but a fullness of existence where every possibility and reality are perfectly integrated. Cusa argues that, although humans are finite beings, they are created in the image of an infinite God, which grants them an infinite potential in their capacity to grow in knowledge, love, and union with God. Christ is the key figure who embodies this connection. As both fully divine and fully human, Christ is the mediator through whom the infinite meets the finite. The incarnation—God becoming human in Christ—represents the ultimate coincidence of opposites. In an act of "self-contraction" God generates through Christ the space for human freedom to act on its potential. Blumenberg describes this conception of incarnation as a system of "synchronized intensifications in the metaphysical triangle of God, cosmos, and man" (*Legitimacy*, 538).

becomes His special and lasting fate."⁶² Put another way, in the language of Jürgen Moltmann,

> Man becomes more human if he is put in the position of being able to abandon his self-deifications and his idolatry. . . . The critical task of theology [is] to take away from anthropology the absolute and totalitarian element and the legalistic view of salvation. Theology only really becomes itself when it agrees with the anthropological criticism of religion and takes seriously the prohibition of images. Conversely anthropology only stands on a basis of reality if it agrees with a critical theology, and respects the wholly other, alongside whom all the self-awareness of man becomes in the end fragments.⁶³

Incarnation holds forth the possibility for an "infinite fortification of human self-respect" because it emphasizes our being made in the image of God and reveals the Absolute is not a hostile, overpowering "Big Other" but rather "on our side." In the history of distancing ourselves from the absolutism of reality, a "contracted," incarnated God to whom we are related not contractually but in terms of care and concern is a momentous step forward. Of course, as Bob Dylan observes, evils can be legitimated through the claim we have "God on our side," but this is difficult to do if one stays connected to a low Christology that begins in the life of Jesus of Nazareth.

According to historian Peter Brown, in the development of doctrine in the church fathers, the movement towards the Chalcedonian formulation was closely connected to "the issue of the solidarity between God and human beings." For example, in the controversy between Cyril and Nestorius, Nestorius worried that by speaking of Christ's two natures in one person, the eternal, immutable, and deathless God was wrongly implicated in suffering. For Cyril, whose position won the day, at stake was

> the guarantee of the solidarity of God with humankind. This was a real and intimate link, not a mere touching of two eternally distinct spheres—the human and the divine. In Christ, God had, indeed, shared in human suffering. To speak of God as having been, indeed, crucified, in the person of Jesus, was to remind him of the shared suffering which bound him indissolubly, almost

---

62. Blumenberg, *Legitimacy*, 595.
63. Moltmann, *Man*, 107–8.

organically, to the human race. He could not forget those with whom he had once shared the universal taste of death.[64]

This is strikingly like aspects of Blumenberg's analysis in *St. Matthew Passion*, and Brown's description of what was at stake for the church fathers in working out the meaning of the incarnation gives pause to Blumenberg's claim that a concern for solidarity "could not have been the [original] intention."[65] On the contrary, the notion of solidarity, and hence that "infinite fortification" of self-respect has a solid foothold in the New Testament.

Still, I have sympathy for old Nestorius who, as Brown describes, was rather sickened by "the ignorant populace of Constantinople [who] danced around bonfires, chanting, 'God has been crucified. God is dead.'"[66] Hans Küng, as mentioned, while acknowledging how Christianity rightly moved beyond Platonic dualism and Aristotelian immovability in favor of a present, active, living God, pulls up short of affirming an identification of the crucified Jesus with God. It isn't clear that the suffering endured by the divine person of the logos necessarily requires God to undergo a process of self-alienation that is generative of a transformation of God's essential nature, along the lines advanced by Hegel. Divine *kenosis* (emptying) is not the same as a change in the divine. The distinction is crucial because it upholds the classical Christian doctrine of the immutability (the impassibility, the apatheia) of God—that God's nature does not change. Kenosis is understood not so much as change or transformation as a self-limitation or self-emptying by Christ in his humanity without implying any alteration in his divine nature.

---

64. Brown, *Rise of Western Christendom*, 119.
65. Blumenberg, *Legitimacy*, 595.
66. Brown, *Rise of Western Christendom*, 119.

Chapter 8

Jung's Mythic Gnosis
A Critique

> The spiritual currents of our time have, in fact, a deep affinity with Gnosticism.
>
> —C. G. Jung, *The Spiritual Problem of Modern Man*

GNOSTICISM IS A CONTESTED, troubled category, partly because it has been central to many scholars seeking to make sense of modernity, especially in influential currents of German thought. Gnosticism was not an autonomous, organized, nameable religious movement of antiquity but rather the name given by nineteenth-century German theologians to a heterogeneous set of texts with a cluster of certain ideas that an emerging Christian orthodoxy deemed heretical. In 1945, a cache of gnostic texts was discovered at Nag Hammadi, Egypt, and many more such texts have been discovered since, revolutionizing and complicating the study of Gnosticism and early Christianity.[1]

As William Styfhals has discussed, a generation of scholars the likes of Jacob Taubes, Hans Blumenberg, Eric Voegelin, Hans Jonas, Odo Marquard, and Gershom Scholem deployed various conceptions of Gnosticism in analyzing and reflecting on the nature of modernity and secular culture. Generally, the idea has been to proffer that modernity is in some

---

1. The briefest of excursions into surveying scholarship on Gnosticism might include Trompf et al., eds., *Gnostic World*; Meyer, ed., *Nag Hammadi Scriptures*; Corrigan and Rasimus, eds., *Gnosticism, Platonism*; Lampe, *From Paul to Valentinus*.

sense "gnostic," and this helps us understand modernity's pathologies. Before these thinkers, the theologians and church historians August Neander and Ferdinand Baur played their part in the reception of gnostic texts into modern Christian historiography. Hans Urs von Balthasar thought Gnosticism allowed us to make sense of German idealism, while Eric Voegelin saw it as foundational to certain modern political movements. Closer to the present, the influential literary critic Harold Bloom fancied himself a gnostic, and endeavored to convince readers that both William Blake and Percy Bysshe Shelley were gnostics. Cyril O'Regan has defended, advanced, and popularized the idea that the modern era is thoroughly rooted in gnostic patterns of thought. Gnosticism has been a favorite of romantics, artists, and seekers of various stripes, including W. B. Yeats, Madam Blavatsky, and our focus in this chapter, C. G. Jung.[2]

Whether philosophically inclined scholarship has done justice to Gnosticism as a historical phenomenon in the era of early Christianity and whether modernity is to be considered in some sense gnostic are complex questions. This chapter is a dip into a vast sea of scholarship. Our way into the conversation around the relationships between Christian thought, Gnosticism, and the trajectory of modernity is the work of C. G. Jung, refracted through Blumenberg's interpretation of modernity as a "second overcoming of Gnosticism," the first overcoming having been resolved (though imperfectly so, in Blumenberg's analysis) via Augustine's theology of original sin.

One of the most influential scholarly works on Gnosticism was published by Hans Jonas, *Gnosis und spätantiker Geist (Gnosticism and the Spirit of Late Antiquity)*. Jonas's work will be used here as a baseline for thinking about Jung's project of revivifying Christianity through his encounter with gnostic thought. Jonas offers a philosophical interpretation of the gnostic phenomenon, whose "important characteristics . . . were its dualism and its existential sense of alienation."[3] For Jonas, a gnostic worldview is fundamentally flawed, since the dualistic conception of the world mired in evil, separated from the authentic divine, is a nihilistic world, one in which there can be "no spiritual investment in this world," which is how Jonas conceived the gnostic position in antiquity. Rather, what was invested in was an attempt at *gnosis*, the desire to know an absent, hidden God through esoteric means vouchsafed

2. See Smith, "Modern Relevance of Gnosticism"; O'Regan, *Gnostic Return in Modernity*.

3. Styfhals, *No Spiritual Investment*, 10.

for an enlightened few: esoteric knowledge; dualistic cosmology; salvific knowledge; initiatory secrecy—these were the hallmarks of gnostic thought and culture. As Styfhals observes, this conception of Gnosticism as divine absence and worldly nihilism, for all its limits, is useful given its influence in shaping postwar German thinking. Styfhals mentions Jung only in passing but given Jung's deep concern to address the religious crisis of modern, Christian Europe and to do so through "gnostic" means he is well-worth consideration.

Jung conceives modernity as a replay of antiquity, prompting a search, through various psychogenic means, for a saving knowledge. Jung highlights the

> widespread and ever-growing interest in all sorts of psychic phenomena, including spiritualism, astrology, Theosophy, parapsychology, and so forth. The world has seen nothing like it since the end of the seventeenth century. We can compare it only to the flowering of Gnostic thought in the first and second centuries after Christ. The spiritual currents of our time have, in fact, a deep affinity with Gnosticism.[4]

It is fair to place Jung's "analytical psychology" in this camp as well. Far from simply studying gnostic texts and trying to understand them psychologically, Jung has a "deep affinity" for gnostic thought and he reads gnostic texts as precursors to his own psychological theories. "From various hints dropped by Hippolytus," writes Jung, "it is clear beyond a doubt that many of the Gnostics were nothing other than psychologists."[5] Robert Segal is surely correct when he observes there is "a much sturdier basis for touting Jung as a Gnostic than for touting virtually any of the other persons [often] named"[6] as part of a modern turn to or embrace of gnostic beliefs and sensibilities.

Therapeutics and Theory

Jung was appointed as a clinician at Zürich's Burghölzli psychiatric clinic, in 1900, where he cared for people suffering acute psychoses. But in his later private practice, he mainly worked with patients suffering from a *neurosis*, which he describes as "an inner cleavage—the state of being at

---

4. Jung, "Spiritual Problem," CW 10, par. 169.
5. Jung, *Aion: Researches into the Phenomenology*, CW 9, par. 347.
6. Segal, *Gnostic Jung*, 7.

war with oneself."[7] About one third of Jung's patients suffered "from no clinically definable neurosis, but from the senselessness and emptiness of their lives [which Jung] described as the general neurosis of our time."[8] Many of Jung's patients were in middle age and socially well adjusted; yet they suffered from the feeling of being stuck and experienced a good deal of anxiety and psychic dislocation. These patients were in all respects normal but "they could find no meaning in their lives or were torturing themselves with questions which neither our philosophy nor our religion could answer. Some of them perhaps thought I knew of a magic formula, but I soon had to tell them that I didn't know the answer either."[9] In other words, Jung's patients were dealing with religious or spiritual crises.

Taking dreams as a transpersonal source of insight, Jung's patients, like Jung himself, would work with dream images through painting, dance, writing, fantasy, what Jung called "active imagination." This process generated a wealth of symbolic material, which the patient would seek to understand in terms of his or her own life. It was often the case, claims Jung, that this therapeutic process led to a culminating dream or vision that communicated to the patient "an impression of the most sublime harmony." Such an experience was "a turning point in the patient's psychological development. It [was] what one would call—in the language of religion—a conversion . . . as though at the climax of the illness, the destructive powers were converted into healing forces."[10] As a therapist, Jung took a pragmatic approach to healing the suffering of those persons with whom he worked. But as a psychologist, Jung sought to give a unity and framework to the experiences and observations he was making, by constructing a model of the structure and dynamics of the psyche.

In Jung's model, a personal and superficial layer of the unconscious rests upon a deeper layer "which does not derive from personal experience but is inborn." This deeper layer Jung calls the *collective unconscious*, consisting of "contents and modes of behavior that are more or less the same everywhere and in all individuals." The collective unconscious constitutes "a common psychic substrate of a suprapersonal nature which is present in everyone of us."[11] A correlate of Jung's hypothesis of the collective uncon-

7. Jung, "Psychotherapists or the Clergy," CW 11, par. 522.
8. Jung, "Aims of Psychotherapy," CW 16, par. 83.
9. Jung, "Psychotherapists or the Clergy," CW 11, par. 515.
10. Jung, "Psychology and Religion, CW 11, par. 110; "Psychotherapists or the Clergy, CW 11, par. 534.
11. Jung, "Archetypes of the Collective," CW 9i, par. 3.

scious is the concept of the *archetype*. Archetypes are the psychic images of biological predispositions within the human organism that have emerged over millennia of evolutionary development, illuminated by the comparative study of mythology, dreams, and religious symbols: certain motifs, symbols, themes, and forms become apparent. These predispositions are in a sense blueprints of the life experience of the human species. Instincts "form very close analogies to the archetypes," writes Jung, "so close, in fact, that there is good reason for supposing that the archetypes are the unconscious images of the instincts themselves, in other words, that they are patterns of instinctual behavior."[12] Jung identified archetypal figures (such as the shadow, the anima, the wise old man, the child), archetypes of transformation (such as birth, death, separation), and archetypal objects (such as the sun, moon, wind, fish, snakes).

One archetype crucial to Jung's psychology of religion is the *archetype of the self*. The self is what Jung calls the "archetype of archetypes," meaning that point around which all other archetypes unify and cohere: the self is the archetype of wholeness, unity, totality. Whereas the ego is the center of consciousness, the self is the center and circumference of an individual's psyche, which in its totality embraces both ego consciousness and the unconscious. Just as important as these structural considerations is a "physiology" of the psyche, which Jung develops through the concept of *individuation*.

By individuation Jung means "the process by which a person becomes a psychological 'in-dividual,' that is, a separate, indivisible unity or whole." "The psyche consists of two incongruous halves which together should form a whole."[13] The problem or task of individuation is to integrate and harmonize the conscious and unconscious aspects of the psyche. Jung claims that the psyche is a *self-regulating system* with a *compensatory* relationship between ego consciousness and the unconscious. Through the processes of shivering and sweating the body maintains a constant body temperature; similarly, the psyche regulates itself by balancing opposing tendencies within the psyche. Jung holds that the primary process by which psychic self-regulation proceeds is through dreams, which means that the regulating element in the psyche originates in the unconscious:

---

12. Jung, "Concept of the Collective," CW 9i, par. 91.
13. Jung, "Conscious, Unconscious, and Individuation," CW 9i, par. 490, 520.

> Whenever life proceeds one-sidedly in any given direction, the self-regulation of the organism produces in the unconscious an accumulation of all those factors which play too small a part in the individual's conscious existence. For this reason I have put forward the compensation theory of the unconscious as a complement to the repression theory.[14]

In summary, individuation is a developmental process in which the ego integrates purposeful, compensatory contents that well up from the collective unconscious during the unfolding of human life and the development of personality.

Jung is, on the face of it, friendly towards religion, and he examines the psychological dimensions of the core aspects of Christian faith, including reflections on the Trinity, Christology, Mariology, and the sacrament of the Mass. His approach is psychological-phenomenological. He asks no historical or sociological questions of the contents of Christian faith. When we turn to Jung's psychology of religion, the integrating theme is his notion of the *transformation of the God-image* in the Judeo-Christian tradition. Jung's key writings on the God-image, written toward the end of his life, *Aion* (1951) and *Answer to Job* (1952), are more myth than argument or scientific treatise, and so this chapter is an exercise in myth criticism, not a critical study of Jung's use of theory and method in developing an empirical psychology of religion. Of particular interest, given the previous chapters, is Jung's Christology, which he develops in *Aion*.

In the simplest of terms, Jung sees Christological doctrine, narratives, and imagery as a partial or dispersed projection of the contents of the archetype of the self. What is missing in Christian motifs and doctrines, he argues, is the dark side of our own inner nature. This leads to the appearance of the adversary (Satan) and a split and conflict between opposites, which plays itself out in narratives of salvation history. The image of Christ as a being without blemish, necessarily constellates its opposite (compensation) as a demand for psychological balance. Jung takes issue with the traditional theological concept of the *privatio boni*, which asserts that evil possesses no essential substantiality: evil is a "privation of the good." God, traditionally understood as a God "of infinite power, wisdom, and benevolence" is "implicated neither as substance nor as direct cause in the existence or effects of evil."[15] For Jung, this view, to be more in keeping with his (claimed) empirical psychological

14. Jung, "Role of the Unconscious," CW 10, par. 20.
15. Hart, *Theological Territories*, 81.

observations, must be overcome through a transformation of the God image to include the shadow side of God as an integral part of God's totality. For Jung, "in the products of the unconscious, we discover mandala symbols, that is, circular and quaternity figures which express wholeness, and whenever we wish to express wholeness, we employ just such figures."[16] From this perspective, a complete God-image is not a Trinity but a quaternity; a development necessary to Christianity is to integrate unassimilated dimensions of the unconscious that had been projected but left unintegrated in the early Christian era; these elements are variously understood as matter, the feminine, and evil. Here, we see the justification for considering Jung a "gnostic" thinker, as he understands God containing the capacity for evil.

A Myth of Meaning

Decades ago, James Heisig demonstrated that Jung's archetypal theory and empirical claims in his studies of the God-image rest on a shaky foundation.[17] To show that Jung does not advance a scientific argument in *Aion* and *Answer to Job* would be more than redundant—it would be wrongheaded given the aims here: indeed, it would be wrongheaded given Jung's stated aims in these works. I deal here not with Jung the mythologist or Jung the psychologist but with Jung's mythologizing, with his effort to create what Jung's colleague and confidant Aneilla Jaffe called a "Myth of Meaning," the story of "The Individuation of Mankind."[18] *Aion* and *Answer to Job* are the principal fruits of this effort, though the basis of Jung's views had been given expression early on, in the privately published *Septem Sermones ad Mortuos* (1916), as well as in the Red and Black notebooks that Jung worked on for decades, and which have been recently published.

As Blumenberg repeatedly emphasizes, the proper location of myth is existential need, and this is precisely where Jung locates it. Myths are not explanatory but consoling and orientating. The stories and myths Blumenberg takes up—the fall, Prometheus, Odysseus and the sirens, the tower of Babel, Leviathan—these "simply weren't told in order to answer

---

16. Jung, *Memories, Dreams, and Reflections*, 323.
17. Heisig, *Imago Dei*.
18. Jaffe, *Myth of Meaning*.

questions, but rather in order to dispel uneasiness and discontent."[19] Cultures produce and then reproduce—work on, alter, extend, adapt—a set of stock stories and images. And they do so, says Blumenberg, to "kill things," most crucially to "kill time" and "kill fear."[20] Our self-awareness includes conscious knowledge of having been in some sense exiled from nature, and hence of being open to and threatened by an immense, unpredictable word. Myth steps in and channels a debilitating anxiety into nameable fears and hopes. Cultures work on myth, just as they work on other modalities of thinking and knowing, including art, science, and dogma. Myth is "work on the reduction of the absolutism of reality" and this work and its products are givens of human being in the world: we are "always already on this side of the absolutism of reality."[21]

Like Blumenberg, Jung understands myth as a narrative strategy for dealing with pressing existential demands, and he sees in myth renewable resources. "Myth," Jung writes, "confers meaning on the banality of life."[22] *Aion* and *Job* were as much the result of creative mythologizing in the service of meaning as products of empirical science or reasoned argument. The notion that academics engage in the writing of cultural fictions is now widely accepted, and studies of Jung's work could benefit by approaching Jung in this light.

The term "myth" still carries pejorative connotations in colloquial English and in much scholarship. The term is meant to be descriptive but can nevertheless be wielded as a rhetorical weapon to label and denigrate. Such is not my intent here. Reading Jung's work on the God-image as "myth" is not meant as an implicit critique. Rather, calling Jung's *Aion* and *Job* myth is to use a descriptive term that directs our attention to certain features of Jung's thought. By myth then, I mean a culturally important image or set of images using metaphoric symbols in narrative or visual form to establish convictions concerning fundamental values of human existence. Jung's work, I think it is safe to say, is culturally important, despite the tendency in academia to deride the man and ignore the products of his life's labor.[23] It is not *that* Jung wrote myth that should concern

19. Blumenberg, *Work on Myth*, 184,
20. Blumenberg, *Work on Myth*, 34.
21. Blumenberg, *Work on Myth*, 13–15.
22. Jung, *Memories, Dreams, Reflections*, 163.
23. Culture by no means ends at the gates to the academy. Jung's thought, disseminated through the work of popular authors such as Joseph Campbell, Paulo Coelho, and Clarissa Pinkola Estes has reached a wide audience. The religion, mythology, and

us—more accurately, a remythologizing of Christianity—but rather *what* he wrote. Is Jung's myth, in other words, a story worth telling? Is it a good tale? What are its liabilities?

A Treatment for Christianity

From his earliest days as a clinician at Zürich's Burghözli psychiatric clinic and entry into the world of psychoanalysis, Jung imagined the path laid out before him in enthusiastically religious terms. Writing to Freud, in the golden years prior to their irreparable split, Jung responded to Freud's inquiry whether psychoanalysts should join an ethical fraternity with an effusive call to embrace the Dionysian:

> I imagine a far finer and more comprehensive task for ψα than alliance with an ethical fraternity. I think we must give it time to infiltrate into people from many centers, to revivify among intellectuals a feeling for symbol and myth, ever so gently to transform Christ back into the soothsaying god of the vine, which he was, and in this way absorb those ecstatic instinctual forces of Christianity for the one purpose of making the cult and the sacred myth what they once were—a drunken feast of joy where man regained the ethos and holiness of an animal.[24]

Freud demurred, and this letter signified the beginning of the end of their collaborations.

In 1916, in the context of his split with Freud, a world mired in war, and experiments in actively imagining, visually and narratively, the content of his dreams and fantasies, Jung reported a series of unsettling phenomena in his home, which he described as an invasion of "spirits" or "the dead." "I had the strange feeling that the air was filled with ghostly entities. Then it was as if my house began to be haunted."[25] These experiences led him to engage deeply with his unconscious, culminating

---

self-help/psychology sections of major bookstores regularly carry Jungian works. Most major North American and Western European cities have privately funded Jung centers, promoting and studying Jung's thought through seminars, workshops, and other events. "Archetype," "shadow," "wise old man," "anima," "individuation," "God-image"—these terms have filtered into everyday language. The new Philemon Foundation is dedicated to publishing the vast remainder of Jung's corpus beyond what is available in the *Collected Works*. Jung's myth of meaning is a chief competitor in the arena of contemporary new age spirituality.

24. Freud and Jung, *Freud/Jung Letters*, 294.

25. Jung, *Memories, Dreams, Reflections*, 190.

in the creation of the "Seven Sermons to the Dead," a privately printed gnostic text written in the voice of Basilides of Alexandria, which was included as an appendix to *Memories, Dreams, and Reflections*. This text marked Jung's lifelong engagement with Gnosticism, which he came to see as a precursor to his own psychological theories. Jung describes his "descent into the unconscious":

> I wrote these fantasies down first in the Black Book; later, I transferred them to the Red Book, which I also embellished with drawings. It contains most of my mandala drawings. In the Red Book I tried an esthetic elaboration of my fantasies, but never finished it. I became aware that I had not yet found the right language, that I still had to translate it into something else. Therefore I gave up this estheticizing tendency in good time, in favor of a rigorous process of understanding. I saw that so much fantasy needed firm ground underfoot, and that I must first return wholly to reality. For me, reality meant scientific comprehension. I had to draw concrete conclusions from the insights the unconscious had given me—and that task was to become a life work.[26]

Jung worked on these "esthetic elaborations" of his fantasies over a period of some twenty years, but he also wrote more scientific essays that weave together Gnosticism, alchemy (which he saw a bridge between ancient and modern thought), material from his and his patient's fantasies and active imaginings, and the core concepts of analytical psychology.

Jung saw a coherence between the disordered individuals he saw in the consulting room and a culture for whom God was dead. "Christian nations," writes Jung, "have come to a sorry pass; their Christianity slumbers and has neglected to develop its myth further in the course of the centuries." Jung emphasizes, writing in the years after WWII, an age wrestling with the aftermath and ongoing threat of political totalitarianism, that we "need psychology for reasons that involve our very existence," namely, to revivify Christianity through adopting a psychological perspective.[27] For Jung, Christianity is the mythological frame of modern Europe, and yet the Christian "myth has become mute, and gives no answers. The fault lies not in it as it is set down in the Scriptures, but solely in us, who have not developed it further, who, rather,

---

26. Jung, *Memories, Dreams, Reflections*, 188.
27. Jung, *Memories, Dreams, Reflections*, 331.

have suppressed any such attempt."²⁸ A central aim of Jung's analytical psychology then is to "dream the [Christian] myth onwards and give it a modern dress,"²⁹ a work of remythicization though the seemingly scientific language of contemporary psychology.

In his autobiography, Jung tells how he lost faith in the traditional Christianity of his father:

> But in what myth does man live nowadays? In the Christian myth, the answer might be. "Do you live in it?" I asked myself. To be honest, the answer was no. For me, it is not what I live by. "Then do we no longer have any myth?" No, evidently we no longer have any myth. "But then what is your myth—the myth in which you do live?" At this point the dialogue became uncomfortable, and I stopped thinking. I had reached a dead end.³⁰

Jung's writings on the transformation of the God-image represent his efforts to push through this "dead end," yet his commitments and presuppositions, despite his protestations that he no longer lived in "the Christian myth," are fundamentally Christian. Jung was not primarily concerned with doing scholarly work on Jewish, gnostic, and Christian thought and history, but rather with revitalizing the religion that he and many others had grown up with, but that no longer offered significance or meaning. "I am not . . . addressing myself to the happy possessors of faith, but to those many people for whom the light has gone out, the mystery faded, and God is dead."³¹

Jung's eclecticism is far reaching, and he created his religious worldview and personal identity out of a multitude of sources. In the end, however, the religious possibilities and resources available to Jung were subsumed and integrated within Christian symbols. "Our Christian doctrine," he writes, "is a highly differentiated symbol that expresses the transcendent psychic." Therefore, "the premise we start from is and remains Christianity."³² Attention to Jung's use of pronouns show that Jung is writing to his brethren—fellow Christians (largely liberal Protestants) who were living in what Weber described as an era of disenchantment.

---

28. Jung, *Memories, Dreams, Reflections*, 332.
29. Jung, *Psychology of the Child*, CW 9i, par. 271.
30. Jung, *Memories, Dreams, Reflections*, 171.
31. Jung, *Psychology and Religion*, CW 11, par. 148.
32. Jung, *Aion*, CW 9ii, par. 270.

Though Jung claims in the foreword to *Aion* that he is "not making a confession of faith or writing a tendentious tract," the ensuing discussion reveals otherwise. When Jung writes that Christ "exemplifies the archetype of the self," and that the self is "the archetype which it is most important for modern man to understand,"[33] he is claiming that Christ and Christianity are of fundamental importance to the spiritual needs of modern men and women. Jung's claim of close parallels between the self archetype and the figure and image of Christ, far from a conclusion of reasoned research and argument, is principally a confession of faith. Jung, despite his special pleading, did indeed live in the Christian myth, or a version of it. His implicit value commitments are to the Christian faith:

> It is only natural that I should constantly have revolved in my mind the question of the relationship of the symbolism of the unconscious to Christianity as well as to other religions. Not only do I leave the door open for the Christian message, but I consider it of central importance for Western man. . . . It needs, however, to be seen in a new light, in accordance with the changes wrought by the contemporary spirit. Otherwise, it stands apart from the times, and has no effect on man's wholeness. I have endeavored to show this in my writings.[34]

What is needed, argues Jung, is that Christianity be remythologized so that it speaks to the modern world.

Through his remythologizing of Christianity Jung was attempting to answer three problems, three "changes wrought by the contemporary spirit." First, the traditional theism of his father's generation could not answer the problem of evil to Jung's satisfaction. "Adam and Eve," reasoned the youthful Jung, "were the first people; they had no parents, but were created directly by God, who intentionally made them as they were. . . . God in his omniscience had arranged everything so that the first parents would have to sin. Therefore it was God's intention that they should sin."[35] Jung's solution to this question of evil was to locate evil as well as good in God, and then, to soften the implication that God is intentionally malicious, to further make God an unconscious force or factor beyond good and evil:

---

33. Jung, *Aion*, CW 9ii, pars. 70 & 422.
34. Jung, *Memories, Dreams, Reflections*, 210.
35. Jung, *Memories, Dreams, Reflections*, 38.

> The naive assumption that the creator of the world is a conscious being must be regarded a disastrous prejudice which later gave rise to the most incredible dislocations of logic. For example, the nonsensical doctrine of the *privatio boni* would never have been necessary had one not had to assume in advance that it is impossible for the consciousness of a good God to produce evil deeds. Divine unconsciousness and lack of reflection, on the other hand, enable us to form a conception of God which puts his actions beyond moral judgment and allows no conflict to arise between goodness and beastliness.[36]

The second problem facing Jung was the relationship between science and religion. Science was the language of modernity, and if Christianity could not speak this language, she was destined to die a quick death. We will return to this theme shortly. Lastly, Jung sought to incorporate the premise of evolution into his project of remythologizing Christianity. Rather than the spirit of evolution being at loggerheads with the myth of a perfect, final revelation, Christianity would become the vehicle of progressive spiritual and psychological development. The transformation of the God-image is thereby a "great drama"[37] in which men and women can participate by travelling the path of individuation, a path that brings to ever greater consciousness the complex nature of the archetype of the self, the God-image within. Jung's remythologizing of Christianity, his work as a doctor of lost souls, may have provided, and continue to provide, individuals with a "view of the world which adequately explains the meaning of human existence in the cosmos."[38]

Some Jungians hold that Jung conducted a successful "treatment" of Christianity, the metaphor suggesting, in keeping with Jung's own view of the matter, that Christianity in modernity is sick.[39] The medicine to bring it back to health is to integrate what Christianity rejected, namely, Gnosticism. Jung saw in gnostic texts not merely a precursor to his own discoveries in psychology, but a body of knowledge capable of reinvigorating the dying Christianity of his ancestors.

---

36. Jung, *Answer to Job*, CW 11, par. 600, n.13.
37. Jung, *Aion*, CW 9ii, par. 404.
38. Jung, *Memories, Dreams, Reflections*, 338.
39. See Stein, *Jung's Treatment of Christianity*.

Three Approaches to Jung's Remythologizing of Christianity

Scholarly studies of Jung's work on the God-image generally run along one of three now rather well-worn paths. Jungian readings tend to take Jung's work at face value, offer little by way of criticism or analysis, and seek to exegetically or hermeneutically extend Jung's ideas. Edward Edinger, for example, in his lectures on *Aion*, comments on a dream of Jung's in which he meets Salome and Elijah and is addressed as "Christ." Jung's dream is taken to mean that Jung

> is the harbinger of a new aeon—what I call and what I think will in the future be called the Jungian aeon. Jung could not have perceived and summarized the content of the aeon of Pisces unless he was already outside it.... Just as Christ was the first person to enter the aeon of Pisces, so Jung is the first to inaugurate the aeon of Aquarius.[40]

In Edinger's work (believe it or not) Jung is a new Christ, with the result being an implicit canonization of Jung's writings—which can be easily quoted, in biblical style, by reference to volume and paragraph number in the Collected Works.

Jungian readings of *Aion* and *Job* have been hampered by several problems. Jungians, like Jung himself, avoid historical-biblical criticism. Second, they have not absorbed critiques of Jung's work on theoretical and methodological grounds, the second prominent path taken in approaching Jung's corpus. Heisig's study is a masterful analysis of Jung's scholarship, and he finds it wanting. Jean Piaget, in an early critique of Jung's work, noted that "Jung has a tremendous capacity for construction, but a certain contempt for logic and rationality.... [Jung is] inclined to be content with too little in the way of proof. The better to understand the reality of which he speaks, he adopts an anti-rationalist attitude, and the surprising comparisons of which he has the secret cannot fail sometimes to disturb the critical reader."[41] But there remains in Jungian circles the assumption that Jung delivered testable scientific hypotheses, rather than seeing such claims as part of the narrative fiction he weaves. Jung himself is partly responsible for this; a double-speak of science and myth pervades his work. Part of the myth, in other words, is that it isn't myth, but science, at the very least a "rigorous process of understanding." What

---

40. Edinger, *Aion Lectures*, 192.
41. Piaget, *Play, Dreams, and Imitation*, 196.

is crucial for Jung is that his works *appears* scientific. Jung's scientific posturing ultimately causes grave difficulties for his myth of meaning, since no myth imagines itself to be a science.

Another problem with Jungian readings of Jung is that while there is recognition that Jung was in some way weaving myth, the conception of myth in Jungian studies tacitly accepts myth's sacredness. John Dourley, for example, writes that Jung's "identification with Joachim [di Fiore] would mean that he saw the unconscious currently working a new myth in the service of the same Spirit, the Self, which had created Christianity but now sought Christianity's completion in its own surpassing."[42] Perhaps this is what Jung "saw," but myth scholarship in recent years has drawn attention to the political and ideological dimensions of myth-making. Locating the emergence of a new myth solely in the workings of a transcendent, collective unconscious has the effect of engendering unconsciousness and diminishing self-reflexivity. Jung's remythologizing of Christianity ranges through the entire history of Christian thought and symbolism, stops off at the prophesies of Nostradamus, plays in the hinterlands of medieval alchemy, incorporates Jewish texts, gnostic texts, ancient dreams, his own dreams, the dreams of patients, astrology, and markings on Egyptian sarcophagi. There might be methodological problems in such an approach.

Jung's narrative is as grand as they come; that is part of its attraction, but also the key feature upon which a third variety of scholarship has fixed. Scholars from various perspectives—cultural studies, critical theory, feminism, post-colonialism—have all raised important issues. What I'm attempting here is to contribute to this third path in the form of myth criticism.

Science?

Jung claims in the prefatory note to *Answer to Job* he is "describing a personal experience [and] carried by subjective emotions." But Jung also wants to convince his readers that there is a reasoned argument behind the book. By the last paragraph, Jung can claim, "It will probably have become clear to the reader that the account I have given of the development of symbolic entities corresponds to a process of differentiation of human

---

42. Dourley, "Jung, Mysticism," 68.

consciousness."[43] *Aion* follows this same rhetorical strategy. Jung opens with the caveat that he writes "as a physician" not "as a scholar" and concludes, in the final paragraph, that his "main concern" in writing *Aion* is to point out "the parallelism or the difference between empirical findings [Jung's psychological theory] and our traditional views [represented in Christian symbols, dogmas, myths]."[44] Personal experience and reasoned "scientific" investigation are harmonized.

Jung openly courts the gnostic and scientific status of the various schools of spiritualism of his day—theosophy, anthroposophy, mediumism, Christian Science, "refurbished versions of kundalini-yoga." These movements signify

> that modern man, in contrast to his nineteenth-century brother, turns to the psyche with very great expectations, and does so without reference to any traditional creed but rather with a view to Gnostic experience. The fact that all the movements I have mentioned give themselves a scientific veneer is not just a grotesque caricature or a masquerade, but a positive sign that they are actually pursuing "science," i.e., knowledge, instead of faith. ... Modern man abhors faith and the religions based upon it.[45]

How are we to understand the paradox between Jung's "subjective emotions" and his claims of scientific objectivity, given that one of the defining features of modern science is precisely the exclusion of subjectivity? It isn't obvious that "gnostic" and "scientific" go hand in hand, though this is what Jung would have us believe.

One way around this tension implicit in Jung's corpus is to say that although Jung is often writing out of his own subjective experience, this experience derives from a universal or objective reality and process. Jung distinguishes between religion and religious creeds. Creeds are "codified and dogmatizied forms of original religious experience." "Religion ... is the term that designates the attitude peculiar to a consciousness which has been altered by the experience of the numinosum."[46] Jung's perennialist view of mystical experience is thus a way of grounding his own subjective experiences in a reality beyond himself. Knowledge of this objective reality (or the "objective psyche," as Jung phrases it) is

---

43. Jung, *Answer to Job*, CW 11, par. 758.
44. Jung, *Aion*, CW 9ii, 479.
45. Jung, "Spiritual Problem," CW 10, 171.
46. Jung, "Psychology and Religion," CW 11, par. 9–10.

known through individual experience, but this experience, conceived as pure and unmediated, thus becomes data for making claims about transpersonal processes. In Jung's hands, the rhetoric of experience serves to shutdown critical discussion: "Religious experience is absolute; it cannot be disputed. You can only say that you have never had such an experience, whereupon your opponent will reply: 'Sorry, I have.' And there your discussion will come to an end."[47] But the discussion need not come to an end; critique of the claims and implications emerging from an individual's experience ought to be fair game. This is especially so when the claim to an absolute experience is used to justify (seemingly) empirical claims, as Jung wants to do.

Despite the rhetorical move of claiming to write not as a scientist but as a doctor, Jung is making scientific claims, truth claims. Jung's often tries to defend himself against the charge that he is a metaphysician, theologian, or mystic, and claims that his psychological theory is a work of science, though at times he lets his guard down:

> The Church still has a little power left, but she pastures her sheep on the ruins of Europe. Her message works, if one knows how to combine her language, ideas, and customs with an understanding of the present. But for many she no longer speaks the language of the present, but wraps her message in sacrosanct words hallowed by age. What success would Paul have had with his preaching if he had to use the language and myths of the Minoan age in order to announce the gospel to the Athenians?[48]

Here, Jung sees himself as modern day Paul, translating a reading of the Gospels into the language of those he wishes to reach. In Jung's context, this new language is that of science, an empirical or phenomenological psychology. Jung's narrative of the transformation of the God-image need not be scientific, but it must at least convey that appearance, so seems to run Jung's reasoning. Following, for example, a psychological paraphrase of a section of Ignatius's *Spiritual Exercises*, Jung comments: "This paraphrase not only sounds rationalistic but is meant to be so, for despite every effort the modern mind no longer understands our two-thousand-year-old theological language unless it 'accords with reason.'"[49] Jung's psychological concepts therefore are offered not so much as explanatory

---

47. Jung, "Psychology and Religion," CW 11, par. 167.
48. Jung, *Aion*, CW 9ii, par. 274.
49. Jung, *Aion*, CW 9ii, par. 254.

devices, probing the psychological background of religious phenomenon, but as translations of religious imagery, doctrines, and theological concepts into a new language. The "psychological equivalent," for example, of the "*decensus ad infernos*, the descent of Christ's soul into hell," is said by Jung to be "the integration of the collective unconscious which forms an essential part of the individuation process."[50] Such sleight of hand—the pouring of old wine into new skins—gives the Christian myth a facticity that it has traditionally relied upon.

Jung, in the introduction to his autobiography, tells us that he can "only 'tell stories.' Whether or not the stories are 'true' is not the problem. The only question is whether what I tell is *my* fable, *my* truth."[51] But clearly Jung is not content to leave it at that. On the one hand, Jung wants to avoid making universal claims and to speak his truth; on the other hand, he offers the transformation of the God-image as an empirically derived theory. Jung's writings on Christianity, he claims, are not the result of faith or apologetics, but of empirical science; when this fails, they are the product of unquestionable experience. Christianity is offered by Jung as the best possible expression of the psychological dynamics Jung claims to have discovered. The archetypal processes of individuation can be described "with an exactness and impressiveness far surpassing our feeble attempts" through recourse to the "Christian tradition."[52] Here, Jung puts the cart before the horse, with the result that the universalistic tendency within Christianity finds its way, willy nilly, into Jung's myth-making.

Though Jung at times argues his ideas are grounded in primary processes—"nature," rather than "art"—his narrative of the transformation of the God-image is the result of historic circumstance, reflection, and selection. Jung, I suggest, would have us believe that the universe is really how he sets it up; or, at least, he feels compelled to seduce his readers into thinking so. A true fictive religiosity would apply the acid of irony and iconoclasm more playfully to itself. In Lonnie Kliever's theorizing, "'fictions' are not hypotheses whose truth remains in doubt for the present. 'Fictions' are symbolic constructs which cannot be verified and hence cannot be true."[53] Jung's fiction of the transformation of the God-image is framed as an empirically tested and proven hypothesis; it is a fiction that

50. Jung, *Aion*, CW 9ii, par. 12.
51. Jung, *Memories, Dreams, Reflections*, 3.
52. Jung, *Aion*, CW 9ii, par. 79.
53. Kliever, "Fictive Religion," 658.

doesn't and can't recognize itself as such, and such fictions, aside from being intellectually dishonest, can be dangerous.

Jung's claims regarding the transformation of the God-image are rooted in an evolutionary paradigm. "For behind all this [transformation of the God-image] looms the vast and unsolved riddle of life itself and evolution in general, and the question of overriding importance in the end is not the origin of evolution but its goal."[54] Adopting a stage model of religious evolution popular in the nineteenth and early twentieth centuries, Jung conceives three fundamental God-images in the history of Western thought: a God of wrath and unconscious blindness exemplified by Yahweh; a God of love and one-sided perfectionism exemplified in the New Testament and early Christian dogma; and a God of wholeness that heals divisions between good and evil, spirit and matter, and the masculine and feminine. This theory is not merely specious, it has underwritten colonial paradigms and practices.

The emergence of Christ as a collective symbol at the onset of the Christian era marks for Jung a profound change in the psychic situation in late antiquity and a monumental step in the evolutionary development of the God-image. "Christ," claims Jung, "exemplifies the archetype of the self." That is, the complex nature of the archetype of the self first manifests itself historically through projection at the beginning of the Christian era. The withdrawal and integration of projections is the path of psychological development. Christianity is therefore of utmost importance to Western civilization since the ongoing "assimilation and integration of Christ into the human psyche"—which includes overcoming the Christ-Antichrist antithesis found in early Christian symbolism and dogma—"results in the growth of the personality and the development of consciousness."[55]

The crucial point here is that Jung isn't simply tracing changes in God-images in the Judeo-Christian tradition—he is claiming a progressive, developmental process. There are difficulties with such a view. Jung quite clearly believes that monotheistic religion represents a psychological and moral advance over polytheism,[56] an idea that has received a good deal of critical attention, not least from the post-Jungian James Hillman.[57] As part of his evolutionary framework, Jung relies on a questionable

---

54. Jung, *Aion*, CW 9ii, par. 279.

55. Jung, *Aion*, CW 9ii, par. 70; 43; 221.

56. Christianity is a "thin wall" that "separates us from pagan times" (*Aion*, CW 9ii, par. 272).

57. See Hillman, *Revisioning Psychology*.

psychological version of Ernst Haeckel's biological notion that ontogeny recapitulates phylogeny. "The anima/animus stage [of psychological development] is correlated with polytheism, the self with monotheism."[58] Jung not only considers monotheistic religion a psychological and moral advance over polytheism, Christianity is portrayed as a developmental advance over Judaism, and here Jung begins to tread on politically, theologically, and historically sensitive ground:

> It is only the careful and farsighted preparations of Christ's birth which shows us that omniscience has begun to have a noticeable effect on Yahweh's actions. A certain philanthropic tendency makes itself felt. The "children of Israel" take something of a second place in comparison with the "children of men."[59]

But to get this line of reasoning to work, Jung fails to consider all the evidence. His is not a Christology from below, and, for all the claims to be working scientifically, Jung is not the least interested to engage with historical Jesus research, or historical research generally. Jung does not discuss the Old Testament concern for the poor, the needy, the widow, the orphan, the robbed and the oppressed, as found in the prophets, and how these correlate (or fail to correlate) with prevailing God-images. A "philanthropic tendency" is certainly found in the book of Jonah, and Abraham pleads with God to spare Sodom and Gomorrah: "Shame on you if you did such a thing, to slay the just with the wicked, letting the just fare like the wicked! Shame on you if the judge of the whole earth should not do right" (Gen 18:25). Jung points to precisely such passages as evidence for his picture of the wrathful Yahweh. But does Abraham, one of the "children of Israel," really take a back seat to the "children of men" who, among others things, call "the Jews" a "brood of vipers" (Matt 12:34)? Even if we grant that in the New Testament God is related to through the language love in a different, even unique valence to the Hebrew Bible—and Jung doesn't attempt to prove this notion, he simply assumes it—is there a correlation with an increased "philanthropic tendency" or personality development among those in the early Christian community? How would we go about actually demonstrating this? In the end, Jung's argument for a transformation in the God-image from wrath and unconscious blindness to benevolent love is dependent on a liberal amount of proof-texting. Jung is by no means oblivious to the many New Testament passages that

58. Jung, *Aion*, CW 9ii, par. 427.
59. Jung, *Answer to Job*, CW 11, 637.

don't fit his developmental model. Thus, when claiming that, "the seven-horned ram [of the Apocalypse] is just about everything that Jesus appears not to be," Jung, in a footnote, comments, "That is, if we disregard passages like Matt. 21:19 and 22:7 and Luke 19:2,7."[60] But why disregard these (and other similar) passages, several of which I pointed to above in the discussion of Christian violence?[61]

Jung's liberal Protestant milieu is clearly present in his remythologizing of Christianity as a religion of love. Jung's comments on Revelation are of interest here:

> There grew up a terrifying picture that blatantly contradicts all ideas of Christian humility, tolerance, love of your neighbor and your enemies, and makes nonsense of a loving father in heaven and rescuer of mankind. A veritable orgy of hatred, wrath, vindictiveness, and blind destructive fury that revels in fantastic images of terror breaks out and with blood and fire overwhelms a world which Christ had just endeavored to restore to the original state of innocence and loving communion with God.[62]

Jung goes onto to attempt an explanation of the "unchristian" ethos of John's Revelation through a psychological analysis of its author. Whatever in the Christian tradition betrays the notion of Christianity as a religion of love Jung summarily dismissed as being foreign to Christian thought.

To repeat, one of Jung's central claims is that the ongoing "assimilation and integration of Christ into the human psyche" results in "the growth of the human personality and in the development of consciousness."[63] Is this a psychological, historical, or theological claim? Were early Christians somehow more conscious than those that remained Jews? Did they possess a more developed personality? If so, what, precisely, does such a claim mean? If someone fails to assimilate Christ into her psyche, does this somehow correlate with a diminished personality and consciousness?

The latent anti-Semitism found in Jung's writings is perhaps the most contentious issue with which any discussion of the Jungian myth must grapple. Within the Jungian community, Andrew Samuels is to be commended for raising and struggling with the question of the relationship

---

60. Jung, *Aion*, CW 9ii, par. 167, & n.12.

61. See, for example, Mark 3:29; 6:11; 9:43-48; Matt 3:12; 5:22, 29; 8:12; 10:15; 22:13-14; 23:33; 24:51; 25:30, 41; Luke 3:17; 12:5; 13:27; 16:19-31.

62. Jung, *Answer to Job*, CW 11, par. 708.

63. Jung, *Aion*, CW 9ii, 346.

between Jung's views on national or ethnic psychology and the National Socialist movement.[64] It is arguable whether Jung's work sponsors a myth of more inclusive embrace, a notion that Dourley advocates.[65] Jung's myth of transformations in the God-image depends on the transposition of a theological idea—namely, that Judaism is a precursor to a more developed, comprehensive truth—into a dubious scientific claim. Christianity has long defined itself against Judaism, and this practice has historically been linked to anti-Jewish invective. Jung fails to extricate himself from the ultimately pernicious notion that Christianity represents the historical fulfillment or completion of Judaism. Jung's imaginative or mythological conception of history is decidedly evolutionary, and this untroubled notion leads (historical-critical questions aside) to Jung sliding theological claims through the back door in the guise of psychological dynamics.

Gnostic "Art Myth"

Jung knew he was writing myth and he used the rhetoric of experience and the language of science as integral parts of his remythologizing of Christianity. This later point needs some further clarification and elaboration.

It is part of Jung's myth that it isn't myth. The tendency in approaching Jung's work on the God-image is to treat this writer of stories as the writer of history or of psychological theory, to imagine that what is being offered is reasoned argument rather than narrative fiction; in being so seduced we forget to remember the fictive quality of Jung's myth-making. Let us state that Jung, despite his protestations to the contrary,[66] was a myth-maker, and one of some talent, and we should leave allusions to the workings of the collective unconscious where they belong—inside Jung's myth. In antiquity, facts were not things discovered but things made and Jung's agency in the making of his myth of meaning need not necessitate putting him on the shelf for good. The

---

64. Samuels, "Jung and Antisemitism" and "New Material Concerning Jung."

65. See Dourley, "Jung, Mysticism." Dourley points to Jung's embracing of the feminine in the dogma of the assumption as an example of Jung's inclusivity. But the question of the feminine in Jung's thought is a double-edged sword, as many feminist critiques of Jung's work have pointed out. The anima, as the image of the feminine in the male psyche does, on purely theoretical grounds, lead to the conclusion, as Hillman puts it, quoting Jung, that "Woman has no anima, no soul" (in Hillman, *Anima*, 59).

66. "It is not we who invent myth, rather it speaks to us a Word of God" (Jung, *Memories, Dreams, Reflections*, 340).

idea that anthropologists and sociologists write culture, religionists write religion, and Jung was writing myth ought to be old hat by now; let everyone write away, and endeavor to write well, with some regard for self-reflexivity. Either naively treating Jung's work as the empirical discovery of relations between the history of Christianity and psychological dynamics or simply shrugging him off because his work is a construction point to our inability to imagine the workings of culture. It is *what* is made not *that* it is made that ought to be of concern in myth criticism.

In Jung's case, myth masquerading as reasoned argument (or revelation mediated through the archetypes of the collective unconscious) is part of what was made, and this fact itself needs critique, not because it means Jung's work is ultimately untrue, but because it locates his myth in the realm of *verum* to begin with.[67] This move owes its origins, I suggest, to the tacit Christian emplotment of Jung's thought; the Christian myth is something more than myth—it is real, true, factual, historical, realism, and so on. Jung felt compelled to locate his myth within the realm of *logos* and this is its downfall, for it puts us in the double bind of at once affirming (or denying) its truth while realizing it stands outside the realm of truth; it involves, in other words, a self-deception. Jung's countryman and contemporary Karl Barth, by way of comparison, rejected the notion of nineteenth-century liberal theology that Christianity was one religion among many, that it was at root a cultural fiction, myth, or legend. Jung also rejects this notion, but his solution is more deceptive than that of Barth, for Jung encourages us to believe in his myth of the transformation of the God-image based on how it (seemingly) accords with reason, argument, and "empirical" evidence, rather than based on a confessional stance, a stance nevertheless implicit in Jung's work.

Jung's work on the God-image, his "myth of meaning," is far closer to fiction or art than to argument. In *Memories, Dreams, Reflections* Jung relates his shock at a dream figure's suggestion that his fantasies were art. Jung, recognizing at this point that his fantasies had "nothing to do with science," clung to the notion that his fantasies and their implications were rooted in "nature," that is, spontaneous, natural processes stemming from the transpersonal workings of the objective psyche.[68]

---

67. As Paul Veyne has discussed, for the Greeks, myth was "from the very outset ... situated beyond the alternative between truth and falsehood" (*Did the Greeks Believe*, 23). Jung, by framing his myth-making as argument, situates himself inside this alternative.

68. Jung, *Memories, Dreams, Reflections*, 185–86.

Jung makes this move, I suggest, because art entails conscious elaboration (whatever unconscious elements may also be present), a notion he required excised from his "myth of meaning" because it would then be unscientific and hold no meaning. In his writings on the Christian God-image, Jung toys with but in the end rejects the possibility of what Lonnie Kliever calls "fictive religion."

In *Work on Myth*, Blumenberg distinguishes between "fundamental myths" and "art myths." These two types of myths serve different purposes and originate from different sources, reflecting the varied ways in which human beings use stories to understand and navigate their world. A fundamental myth is a narrative that provides the foundational framework for a culture or civilization. These myths are deeply embedded not in a collective *un*conscious but in the collective *consciousness;* they are integral to the way a society understands itself, its origins, and its place in the universe. Fundamental myths address profound existential questions, offering explanations for the nature of reality, the human condition, and the origins of society. In contrast, an art myth does not serve the same foundational or explanatory role as a fundamental myth. Instead, it emerges from the realm of creation, often crafted by an individual rather than arising from the collective cultural consciousness. Art myths are deliberately created or reshaped, often with a clear awareness of their fictional nature. Rather than claiming to explain the fundamental truths of existence, art myths are more concerned with exploring, expressing, or even critiquing social realities. These myths are found in literature, theater, and other forms of art, where mythic elements are used as tools for creative exploration and expression.

A fundamental myth "cannot be allowed to fall under the suspicion that it is an artifact." It must remain a "psychological product of nature" that "could not have been invented"; myth is a "Darwinism in the realm of words." Blumenberg even cites Jung in this regard, a passage from *Memories, Dream, Reflections,* where Jung understands the flood of images in his dreams and fantasies as "the Word of God," a revelation unsullied, writes Jung, by the "arbitrary operation of our will."[69] Such a perspective makes a certain sense in the case of antique myths, whose origins are lost in time. But in an era where, as Goethe said, "No one is a hero to their valet," eyebrows raise when we read Jung claim his dreams are the Word of God. Moreover, one of the features of fundamental myths

---

69. Blumenberg, *Work on Myth*, 128. See Jung, *Memories, Dreams, Reflections,* 340.

is the economy of style, a condensation that does not in any way lead to a hollowing out of significance and complexity. More words do not equal more profundity. Jung's garrulous style not-withstanding, the rag-tag way he cobbles together his source material leaves the reader unable to follow the argument, if there is an argument.

Jung's myth of meaning is closer to an art myth than a fundamental myth; the informing method, the substance, and the social context and setting in which it was Jung's myth was generated closely resemble Blumenberg's description of "gnostic art myth":

> The weakness of the Gnostic art myth: It belongs to an arcane literature that remains withdrawn from the discipline exercised by an audience. That allows it to take on the character of unbridled prolixity, of fanciful proliferation, which is not subject to any process of selection. The myth that is given out as "secret teachings" does have variants, but they were clearly not exposed to any process of comparison. The litany and the piling up of repetitions that can be imposed on a small sworn group do not encounter any threshold of boredom and indifference because even being tortured by them strengthens one's consciousness of being among the chosen. That is well known from totalitarian systems, where the speeches of leading functionaries can be just as long as they are boring, as though there had never been such a thing as rhetoric—rhetoric being a skill needed by those who are still seeking power. It is also generally true, in connection with ritual and texts associated with worship, that one wants to be able to show what one endures "for the cause." So the Gnostic art myth degenerates under the hothouse treatment that is accorded to it as a result of the sanction that lies on it and that keeps it distant from any "judgment of taste."[70]

Overcoming Gnosticism

On the road to the formation of Christian dogma, early Christian thinkers faced two key challenges. First, as Christianity moved out from Palestine it encountered Greek philosophical culture. This was not simply philosophy in the intellectual sense but an integral aspect of religious life. Through Neoplatonism, the Platonic, Aristotelian, and Stoic traditions were unified in a system that "was philosophic and religious at the

---

70. Blumenberg, *Work on Myth*, 209.

same time."[71] If Christianity was to survive it would have to evoke the existential meaning and philosophic wisdom of its competitors while at the same time remaining true to its founding event—the life, death, and resurrection of Jesus, understood as the well-spring of redemption. The second challenge was Gnosticism, that widespread current of abjuring a spiritual investment in the world, which colored Judaism, Greek philosophy, Roman law, and Christian theology.[72]

Suffering is a great enigma. The ancient world posed the problem of why there is so much "bad" in the world. Metaphysically speaking, we find the problem in Plato, who made a distinction between our world of appearances (matter and the senses) and the ideal world of forms (spirit and thought); with such a distinction in place, our world is a "fallen" one, with matter and the body conceived as prisons of some sort. This metaphysical view has rather solid support in the form of the daily news, natural disasters, and terminal illnesses. In gnostic thought, the cosmos in its entirety is one huge wrong turn. In this view, there is no need for a theodicy (the attempt to justify or understand the creator God in light of our fallenness), since for the gnostic "the good God has never had anything to do with the world."[73] Such a move does little to ward off the experience of the absolutism of reality, little to help create a feeling of basic trust in a world we must necessarily inhabit.

At issue is what may be described as the gnostic drama or gnostic myth, and the manner Gnosticism sought to incorporate the event of Jesus into this drama. The God of Genesis, of creation, of the Old Testament is not the highest God but a *demiurge*, a fallen god ignorant of the higher realm above and rooted in an evil principle. It is this demiurge that is the creator of the material world. But during this creation spiritual elements became trapped in material bodies. These souls are unaware of their true spiritual nature and a savior is required to bring the true knowledge that can deliver them back to the heavenly realm. Jesus is by no means God, for the highest God is transcendent, unknowable, and invisible. Rather, this saving power descends to earth and adopts the body of Jesus to reveal liberating knowledge to those few *pneumatikoi* who had become trapped in the material realm. The man Jesus who suffered and was crucified was in no way divine for a divine being could never suffer or die.

---

71. Tillich, *History of Christian Thought*, 50
72. Tillich, *History of Christian Thought*, 33
73. Blumenberg, *Legitimacy*, 129.

Irenaeus was one who sought to combat this gnostic narrative. He saw a partly Christian, partly pagan myth and theology as more dangerous than something completely outside of the Christian tradition. These gnostics "alter the scriptural context and connection, and dismember the truth as much as they can. By their perversions and changes, and by making one thing out another, they deceive many with their specious adaptations of the oracles of the Lord." Whereas a thinker like Marcion sought to sever New Testament texts from Hebrew scripture, Irenaeus wanted to ensure that the Christian message remain rooted in Jewish tradition. God the Father spoken of by Jesus is the God of creation revealed in the Hebrew scriptures:

> The rule of truth we hold is that there is one God Almighty, who made all things by his word, and fashioned and formed that which has existence out of that which had none.... The Father made all things by him, both visible and invisible.... And such he did not make by angles or by any powers separated from His thought.... Above Him there is no other God.

Furthermore, this creation was not fallen as the gnostics suggest but an emanation of God. God did not introduce spirits into a preexistent material world; there were not two principles as suggested by the dualism of the gnostics but one. Creation is not the "fruit of defect" as the gnostic have it but the creation of the True and Almighty God. Exercising free will God created the world, and it is a world of order in which the spiritual, celestial, angelic, psychical, and earthly elements are all divine and part of his harmonious creation.[74] Jesus is understood within Gnosticism as the "receptacle of Christ" but not Christ himself. For Irenaeus, the gnostics erred in refusing the idea of the incarnation.

What was at stake in Irenaeus's battle with the gnostics? For Irenaeus, what is needed is a religion that can thrive in this world and the gnostics did not offer one. The gnostics degraded the material world, and they did so for the purpose of salvation. The theology of Irenaeus is an affirmation of the world; for all its pain and suffering, it is good because it comes of God. God is not beyond us and untouchable; we are related to God: as we suffer so he suffered; and as he lives so we live. The entirety of the efforts within Christian thought to refute Gnosticism were aimed at

---

74. Quotations from Irenaeus's *Against Heresies* are drawn from Kerr, *Readings in Christian Thought*, 30–32.

protecting or retrieving the dignity of the ancient idea of a *cosmos* within the Christian system of incarnational thinking.

Blumenberg devotes considerable attention to gnostic thought, as well to Christian attempts to overcome it. He offers a critique of Gnosticism, rooted in the principles of his philosophical anthropology. Central to Blumenberg's anthropology is the active role of we play in constructing meaning and order. It focuses on the creative and adaptive capacities of human beings to deal with their existential conditions. This perspective values human ingenuity, resilience, and the effort to impose order and meaning on an otherwise hostile and indifferent reality, our capacity to resist the absolutism of reality. From this perspective the gnostic view is intolerable. Gnosticism's dualism denigrates the material world as inherently evil or flawed, and so emphasizes escape from the world rather than engagement with it. Little wonder there is next to no social-political or historical analysis in Jung's writings, nor an engagement with eschatology and salvation history. Gnosticism undermines human creativity and adaptive effort to make a home in the world, though at least, unlike Jung, the gnostics held there was something that we needed saving from. Sin is not mentioned in *Aion*; Jung's myth-making is therapeutic, focused on self-development and wholeness, not matters of freedom, emancipation, and history. Furthermore, gnostic thought implies that human progress and the search for knowledge within the material world are futile, with knowledge only available via revealed secret teachings. This perspective is antithetical to Blumenberg's view that human history is a continuous project of overcoming and adapting to the absolutism of reality. In Blumenberg's framework, the human response to the absolutism of reality needs be constructive—creating myths, religions, and philosophies that help humans navigate and mitigate the harshness of reality. Gnosticism's response, however, is withdrawal from and rejection of the world, rather than constructive engagement. As such, Blumenberg, not unlike the church fathers, sees Gnosticism as defeatist. Jung, for his part, enfolds evil into the Absolute; this is an approach to dealing with the problem of suffering that simply makes it disappear. Compensation theory, which moves us to reflect on and integrate alienated or undeveloped aspect of ourselves, when applied to the social world, crumbles as a house of cards.[75]

---

75. See Žižek, *Less Than Nothing*, 299–305, for a devastating critique of the social-political implications of Jung's compensation theory.

The great synthesis of efforts to overcome Gnosticism is found in the thought of Augustine. Initially an adherent of Manichaeism, a form of Gnosticism, Augustine later rejected its dualistic cosmology. He sought to defend the goodness of the world and its creator by developing a theodicy that attributed the existence of evil not to an evil demiurge but to the corrupted free will of human beings. Deficiencies in the world are not to be laid before God but by assumed by people. This new conception of freedom came twined with the assigning of guilt. In placing the burden of the goodness of world on us, Augustine unburdened God of responsibility for evil and suffering. Generally, ancient philosophical systems did not distinguish the bad things we do from the bad we encounter: Augustine did just that. The bad we encounter is the bad we have done. Of course, this is a difficult position to maintain in the face of so-called "natural evil," in the form of a hurricane or a cancer. Suffering is the greatest objection to all forms of theism that place faith in a loving God. Suffering has the quality of a mystery, and forces the choice, discussed earlier, between nihilism and a trusting faith. Jung doesn't only side-steps the problem of suffering. His "pseudo-Hegelianism"[76] can make room for all sorts of evil to be seen as a part of an unfolding process where the "bad" viewed from enough distance, becomes part of a pattern of balanced harmonies.

Blumenberg argues that Augustine's solution was ultimately insufficient. By transposing the responsibility for evil onto humanity's free will, Augustine did not eradicate the gnostic conception of a fundamentally evil world. Instead, he merely shifted the locus of responsibility, thus perpetuating a worldview where the inherent evil of the world remained unchallenged. This transference placed an enormous moral burden on humanity, implying that evil is a direct consequence of human actions, yet this did not fully absolve God of responsibility for the creation of a world in which evil could exist. Again, these difficulties are especially apparent in the case of so-called "natural evil," which seems to take place regardless of our will.

A solution here is to interpret the incarnation not as necessary to deal with the problem of sin but as a means of completing creation: through the incarnation, we become related to a God of solidarity, concern, and care. In adapting the logos doctrine to the event of Jesus and in the fight to safeguard the Christian message against gnostic elements, the same theme presents itself: the union of the spiritual and the material.

---

76. Žižek, *Less Than Nothing*, 300.

"Man is in every respect the formation of God," writes Irenaeus, "and therefore he [Jesus Christ] recapitulates men into himself, the invisible becoming visible, the incomprehensible comprehensible, the one superior to suffering becoming subject to suffering, and the Word becoming man."[77] In Jesus as the Christ, the logos comes home, so to speak, and what is more, to its proper home—human life.

If gnostics of old felt alienated from the outer, material world, which was understood to be an evil, fallen world having nothing whatsoever to do with the true God, moderns like Jung feel alienated from their true selves, lost and wandering in a spiritual wasteland produced by a culture that had embraced positivism and technocratic, instrumental rationality and consumption, abandoning inner, spiritual needs and capacities. For the gnostics of old it is ignorance that keeps us tied to a fallen material realm, a state that may be overcome through acquiring wisdom, understood as knowledge of the starkly dualistic state of cosmic ocean in which we swim, a knowledge that frees us from unconscious bondage to matter. For modern gnostics like Jung we can reorient, redress, rebalance our one-sided culture of "single vision" (Blake) by (re)discovering the hidden, inner image of God that is the basis for our very self. While gnostics of old separated divinity into two antithetical gods embodying truth and falsehood, good and evil, redemption and wrath, spirit and matter, modern gnostics work to harmonize, to make whole, to balance these differentiated potentials. Jung holds that although Christ is a symbol of the self, the Christ figure is not a totality, as it "lacks the nocturnal side of the psyche's nature, the darkness of the spirit, and is also without sin. Without the integration of evil there is no totality." Christ "suffers, so to speak, from the violence done to him by the self."[78] God, in Jung's theorizing, is both evil and masochistic. No doubt those who are persecuted, tortured, humiliated, and executed by the state experience profound psychological distress, and we ought to try and understand what oppressive forms of colonial violence do to both victims and perpetrators. But is any of this gnostic mythicizing of Christ symbolism helpful in such in endeavor? Is the cross the locus of individuation and the development of personality, or a symbol of keeping faith with failure, and hence keeping faith with the hope of liberation, reconciliation, and justice? Jung's obliviousness to history, politics, and social dynamics is in keeping with the gnostic's refusal

---

77. Quoted in Kerr, *Readings in Christian Thought*, 36
78. Jung, "Psychological Approach," CW 11, par. 232–33.

of any "spiritual investment in this world" that brings with it a social and political investment.

Should we really aim, as Jung would have it, to balance good and evil? Or should we work for more the former, and less of the latter? Shall we "integrate" and "become whole," or shall we follow the spirit of eschatology embodied in the words of Martin Luther King Jr.: "we shall overcome?"

Coda: "When Did We See Thee Hungry?"

> *Justice towards the evolving god.*—When the entire history of culture opens up before our gaze as a confusion of evil and noble, true and false conceptions, and at the sight of this surging of the waves we come to feel almost seasick, we are then able to grasp what comfort there lies in the idea of an evolving god: the transformations and destinies of mankind are, according to this idea, the ever increasing self-revelation of this god, it is not all a blind mechanism, a senseless, purposeless confused play of forces. The deification of becoming is a metaphysical outlook—as though from a lighthouse down on to the sea of history—in which a generation of scholars too much given to historicizing found their consolation; one ought not to get annoyed at it, however erroneous that idea may be. Only he who, like Schopenhauer, denies the fact of evolution, will likewise feel nothing of the wretchedness of this surging of the waves of history, and because he knows and feels nothing of that evolving god or of the need to suppose his existence may fairly give vent to his mockery.
>
> —Friedrich Nietzsche, *Human All Too Human*

THE IDEA OF AN evolving (or transforming) God is commonly associated with German idealism. Schelling could never quite make up his mind on the matter. In his middle period, he inscribed difference, flux, and change into the very heart of the Absolute. As Sean McGrath describes, Schelling conceives the absolute as "in process, giving birth to itself as a divine personality by means of duality, multiplicity, and history." Later, he reversed course to reject the notion that the Absolute has any need of historical development.[1] For Nietzsche, the "idea of the evolving God" offers tremendous comfort in face of the flux and chaos of history. Becoming, writes Nietzsche, is "deified" and however absurd the notion of an Absolute changing might be, it provides a necessary consolation against the fear that our destinies are merely the result of a "blind mechanism, a senseless, purposeless confused play of forces." However "erroneous" the idea of "the evolving god" might be, "one ought not to get annoyed at it."[2] The young Schelling is to be credited with inventing "historical immanentism"—the notion that God is not "whole, complete, or perfectly actual being," but rather a work in progress. Hegel said the same, Nietzsche understood its appeal, and process theology ran with the idea.

The notion of an evolving God could likely never have gotten off the ground were there not hints of it in Scripture—and there are plenty. The Almighty regrets he made Saul king. The LORD first desires his "wrath to burn hot" against the idolaters in the gold calf episode, but then changes his mind owing to the pleas of Moses; the LORD, we read, "repented of the evil which he thought to do to his people" (Exod 32:14). But this was but a temporary metanoia, and the LORD winds up commanding the sons of Levi to put to the sword some three thousand of their own people. Witnessing human wickedness and an earth filled with violence, he rains down the devastation of the great flood; but then, surveying the damage, promises to never react that way again. God, we learn, first gives precise instruction on how to perform sacrifice; later, for example in Hosea, he desires "steadfast love and not sacrifice" (Hos 6:6). Deuteronomy allows for divorce with a certificate, and there seems no implied moral judgment; in Malachi, the LORD pronounces, "I hate divorce" (Mal 2:16). As Jack Miles has demonstrated, one can productively read the Bible as a "biography" of God, a god who, like people, changes and develops. God invents religion, only to become rather weary of the whole sorted affair.

Of course, we might reasonably ask if, when we encounter the word "God" in the Bible (or elsewhere), are we encountering God as such, assuming God exists, or human attempts to understand or represent God, attempts that run the gamut from "not even close" to accurately uncovering and articulating some aspect of an ultimate, unchanging, eternal reality? Traditional doctrine has emphasized God's constancy

---

1. McGrath, *Dark Ground of Spirit*, 6.
2. Nietzsche, *Human, All Too Human*, 238.

and perfection. Is it God who needs changing or ourselves? If it is God, it is difficult to know what effect we mere mortals could actually have, God being God. After demanding an account from God as to why he suffers, a demand that provokes a hauntingly poetic outburst—a flood of words that can reasonably be termed a harangue—Job replies, not without a hint of irony, "Behold, I am of small account; what shall I answer thee? I lay my hand on my mouth." This prompts even more haranguing until Job (the irony now truly palpable) responds with "I have uttered what I did not understand, things too wonderful for me, which I did not know" (Job 40:4; 42:3). How else can one respond to someone who refuses to answer a serious question by going on at length about how great he is? How much does the book of Job reveal to us of God, if God exists? Perhaps Job is not about God at all, but about, as Girard has powerfully argued, scapegoating.

But if it is we who need to change, the only true reason we could offer for advocating and advancing a particular direction is the faith that we are pursuing King's bending arc, drawn to a power calling us to align ourselves ever closer to matters of justice and truth, goodness and beauty. In David Bentley's Hart presentation of Greek Christianity, God's unchanging nature is what guarantees the constancy of divine love, goodness, and truth. Otherwise, change is random at worst, pragmatic at best. This also ensures that God's relationship with the world is not one of mutual influence or dependency, but rather one where God freely creates, sustains, and redeems without being altered by his creation. If God could change, he would be contingent and dependent, rather than the necessary and independent foundation of all that exists. This immutability also underpins God's other attributes, such as his omniscience, omnipotence, and eternal nature. Since God is outside of time, he is not subject to the processes of becoming or change that characterize created beings. Again, this may not be the correct view of God's nature, but it certainly isn't stupid one. It is worthy of our deep contemplation. Could there really be any progress without God?

The universe may well be in evolution; there is every indication that it is. No contemporary faith can avoid relating to the modern understanding of becoming, which is rooted in the sciences of astrophysics, biological evolution, paleontology, anthropology and archeology, and the study of history: we live no longer in a cosmos but a cosmogenesis. We can appreciate and dignify, with Nietzsche, the "deification of becoming," but still see it as "erroneous." For Nietzsche, this is because the idea that the universe as "headed somewhere" is a fiction; but it is no less a fiction than the view there is no Omega point: both are fictions, which is to say both are positions of faith.

In the medieval worldview, there was a subtle but meaningful connection between faith and fiction. Both faith and fiction involved an act of shaping or forming an understanding or perception that transcended the immediately apparent or the empirically verifiable. For Aquinas, faith was not merely a rational assent to certain doctrines but also an engagement of the imagination. Believers were called to give form to their understanding of divine truths that could not be directly seen or fully comprehended. This act of shaping belief through imagination was, in many ways, parallel to how fiction creates narratives that go beyond the literal or the observable.[3]

We need not follow Jung and postulate a changing God to deal with matters of change in ourselves and evolution in the universe. For a speculative philosopher like Žižek, his atheism requires enfolding a gap, a limit, finiteness, and negativity inside of Being itself, since there is no Other to whom we can relate.[4] No drive to wholeness—just a "cut" that bars any claims to totality. But, again, Žižek doesn't know any better than you or me whether the Absolute exists: atheism is a position he takes up, which then requires a certain kind of analysis in order to be consistent. It is an analysis worth reading and absorbing. But it is, in the end, a view of truth, not truth itself, and there is something that urges us beyond what is, in the end, a form of constructivism, and hence relativism.

In the New Testament, the metaphors linking God and Christ are not the categories of Greek metaphysics but more immediate, more sensate, and familial: "You are the Christ, the Son of the living God." Peter utters these words, in response to the question Jesus puts to him: "But who do you say I am?" (Matt 16:15). The adjective used here describing a "living" God might be seen as a progenitor of evolutionary, cosmogenic thinking. This need not mean God evolves but that God is in evolution, or, that this "living" God is a God of evolution. In some fashion, it provokes the realization that creation is not instantaneous but unfolding; even more, that the "directionality" of this unfolding depends on us. We "see" the "King" when we feed and clothe people, when we visit those in prison, when we welcome strangers (Matt 25).

---

3. On this relationship between faith worlds and fictive worlds, see Plate, *Religion and Film*.

4. See Žižek, *Christian Atheism*.

Jesus is not God—he is the Son, or, in Greek metaphysics, his *ousia* (essence) is to be "consubstantial with the Father"—which means he is representative of (he embodies) the nature, character, will, and passion of God. Jesus, himself a metaphorician (among other things), is a metaphor of God: this is that. God as "prime mover" or uncaused cause means God is "independent of his work, and in consequence, without any definable basis to his immanence." In an evolutionary conception, through which we must now necessarily think, the contrary is true: "God is not conceivable . . . except in so far as he coincides with . . . but without being lost in, the center of convergence of cosmogenesis."[5] On the road to Emmaus, in the offering of a meal to a stranger, he makes himself known, a parable of resurrection (Luke 24:13–35). "Our capacity to love" is the convergence point around and through which "nature is finally held together" in a "gravitation" towards the "living God."[6]

Teilhard places God in evolutionary processes. God is not some distant "efficient cause" of creation who, once he wound the clock and pushed the pendulum takes a long cosmic break as matters unwind. This does not mean that God evolves, but that he is within creation, a God of creation. And, in saying God is the "First Cause," this "first" is "not a retro, in the light of the origin of things." Rather, God is the "First principle," out "ahead" of creation "and draws it to himself."[7] The Word becoming flesh, God in Christ—these metaphors mean that God's will, character, and person were embodied in the life of a person, in Jesus of Nazareth; philosophically and theologically, this means replacing an ontology of essence or being with one of participation and relation—what Teilhard terms *Uniri*, "to be, to unite, to be united."[8]

> Our Father who art in heaven,
> Hallowed be thy name.
> Thy kingdom come.
> Thy will be done,
> On earth as it is in heaven. (Matt 6:9–10)

---

5. Teilhard, *Christianity and Evolution*, 239.
6. Teilhard, *Christianity and Evolution*, 239–40.
7. Küng, *Does God Exist?*, 174. See also Illich, *Rivers North*, 71–73.
8. Teilhard, *Christianity and Evolution*, 227.

Bibliography

Abelard, Peter. *Commentary on the Epistle to the Romans*. Translated by Stephen R. Cartwright. Washington, DC: The Catholic University of America Press, 2011.
Addison, Heather. "Cinema's Darkest Vision: Looking into the Void in John Carpenter's *The Thing* (1982)." *The Journal of Popular Film and Television* 41 (2013) 154–66.
Alter, Robert. *Genesis: Translation and Commentary*. New York: Norton, 1997.
———. *The Hebrew Bible, Volume 3, The Writings: A Translation with Commentary*. New York: Norton, 2019.
Anderson, Gary A. *Sin: A History*. New Haven, CT: Yale University Press, 2010.
Anholt, Robert R. H., and Trudy F. C. Mackay. "Genetics of Aggression." *Annual Review of Genetics* 46 (2012) 145–64.
Anselm. *Cur Deus Homo*. Translated by Sidney Norton Deane. https://sacred-texts.com/chr/ans/ans115.htm.
———. "Why God Became Man." In *Anselm of Canterbury: The Major Works*, edited by Brian Davies and G. R. Evans, 260–356. New York: Oxford, 2008.
Aquinas, Thomas. *Summa Theologiae*. https://www.newadvent.org/summa/.
Arbel, Daphna, et al., eds. *Not Sparing the Child: Human Sacrifice in the Ancient World and Beyond*. London: Bloomsbury T&T Clark, 2015.
Assmann, Jan. *The Price of Monotheism*. Translated by Robert Savage. Stanford, CA: Stanford University Press, 2009.
Astell, Ann W., and Sandor Goodhart, eds. *Sacrifice, Scripture, and Substitution: Readings in Ancient Judaism and Christianity*. Notre Dame, IN: University of Notre Dame Press, 2011.
Auden, W. H. (Wystan Hugh). *The Age of Anxiety: A Baroque Eclogue*. London: Faber and Faber, 1948.
Augustine, Saint. *The Retractions*. The Fathers of the Church 60. Washington, DC: Catholic University of America Press, 2010.
Behr, John. *Origen: On First Principles*. New York: Oxford University Press, 2019.
Berger, Peter L. *The Sacred Canopy: Elements of a Sociological Theory of Religion*. New York: Anchor, 1990.
Biale, David. *Blood and Belief: The Circulation of a Symbol Between Jews and Christians*. Berkeley, CA: University of California Press, 2008.
Black, Max. "Metaphor." *Proceedings of the Aristotelian Society* 55 (1954) 273–94.

———. *Models and Metaphors: Studies in Language and Philosophy by Max Black*. Ithaca, NY: Cornell University Press, 1962.
Blumenberg, Hans. "An Anthropological Approach to the Contemporary Significance of Rhetoric." In *History, Metaphors, Fables: A Hans Blumenberg Reader*, edited, translated, and with an introduction by Hannes Bajohr et al., 177–208. Ithaca, NY: Cornell University Press, 2020.
———. "Beobachtungen an Metaphor." *Archiv Fur Begriffsgeschite* 15 (1971) 161–214.
———. *Beschreibung Des Menschen*. Frankfurt: Suhrkamp Verlag, 2014.
———. "Kant und Die Frage Nach Dem 'Gnädigen Gott.'" *Studium Generale* 7 (1954) 554–70.
———. *The Legitimacy of the Modern Age*. Studies in Contemporary German Social Thought. Cambridge: MIT Press, 1983.
———. *Paradigms for a Metaphorology*. Translated by Robert Savage. Ithaca, NY: Cornell University Press, 2016.
———. *The Readability of the World*. Translated by Robert Savage and David Roberts. Ithaca, NY: Cornell University Press, 2022.
———. *Shipwreck with Spectator: Paradigm of a Metaphor for Existence*. Translated by Steven Rendall. Cambridge: MIT Press, 1996.
———. *St. Matthew Passion*. Translated by Helmut Müller-Sievers and Paul Fleming. Ithaca, NY: Cornell University Press, 2021.
———. *Wirklichkeiten in Denen Wir Leben*. Stuttgart: Reclam, 1986.
———. *Work on Myth*. Cambridge: MIT Press, 1985.
Boccaccini, Gabriele. *Paul's Three Paths to Salvation*. Grand Rapids: Eerdmans, 2020.
Booth, Wayne C. "Metaphor as Rhetoric: The Problem of Evaluation." *Critical Inquiry* 5 (1978) 49–72.
Borg, Marcus, and John Dominic Crossan. *The First Paul: Reclaiming the Radical Visionary Behind the Church's Conservative Icon*. New York: HarperOne, 2010.
Bowler, Kate. *Blessed: A History of the American Prosperity Gospel*. New York: Oxford University Press, 2013.
Brock, Rita Nakashima, and Rebecca Ann Parker. *Saving Paradise: How Christianity Traded Love of This World for Crucifixion and Empire*. Boston: Beacon, 2008.
Brown, Peter. *The Rise of Western Christendom: Triumph and Diversity, A.D. 200–1000*. 10th anniversary rev. ed. Chichester, UK: Wiley-Blackwell, 2013.
Buber, Martin, and Leora Batnitzky. *Eclipse of God: Studies in the Relation Between Religion and Philosophy*. Princeton: Princeton University Press, 2015.
Bunch, Ryan. *Oz and the Musical: Performing the American Fairy Tale*. New York: Oxford University Press, 2023.
Burke, Kenneth. *A Grammar of Motives*. New York: Prentice-Hall, 1945.
Burke, Peter. "The Rise of Literal-Mindedness." In *Words: Religious Language Matters*, edited by Ernst van den Hemel and Asja Szafraniec, 364–75. New York: Fordham University Press, 2016.
Burkert, Walter, et al. *Violent Origins: Walter Burkert, René Girard, and Jonathan Z. Smith on Ritual Killing and Cultural Formation*. Edited by Robert G. Hamerton-Kelly. Stanford: Stanford University Press, 1988.
Burns, J. Patout. "The Concept of Satisfaction in Medieval Redemption Theory." *Theological Studies* 36 (1975) 285–304.
Chafetz, Janet Saltzman. *Sex and Advantage: A Comparative Macro-Structural Theory of Sex Stratification*. Lanham, MD: Rowman & Littlefield, 1984.

Chirichigno, Gregory C. *Debt-Slavery in Israel and the Ancient Near East*. London: Bloomsbury T&T Clark, 2009.
Chomsky, Noam. *What Kind of Creatures Are We?* New York: Columbia University Press, 2015.
Conolly, Jez. *The Thing*. Leighton Buzzard, UK: Auteur, 2014.
Cormac, Earl R. Mac. *A Cognitive Theory of Metaphor*. Cambridge: MIT Press, 1990.
Corrigan, Kevin, and Tuomas Rasimus, eds. *Gnosticism, Platonism and the Late Ancient World: Essays in Honour of John D. Turner*. Leiden: Brill, 2013.
Crossan, John Dominic. *The Birth of Christianity: Discovering What Happened in the Years Immediately After the Execution of Jesus*. New York: HarperOne, 1999.
———. *The Historical Jesus: The Life of a Mediterranean Jewish Peasant*. New York: HarperOne, 2010.
———. *How to Read the Bible and Still Be a Christian: Is God Violent? An Exploration from Genesis to Revelation*. New York: HarperOne, 2016.
———. *Jesus: A Revolutionary Biography*. San Francisco: HarperSanFrancisco, 1994.
———. *The Power of Parable: How Fiction by Jesus Became Fiction About Jesus*. New York: HarperOne, 2013.
Cumbow, Robert C. *Order in the Universe: The Films of John Carpenter*. Lanham, MD: Scarecrow, 2000.
Dawkins, Richard. *The God Delusion*. New York: Bantam, 2006.
Debray, Regis. *God: An Itinerary*. New York: Verso, 2004.
Derrida, Jacques. *Margins of Philosophy*. Translated by Alan Bass. Chicago: University of Chicago Press, 1984.
Dodds, Eric R. *The Greeks and the Irrational*. 2nd ed. Berkeley: University of California Press, 2004.
Donald, Merlin. *Origins of the Modern Mind: Three Stages in the Evolution of Culture and Cognition*. Cambridge: Harvard University Press, 1993.
Dourley, John P. "Jung, Mysticism and a Myth in the Making." *Studies in Religion* 30 (2001) 65–78.
Dupuy, Jean-Pierre. *On the Origins of Cognitive Science: The Mechanization of the Mind*. Cambridge: MIT Press, 2009.
Dyson, Freeman J. *Birds and Frogs: Selected Papers Of Freeman Dyson, 1990–2014*. London: World Scientific, 2015.
Eagleton, Terry. *Holy Terror*. New York: Oxford, 2005.
———. *The Illusions of Postmodernism*. Malden, MA: Blackwell, 1996.
———. *Reason, Faith, and Revolution: Reflections on the God Debate*. New Haven, CT: Yale University Press, 2009.
———. *Why Marx Was Right*. New Haven, CT: Yale University Press, 2018.
Eco, Umberto. *Semiotics and the Philosophy of Language*. Bloomington, IN: Indiana University Press, 1986.
Edinger, Edward F. *Aion Lectures: Exploring the Self in C. G. Jung's Aion*. Toronto: Inner City, 1996.
Ehrman, Bart D. *Did Jesus Exist? The Historical Argument for Jesus of Nazareth*. New York: HarperOne, 2013.
———. *Jesus Interrupted: Revealing the Hidden Contradictions in the Bible (And Why We Don't Know About Them)*. New York: HarperOne, 2010.
Eisen, Arnold. "Covenant." In *Contemporary Jewish Religious Thought: Original Essays on Critical Concepts, Movements and Beliefs*, edited by Arthur A. Cohen and Paul Mendes-Flohr, 107–12. New York: Scribner's Sons, 1987.

Erikson, Erik H. *Childhood and Society: The Landmark Work on the Social Significance of Childhood.* 2nd ed. New York: Norton, 1993.
Eusebius. *The Ecclesiastical History.* Portsmouth, NH: Heinemann, 1975.
Feldman, Karen S. *Binding Words.* Chicago: Northwestern University Press, 2006.
Fisher, Mark. *Capitalist Realism: Is There No Alternative?* New York: Zero, 2009.
Flusberg, Stephen J., et al. "War Metaphors in Public Discourse." *Metaphor and Symbol* 33 (2018) 1-18.
Freud, Sigmund, and C. G. Jung. *The Freud/Jung Letters: The Correspondence Between Sigmund Freud and C. G. Jung.* Abridged paperback ed. Edited by William McGuire, translated by R. F. C. Hull and Ralph Manheim. New Haven, CT: Princeton University Press, 1994.
Fromm, Erich, and Karl Marx. *Marx's Concept of Man: Including "Economic and Philosophical Manuscripts."* London: Bloomsbury Academic, 2013.
Frye, Northrop. *The Educated Imagination and Other Writings on Critical Theory 1933-1963.* Toronto: University of Toronto Press, 2006.
Gadamer, Hans-Georg. *Philosophical Hermeneutics.* 30th anniversary ed. Edited by David E. Linge. Berkeley: University of California Press, 2008.
Gasset, José Ortega Y. *The Dehumanization of Art and Other Essays on Art, Culture, and Literature.* New Haven, CT: Princeton University Press, 2019.
Geertz, Clifford. *The Interpretation of Cultures: Selected Essays.* New York: Basic, 1973.
———. *Negara: The Theatre State in 19th Century Bali.* New Haven, CT: Princeton University Press, 1981.
Gehlen, Arnold. *Man: His Nature and Place in the World.* New York: Columbia University Press, 1988.
Gilders, William K. *Blood Ritual in the Hebrew Bible: Meaning and Power.* Baltimore, MA: Johns Hopkins University Press, 2004.
Gillespie, Michael Allen. *Nihilism Before Nietzsche.* Chicago: University of Chicago Press, 1996.
Girard, René. *I See Satan Fall.* Maryknoll, NY: Orbis, 1999.
———. *The One by Whom Scandal Comes.* Translated by Malcolm B. DeBevoise. East Lansing, MI: Michigan State University Press, 2014.
———. *Things Hidden Since the Foundation of the World.* Translated by Stephen Bann and Michael Metteer. Stanford: Stanford University Press, 1987.
———. *Violence and the Sacred.* Translated by Patrick Gregory. Baltimore, MA: Johns Hopkins University Press, 1979.
Glasberg, Elena. "Who Goes There? Science, Fiction, and Belonging in Antarctica." *Journal of Historical Geography* 34 (2008) 639-57.
Goldman, M. Review of *The God Gene: How Faith Is Hardwired into Our Genes* by Dean Hamer. *Nature Genetics* 36 (2004) 1241.
Gould, Stephen Jay. *Full House: The Spread of Excellence from Plato to Darwin.* New York: Three Rivers, 1997.
Gurney, John. *Brave Community: The Digger Movement in the English Revolution.* Manchester: Manchester University Press, 2012.
Häkkinen, Sakari. "Poverty in the First-Century Galilee." *Hervormde Teologiese Studies* 72 (2016) 1-9.
Hamer, Dean H. *The God Gene: How Faith Is Hardwired into Our Genes.* 1st ed. New York: Doubleday, 2004.
Harman, Graham. *Object-Oriented Ontology.* New York: Pelican, 2018.

———. "Undermining, Overmining and Duomining: A Critique." In *Add Metaphysics*, edited by Jenna Suleta, 40–51. Espoo, Finland: Aalto University Design Research Laboratory, 2013.

Hart, David Bentley. *The Experience of God: Being, Consciousness, Bliss*. New Haven, CT: Yale University Press, 2014.

Hauser, David J., and Norbert Schwarz. "The War on Prevention: Bellicose Cancer Metaphors Hurt (Some) Prevention Intentions." *Personality and Social Psychology Bulletin* 41 (2015) 66–77.

Hegel, G. W. F. *Hegel: Lectures on the Philosophy of Religion. Volume III: The Consummate Religion*. Edited by Peter C. Hodgson. New York: Oxford University Press, 2008.

Heisig, James W. *Imago Dei: A Study of C. G. Jung's Psychology of Religion*. Plainsboro, NJ: Associated University Press, 1979.

Hemel, Ernst van den, and Asja Szafraniec. *Words: Religious Language Matters*. New York: Fordham University Press, 2016.

Hesse, Mary B. *Models and Analogies in Science*. Notre Dame, IN: University of Notre Dame Press, 1966.

Hillman, James. *Anima: An Anatomy of a Personified Notion*. Thompson, CT: Spring, 1998.

———. *Revisioning Psychology*. New York: Harper Perennial, 1992.

Hitchens, Christopher. *God Is Not Great: How Religion Poisons Everything*. New York: Twelve, 2007.

Hobbes, Thomas. *Leviathan*. Edited by J. C. A. Gaskin. New York: Oxford Classics, 2008.

Hogg, Michael A., and Danielle L. Blaylock, eds. *Extremism and the Psychology of Uncertainty*. Chichester, UK: Wiley-Blackwell, 2012.

Homer. *The Iliad*. Translated by Robert Fagles. New York: Penguin, 1998.

Hudson, Michael. *. . . And Forgive Them Their Debts: Lending, Foreclosure and Redemption from Bronze Age Finance to the Jubilee Year*. Dresden: Islet, 2018.

Illich, Ivan. *The Rivers North of the Future: The Testament of Ivan Illich*. Toronto: House of Anansi, 2005.

Jaffe, Aniela. *Myth of Meaning*. Einsiedeln, CH: Daimon, 1984.

James, William. *The Varieties of Religious Experience*. New York: Mentor, 1958.

Jean, Piaget. *Play, Dreams, and Imitation in Childhood*. New York: Norton, 1962.

Jensen, Morton. "Climate, Droughts, Wars, and Famines in Galilee as a Background for Understanding the Historical Jesus." *Journal of Biblical Literature* 131.2 (2012) 307–24.

John Paul II. "General Audience." Vatican Website. July 21, 1999. http://w2.vatican.va/content/john-paul-ii/en/audiences/1999/documents/hf_jp-ii_aud_21071999.html.

Johnson, Mark, ed. *Philosophical Perspectives on Metaphor*. Minneapolis, MN: University of Minnesota Press, 1981.

Jones, James William. *Can Science Explain Religion? The Cognitive Science Debate*. New York: Oxford University Press, 2016.

Jung, C. G. *The Collected Works of C. G. Jung*. 20 vols. New Haven, CT: Princeton University Press, 1953–79.

———. *The Gnostic Jung: Selections from the Writings of C. G. Jung and His Critics*. Edited by Robert A. Segal. New Haven, CT: Princeton University Press, 1992.

———. *Memories, Dreams, Reflections*. Edited by Aniela Jaffe. Translated by Clara Winston and Richard Winston. New York: Vintage, 1989.

Kant, Immanuel. *Religion Within the Boundaries of Mere Reason: And Other Writings*. Translated by Allen Wood and George di Giovanni. New York: Cambridge University Press, 1998.

Kaufmann, Walter, and Ivan Soll. *Goethe, Kant, and Hegel*. Discovering the Mind 1. 1st ed. Piscataway, NJ: Transaction, 1991.

Kerr, Stephen T. *Readings in Christian Thought*. Nashville, TN: Abingdon, 1990.

King, Martin Luther, Jr. *A Testament of Hope: The Essential Writings and Speeches*. New York: HarperOne, 2003.

King, Robert Alan. "The Story of Jonah as Allegory, Parable or History?" Bible Commentator, Jun. 18, 2017. https://biblecommentator.com/jonah-allegory-parable-history/.

Kliever, Lonnie D. "Fictive Religion: Rhetoric and Play." *Journal of the American Academy of Religion* 49 (1981) 657–69.

Koryakin, Sergey. "Abandoning Penal Substitution: A Patristic Inspiration for Contemporary Protestant Understanding of the Atonement." *Religions* 12 (2021) 785. https://doi.org/10.3390/rel12090785.

Kotsko, Adam. *Neoliberalism's Demons: On the Political Theology of Late Capital*. Stanford, CA: Stanford University Press, 2018.

Kövecses, Zoltán. *Metaphor in Culture: Universality and Variation*. New York: Cambridge University Press, 2006.

———. *Where Metaphors Come From: Reconsidering Context in Metaphor*. New York: Oxford University Press, 2015.

Kruijff, S., and C. Van Zweden. "The Harmful Impact of the Rhetoric 'War on Cancer.'" *European Journal of Surgical Oncology* 43 (2017) 963–64.

Kuhn, Thomas. *The Structure of Scientific Revolutions*. Chicago: University of Chicago Press, 1962.

Küng, Hans. *Christianity: Essence, History, and Future*. New York: Continuum, 1995.

———. *Does God Exist? An Answer for Today*. New York: Doubleday, 1980.

———. *On Being a Christian*. Glasgow: Collins' Sons, 1986.

———. *What I Believe*. London: Bloomsbury Academic, 2010.

Lakoff, George, and Mark Johnson. *Philosophy in the Flesh*. New York: Basic, 1999.

Laland, Kevin N., et al. "How Culture Shaped the Human Genome: Bringing Genetics and the Human Sciences Together." *Nature Reviews. Genetics* 11 (2010) 137–48.

Lampe, Peter. *From Paul to Valentinus*. Edinburgh: T&T Clark, 2003.

LeDrew, Stephen. *The Evolution of Atheism: The Politics of a Modern Movement*. New York: Oxford University Press, 2016.

Leibniz, Gottfried Wilhelm. "The Principles of Nature and Grace, Based on Reason." In *Philosophical Papers and Letters*, edited and translated by Leroy E. Loemker, 1:636–42. 2 vols. New York: Springer, 1989.

Lepicard, Etienne. "An Alternative to the Cosmic and Mechanic Metaphors for the Human Body? The House Illustration in Ma'aseh Tuviyah (1708)." *Medical History* 52 (2008) 93–105.

Lewis, C. S. *The Case for Christianity*. New York: Macmillan, 1946.

Locke, John. *The Clarendon Edition of the Works of John Locke: An Essay Concerning Human Understanding*. New York: Oxford University Press, 1979.

Lycan, William G. *Philosophy of Language: A Contemporary Introduction*. 3rd ed. London: Routledge, 2018.

Ma, Lin, and Aihua Liu, "A Universal Approach to Metaphors." *Intercultural Communication Studies* 17 (2008) 260–68.

Malabou, Catherine. "Is Psychic Phylogenesis Only a Phantasy? New Biological Developments in Trauma Inheritance." In *Freud and Monotheism: Moses and the Violent Origins of Religion*, edited by Gilad Sharvit and Karen S. Feldman, 177–218. New York: Fordham University Press, 2018.
Man, Paul de. "The Epistemology of Metaphor." *Critical Inquiry* 5 (1978) 13–30.
Mann, Michael. *The Sources of Social Power. Volume 1: A History of Power from the Beginning to AD 1760*. New York: Cambridge University Press, 1986.
Marquard, Odo, and Hannes Bajohr. "Unburdening from the Absolute: In Memory of Hans Blumenberg." *New German Critique* 49 (2022) 225–35.
Maslow, Abraham. *Toward a Psychology of Being*. New York: Van Nostrand, 1962.
May, Rollo. *The Meaning of Anxiety*. New York: Norton, 2015.
McCabe, Herbert. *God Matters*. London: Mowbray, 2000.
———. *God Still Matters*. New York: Continuum, 2002.
McCutcheon, Russell T. *Critics Not Caretakers: Redescribing the Public Study of Religion*. Albany, NY: State University of New York Press, 2001.
McGrath, S. J. *The Dark Ground of Spirit: Schelling and the Unconscious*. London: Routledge, 2012.
Mews, Constant J. "The Lists of Heresies Imputed to Peter Abelard." *Revue Bénédictine* 95 (1985) 73–110.
Meyer, Marvin W., and James M. Robinson. *The Nag Hammadi Scriptures: The Revised and Updated Translation of Sacred Gnostic Texts Complete in One Volume*. New York: HarperOne, 2009.
Midgley, Mary. *Science as Salvation: A Modern Myth and Its Meaning*. London: Routledge, 1992.
Miles, Jack. *Christ: A Crisis in the Life of God*. New York: Vintage, 2002.
———. *God: A Biography*. New York: Vintage, 1996.
Miller, Madeleine S., and J. Lane Miller, eds. *Harper's Bible Dictionary*. New York: Harper and Row, 1952.
Moltmann, Jürgen. *The Crucified God: The Cross of Christ as the Foundation and Criticism of Christian Theology*. New York: Harper & Row, 1974.
———. *Man: Christian Anthropology in the Conflicts of the Present*. London: SPCK, 1974.
Moss, Lenny. "From Representational Preformationism to the Epigenesis of Openness to the World? Reflections on a New Vision of the Organism." *Annals of the New York Academy of Sciences* 981 (2002) 219–29.
———. "Redundancy, Plasticity, and Detachment: The Implications of Comparative Genomics for Evolutionary Thinking." *Philosophy of Science* 73 (2006) 930–46.
Moss, Lenny, and Vida Pavesich. "Science, Normativity and Skill: Reviewing and Renewing the Anthropological Basis of Critical Theory." *Philosophy and Social Criticism* 37 (2011) 139–65.
Myers, Ched. *Binding the Strong Man*. Maryknoll, NY: Orbis, 2008.
Newberg, Andrew, and Eugene d'Aquila. *Why God Won't Go Away: Brian Science and the Biology of Belief*. New York: Ballantine, 2001.
Nietzsche, Friedrich. *The Gay Science: With a Prelude in Rhymes and an Appendix of Songs*. Translated by Walter Kaufmann. New York: Vintage, 1974.
———. *Nietzsche: Human, All Too Human: A Book for Free Spirits*. Translated by R. J. Hollingdale. New York: Cambridge University Press, 1996.
———. *The Portable Nietzsche*. Edited and Translated by Walter Kaufmann. New York: Penguin Classics, 1977.

"Ninety-Eight Cents." *Time*, Nov. 8, 1926. https://time.com/archive/6659905/science-ninety-eight-cents/.

O'Regan, Cyril. *Gnostic Return in Modernity*. Albany, NY: State University of New York Press, 2001.

Origen. *De Principiis*. In *The Ante-Nicene Fathers*. Edited by Philip Schaff. Electronic ed. Garland, TX: Galaxie Software, 2000.

Ortony, Andrew, ed. *Metaphor and Thought*. New York: Cambridge University Press, 1993.

Pahl, Jon. *Empire of Sacrifice: The Religious Origins of American Violence*. New York: New York University Press, 2012.

Parker, Rebecca Ann, and Rita Nakashima Brock. *Saving Paradise: How Christianity Traded Love of This World for Crucifixion and Empire*. Boston: Beacon, 2009.

Pascal, Blaise. *Pensées and Other Writings*. Edited by Anthony Levi. Translated by Honor Levi. New York: Oxford, 2008.

Pelikan, Jaroslav. *Jesus Through the Centuries*. New Haven, CT: Yale University Press, 1999.

Phillips, Charles, and Alan Axelrod, eds. *The Encyclopedia of War*. 5 vols. New York: Facts on File, 2004.

Philo. *Every Good Man Is Free. On the Contemplative Life. On the Eternity of the World. Against Flaccus. Apology for the Jews. On Providence*. LCL 9. Translated by F. H. Colson. Cambridge: Harvard University Press, 1941.

Plate, S. Brent. *Religion and Film: Cinema and the Re-Creation of the World*. New York: Columbia University Press, 2017.

Popper, Karl. *The Logic of Scientific Discovery*. London: Routledge, 2002.

Rappaport, Roy A. *Ritual and Religion in the Making of Humanity*. New York: Cambridge University Press, 1999.

Rasmussen, Ulrik Houlind. *The Memory of God: Hans Blumenberg's Philosophy of Religion*. Copenhagen: University of Copenhagen, 2009.

Rees, John. *The Leveller Revolution: Radical Political Organisation in England, 1640–1650*. New York: Verso, 2017.

Richards, I. A. *The Philosophy of Rhetoric*. New York: Oxford University Press, 1995.

Roberts-Zauderer, Diana L. *Metaphor and Imagination in Medieval Jewish Thought: Moses ibn Ezra, Judah Halevi, Moses Maimonides, and Shem Tov ibn Falaquera*. New York: Palgrave, 2019.

Robinson, James M. *The Nag Hammadi Library in English*. Rev. ed. New York: Harperone, 1990.

Rucker, Rudy. *Mind Tools: The Five Levels of Mathematical Reality*. New York: Dover, 2013.

Samuels, Andrew. "Jung and Antisemitism." *Jewish Quarterly* 41 (1994) 59–63.

———. "New Material Concerning Jung, Anti-Semitism, and the Nazis." *Journal of Analytical Psychology* 38 (1993) 463–70.

Sanday, Peggy Reeves. *Female Power and Male Dominance: On the Origins of Sexual Inequality*. New York: Cambridge University Press, 1981.

Sanday, Peggy Reeves, and Ruth Goodenough, eds. *Beyond the Second Sex*. Philadelphia: University of Pennsylvania Press, 1989.

Schweitzer, Albert. "The Conception of the Kingdom of God in the Transformation of Eschatology." In *The Theology of Albert Schweitzer*, edited by E. N. Mozley, 87–117. Baisongstoke, UK: Macmillan, 1951.

Sloterdijk, Peter. *In The Shadow of Mount Sinai*. Translated by Wieland Hoben. Malden, MA: Polity, 2015.

Slotkin, Richard. *Regeneration Through Violence: The Mythology of the American Frontier, 1600–1860*. Norman, OK: University of Oklahoma Press, 2000.

Smith, Richard. "The Modern Relevance of Gnosticism." In *The Nag Hammadi Library in English*, edited by James M. Robinson, 532–49. San Francisco: HarperSanFrancisco, 1990.

Snow, C. P. *The Two Cultures*. New York: Cambridge University Press, 2012.

Sontag, Susan. *Illness as Metaphor*. New York: Vintage, 1979.

Sprat, Thomas. *The History of the Royal-Society of London for the Improving of Natural Knowledge by Tho. Sprat*. London, 1667.

Stein, Murray. *Jung's Treatment of Christianity: The Psychotherapy of a Religious Tradition*. Asheville, NC: Chiron, 2018.

Stephenson, Barry. "Liminality, Structures, and 'The Problem of the Lie.'" *Liminalities: A Journal of Performance Studies* 17 (2021) 1–10.

Stern, Menahem. *Greek and Latin Authors on Jews and Judaism. Volume 2: From Tacitus to Simplicius*. Jerusalem: The Israel Academy of Sciences and Humanities, 1980.

Styfhals, Willem. *No Spiritual Investment in the World: Gnosticism and Postwar German Philosophy*. Ithaca, NY: Cornell University Press, 2019.

Taves, Anne. "From Religious Studies to Worldview Studies." *Religion* 50 (2019) 137–47.

Taylor, Charles. *The Language Animal: The Full Shape of the Human Linguistic Capacity*. Cambridge: Belknap, 2016.

———. *A Secular Age*. Cambridge: Belknap, 2007.

Taylor, Richard. *Metaphysics*. Englewood Cliffs, NJ: Pearson, 1991.

Teilhard de Chardin, Pierre. *Christianity and Evolution*. Translated by Rene Hague. Boston: Harcourt, 1971.

Tertullian. *De spectaculis*. Translated by T. R. Glover. Cambridge: Harvard University Press, 1931.

Tillich, Paul. *The Ground of Being: Neglected Essays of Paul Tillich*. Selma, NC: Mindvendor, 2015.

———. *History of Christian Thought*. New York: Touchstone, 1972.

———. *Systematic Theology*. 3 vols. Chicago: University of Chicago Press, 1967.

Trompf, Garry W., et al., eds. *The Gnostic World*. London: Routledge, 2020.

Velmans, Max. "Introduction to Monist Alternatives to Physicalism." *Journal of Consciousness Studies* 19 (2012) 7–18.

Veyne, Paul. *Did the Greeks Believe in Their Myths? An Essay on the Constitutive Imagination*. Translated by Paula Wissing. Chicago: University of Chicago Press, 1988.

Voegelin, Eric. *The Ecumenic Age. Volume 4: Order and History*. Baton Rouge: Louisiana State University Press, 1974.

Weinfeld, Moshe. *Social Justice in Ancient Israel and in the Ancient Near East*. Jerusalem: Hebrew University Magnes Press, 2011.

Wertz, Anna. "On the Possibility of Creative Being: Introducing Hans Blumenberg." *Qui Parle* 12 (2000) 3–15.

West, Cornel. *Keeping Faith: Philosophy and Race in America*. London: Routledge, 2008.

White, Eric. "The Erotics of Becoming: Xenogenesis and *The Thing*." *Science-Fiction Studies* 20 (1993) 394–408.

Wilber, Ken. *Sex, Ecology and Spirituality: The Spirit of Evolution*. Boulder, CO: Shamabala, 1995.

Wiley, Tatha. *Original Sin: Origins, Developments, Contemporary Meanings*. Mahwah, NJ: Paulist, 2002.
Wilken, Robert Louis. *The Spirit of Early Christian Thought: Seeking the Face of God*. New Haven, CT: Yale University Press, 2005.
Williams, Rowan. *Eucharistic Sacrifice: The Roots of a Metaphor*. New York: Grove, 1982.
Williams, Thomas. "Sin, Grace, and Redemption." In *The Cambridge Companion to Abelard*, edited by Jeffrey E. Brower and Kevin Guilfoy, 258–78. New York: Cambridge University Press, 2004.
Wright, N. T. *The New Testament and the People of God*. London: SPCK, 1992.
Wright, Robert. *The Evolution of God*. Reprint, Boston: Back Bay, 2010.
Žižek, Slavoj. *Less Than Nothing: Hegel and the Shadow of Dialectical Materialism*. New York: Verso, 2013.

Index

1984 (George Orwell), 20

Abelard, Peter, 148–49, 168
Abraham, 78, 91, 123–24; and Isaac, 78–79, 91, 114, 124
absolutism of reality. *See* Blumenberg
adaptation, 44–45
Aion (C.G. Jung), 187, 193, 209
Alter, Robert, 23
Alsberg, Paul, 40
Anderson, Gary, 94, 95, 111n28
animal sacrifice: in ancient Near East, 88–90; and atonement, 88, 93; Christian reinterpretation of, 88–89; critique of, 87, 92, 113–14; Girard's theory, 91, 119, 141, 146, 167, 215; ; in Hebrew Bible, 6, 66, 76, 91–92; in Homer, 90; Roman *Suovetaurilia*, 89
Annals of the World (James Ussher), 98
Anselm of Canterbury: on atonement and divine honor, 93, 113, 117, 143; Blumenberg on, 143–45; and substitutionary atonement, 142, 146–47
Answer to Job (C.G. Jung), 187, 196
anti-Semitism, 91n13, 125, 202–3
anthropogenesis. *See* hominization
anxiety, 4, 47–50
apatheia. *See* God, impassibility
apocalypticism, 103, 130–31, 133–36

Aquinas, Thomas, 20, 23–24, 216
Arendt, Hannah, 44
Aristotle, 23, 27
Assyrian empire, 102–3, 108
atheism, 5–6, 216
atonement: doctrine of, 62–63; theories of, 112–13; Abelard's exemplarism, 148–49; Anselm's theory, 142–47; Christus Victor, 119–20; ransom theory, 112–13, 120–21, 142; substitutionary, 93, 113, 119, 121, 142, 146–47. *See also* redemption
Atwood, Margaret, 20
Augustine of Hippo, 10, 56, 60–61, 75, 118, 120, 144n41, 146, 183, 210. *See also* original sin
Aulén, Gustaf, 119

Babylonian Empire, 102, 111
Barth, Karl, 3, 164n33
basic trust, 157–58, 207. *See also* faith
Baum, L. Frank, 54
Bentley Hart, David, 164, 187, 215
Berger, Peter, 2
Bible: contradictions in, 7–8, 17; genre of, 15–21; and literalism, 18–19, 21, 25–26, 32–33
Black, Max, 38
bloodguilt, 87, 92

Blumenberg, Hans: absolute metaphors, 3, 8–9, 11–12, 22, 57, 161–62; absolutism of reality, x, 46–50, 52–53, 160–61, 180, 189, 207; on Anselm's atonement theory, 143–45; anthropological approach of, 44–45; on answers preceding questions, 47, 56, 162; on Christian love, 166; on contingency, 50–51; on covenant, 82; Darwinism of words, 70; on the 'death of God,' 178; on distancing, 50–51; on dogma and original sin, 118; on fossil-like nature of metaphor, 56–58; on fundamental myths, 8, 9–10, 205; on God's question to Cain, 177; on Gnostic art myth, 205–6; on the incarnation, 176–80; on Kant's fundamental questions, 160; on metaphorology, 45, 56–58, 76, 161–62; on myth, 52–53, 70–73, 188–89; negative anthropology of, 44, 52; on nominalism, 154–55; on the possibility of God's return, 155, 178; on reason, 58; on retrieval of past possibilities, 155; on the second overcoming of Gnosticism, 183; on theological absolutism, 145, 147, 178
Boccaccini, Gabriele, 89
body, 37, 42, 55, 67; despising of, 6; house metaphor, 30; machine metaphor, 29–30; prison metaphor, 207; suffering, 111–13, 129, 146
Booth, Wayne C., 34
Borg, Marcus, 7
Bowler, Kate, 97, 98n23
Bronze Age, 98–99, 104
Brown, Peter, 180–81
Buber, Martin, 152
Burke, Kenneth, 34
Burke, Peter, 32–33

Cain and Abel, 64, 66–70, 73–74, 78, 84, 94, 104, 111, 177
Calvin, John, 69
care, 167–68, 176–81
Carpenter, John, 63–69
Chalcedon, Council of, 171, 175, 180
change, divine, 7–8, 214–15. *See also* God
Chomsky, Noam, 6
Christ. *See* Jesus Christ
Christianity: as worldview, 11; as revelation vs. construct, 3; early, 83, 88–89, 103–4, 113–14; Jung's remythologizing of, 191–94, 196, 202
Christology: adoptionism, 170–71; from above vs. from below, 179–80; Chalcedonian formula, 171; and the historical Jesus, 168–69; as logos, 172–73; and ontology, 173; and soteriology, 173; Jungian, 187, 193, 200, 211. *See also* descent
Christus Victor, 119–20, 142
Commentary on St. Paul's Epistle to the Romans (Peter Aberlard), 148
climate change, 48–49
conceptual metaphor theory, 36–38
constructivism, 28, 216
contingency, 13, 50–51, 153, 158–59, 163, 164. *See also* distancing
cosmogenesis, 215, 217
covenant: and divine negotiation, 82, 151, 179; in Hebrew Bible, 78–79; promises and obligations of, 79; sanctions in, 80; logic of, 108, 112
creation, goodness of, 157
Critique of Pure Reason (Immanuel Kant), 159
creation myths, 51
Cross, the. *See* crucifixion
Crossan, John Dominic, 7, 79, 129, 133; on apocalyptic eschatology, 133, 136; on covenant and sanction, 79, 80, 91n13; on eschatology, 134; on historical Jesus, 136; on nonviolent resistance, 136

INDEX

Crucified God, The (Jürgen Moltmann), 175
crucifixion: and care, 167–68; as central Christian reality, 166; and the cry of dereliction, 175; and God's suffering, 174–75; Hegel's Speculative Good Friday, 176; interpretations of, 167; as God's solidarity, 180–81; as sacrificial atonement, 88–89, 112–13, 128, 146. *See also* atonement, exemplarism
culture: as adaptive response, 41–42, 44, 51; and distancing, 51; gene-culture process, 42; and instinctual deficiency, 44, 46–47, 51; as learned behavior, 4; nature and, 5; as solution to human problem, 4; theoretic vs. oral-mythic, 38
Cur Deus Homo (Anselm), 93, 113, 142–47
Cusa, Nicholas of, 165, 178, 179, 179n61
Cyril of Alexandria, 175, 180

Dante Alighieri, 83–84
Darwin, Charles, 28
Darwinism of word. *See* Blumenberg
David, King, 51, 83–87, 102
Davidson, Donald, 35–36, 39
Dawkins, Richard, 5, 25, 33
death of God, 49, 154, 178
debt, as metaphor for sin, 95–96, 111–12
debt-slavery: in ancient Near East, 109; Hebrew Bible laws on, 110–11; and metaphors of atonement, 111–12
Debray, Régis, 150–51
Deleuze, Gilles, 66
de Man, Paul, 27
Derrida, Jacques, 27n22, 32
Descartes, René, 38
descent (theological concept), 171, 173, 177–78
descensus ad infernos, 199
distancing, 6–7, 50–51
Documentary Hypothesis, 81

Dodds, E. R., 132–33
Donald, Merlin, 38
Dourley, John, 196, 203
dualism, 183, 207, 208, 210
Dyson, Freeman, 29n26
Dylan, Bob, 180

Eagleton, Terry, 5, 42, 149, 154, 157, 168
Eco, Umberto, 14, 34–35
eco-anxiety, 48–49
Edinger, Edward, 195
Ehrman, Bart, 17, 168n41, 169, 221
Eisen, Arnold, 79n5, 82
Eliot, T. S., 4
Elohim. See God, names of
empire, 99–102, 109; *See also* Assyrian Empire, Babylonian Empire, Persian, Roman Empire.
Erikson, Erik, 156–57
eschatology: end times, 129–30; vs apocalyptic, 133–34, 136; delay of the *Parousia*, 83, 140; ethical, 136; of historical Jesus, 136, 138–40
evil, problem of, 60–62, 177, 187, 193–94, 207, 209–10
evolution, 28, 40–43, 65–66, 194, 200–201, 214–15, 217. *See also* adaptation, philosophical anthropology
exemplarism, 149
exile, Babylonian, 86, 102, 106
existentialism, 49
extinction, 54

faith: and basic trust, 157, 158; and *fideism*, 158; and fiction, 216; and hope, 165–66; and love, 165–66; as performative, 158; seeking understanding, 158; vs. nihilism, 153–54
feminist theology, 152, 196, 203n65
fideism, 158
Fisher, Mark, 66
forgiveness, 88, 94, 124–25, 149
freedom, and anxiety, 48
Freud, Sigmund, 61
Frye, Northrop, 27

fundamental myths. *See* Blumenberg.
fundamentalism, 19, 31–32

Gadamer, Hans-Georg, 155–56
Geertz, Clifford, 2, 7, 32, 41, 44
Gehlen, Arnold, 40, 45
genre, of religious texts, 15–21
Gillespie, Michael Allen, 154
Girard, René, 91, 119n4, 141, 146n47, 215
Glasberg, Elena, 65
Gnosticism: alienation, 183, 211; Blumenberg's critique of, 209; and the demiurge, 207; as a historical category, 182; Irenaeus's refutation of, 207–8; and Jung, 184, 190–91, 194, 197, 203, 211–12; and modernity, 182–83, 197; and the problem of evil, 207; salvation through knowledge, 183–84
Gnosticism and the Spirit of Late Antiquity (Hans Jonas), 183
Gödel, Kurt, 29, 165
God: as absolute metaphor, 3, 9, 12, 161–62; abstract conceptions of, 154–55; analogical language for, 163–64; arguments for existence of, 158–59; as being vs. Being, 163; biblical conceptions of, 151–52; change in conceptions of, 150–52, 161–62, 213–15; as concept, 1, 11; as condition of possibility, 149, 157; as creator, 163; and care, 177; and contingency, 158–59; death of, 154, 178; and evolution, 214, 215, 217; as first cause, 217; functional existence of, 1–2; as ground of being, 157, 158, 164; impassibility, 174–75, 181; immutability of (*apatheia*), 174–75, 181, 214–15; as infinite, 165; of love vs. wrath, 117, 123–24, 129; as living, 216; mathematical metaphors for, 164–65; names of, 80–82; necessary being, 158–59, 163; nominalist conception of, 154–55, 178–79; not a being, 149, 157, 171; personal metaphors for, 165; passibility of, 174–75, 181; possibility of return of, 155, 178; and process theology, 214; solidarity of with humanity, 180–81; as Trinity, 165; as uncaused cause, 163, 164; and violence, 80, 84, 115, 122–24, 128, 136, 146
God-image, transformation of, 187, 193–94, 199–202, 204
Goethe, Johann Wolfgang, 160–61
Goldstein, Kurt, 50
Gospels, as proclamation vs. biography, 12–13
Gould, Stephen Jay, 30
Guattari, Félix, 66

Harman, Graham, 71–72, 75
Handmaid's Tale, The (Margaret Atwood), 20
Heaven: as state vs. place, 16–17, 20; kingdom of, 16, 53, 55, 57–58
Hegel, Georg Wilhelm Friedrich, 159, 176
Heidegger, Martin, 13
Heisig, James, 188, 195
Hellenism, 102–3
Hillman, James, 32, 200, 203n65
Historical Jesus, 130–31, 136–40, 168–69
historicity, of biblical texts, 17–21, 25–26
Hitchens, Christopher, 5
Hobbes, Thomas, 24–25, 29, 61, 65
hominization, 40, 43, 46.
hope, 151, 159–60, 165–66
Human All Too Human (Friedrich Nietzsche), 213
human nature, 13, 44, 52
Hugh of St. Victor, 142, 148

idolatry, 158n22, 163
Iliad, The (Homer), 90
immanentism, 214
Incarnation: and absolute metaphors, 161–62; Blumenberg's

speculative reading of, 177–78; as completion of creation, 178; and the cross, 174; and fortification of human self-respect, 179–80; and logos, 172–73; and love, 166; and mystery, 171; and participatory ontology, 173; and solidarity, 180–81; theological development of, 170–73
individuation (Jung), 186–87, 194, 199, 200, 211
instinctual deficiency, 41, 44, 46–47, 51
Iron Age, 100–101
Isaiah, 110–11, 113–14
Israel, origins, 100–103

Jaffé, Aniela, 188
James, William, 149, 156
Jefferson, Thomas, 7
Jerome, Saint, 128
Jerusalem, destruction of, 86, 102, 106–7
Jesus Christ: abandonment, experience of, 175–77; and adulterous woman, 62; as door, 21; as truth, 11; critique of institutions, 6–7; on kingdom of heaven, 53, 55, 57–58; miracles of, 19–20; parables of, 16, 19; redemption through, 10; and solidarity, 180; theoretical curiosity of, 58; titles of, 168–70, 172
Job, Book of, 215
Joas, Hans, 15
John Paul II, 16–17, 21, 52
Johnson, Mark, 12, 36–37
Jonah (and the whale), 25
Jonas, Hans, 182–83
Jubilee Year, 111
Judaism, 79n5, 92, 103, 114
Jung, C. G. on the archetype of the self, 186, 193, 200, 211; and Christology, 187, 193, 200, 211; and the collective unconscious, 185–86, 197, 203, 205; on compensation theory, 187, 209, 209n75; critique of, 188, 195–96, 201–3, 209, 211–12; and evolutionary paradigm, 194, 200–201; and Gnosticism, 184, 190–91, 194, 197, 203, 211–12; on the God-image, transformation of, 187, 193–94, 199–202, 204; on individuation, 186–87, 194, 199, 200, 211; and myth-making, 188–89, 192–93, 195, 199, 203–6; on neurosis and meaninglessness, 184–85; and the problem of evil, 187, 193–94, 209–10; on religion and science, 194, 196–99; remythologizing of Christianity, 191–94, 196, 202; on suffering, 209–10; therapeutic approach of, 184–85, 188
justice, 59–60, 79, 82, 104, 107, 111–15, 134–38, 151; and cosmic balance, 167; and God's honor, 146–48, 151, 215; and King's moral arc, 151, 153, 156, 215; retributive or distributive, 115, 126, 128

kairos, 173
Kant, Immanuel, 2, 159–60
Kaufmann, Walter, 161
kenosis, 181
Kierkegaard, Søren, 11
King, Martin Luther, Jr., 151, 215
Kliever, Lonnie, 199, 205
Kotsko, Adam, 59
Kuhn, Thomas, 28
Küng, Hans, 13n17, 128–29, 138, 146, 162n29, 166, 174, 174n52, 176n55, 181

Lakoff, George, 12, 36–37
Lamentations, Book of, 106–7
Lament of Ur, 104–5
Language: and anthropogenesis, 43–44, 46; constitutive-expressive theory, 39; designative-instrumental theory, 39; and lying, 44; and subjunctive space, 43

Language Animal, The (Charles Taylor), 39
Lebenswelt (lifeworld), 4, 12, 57–58
Leibniz, Gottfried Wilhelm, 153, 164
Lennon, John, 1, 9, 11–12
Leviathan (Thomas Hobbes), 29
Lewis, C. S., 129
literal-mindedness, rise of, 32–33
literalism. *See* Bible
Locke, John, 24, 61
logocentrism, 27n22, 32
logos, 10, 12, 27, 33, 52, 58, 165, 170, 172–73, 181
Lord's Prayer, 96
love, 165–66, 167–68, 180
Löwith, Karl, 60
Luther, Martin, 24, 69, 119, 176
Lying. *See* language
Lycan, William G., 35–37

Maimonides, 18
Malabou, Catherine, 42n5
manichaeism, 210
Mann, Michael, 100
Marquard, Odo, 120
Marx, Karl, 6, 61
Maslow, Abraham, 51–52
McCabe, Herbert, 168, 171, 176n55
McCutcheon, Russell, 33
McFague, Sallie, 12
McGrath, Sean, 213
Memories, Dreams, Reflections (C.G. Jung), 191, 204–5
metaphor: in Aristotle, 23; brain-as-computer, 28, 31; cognitive function of, 15, 22, 34–39; conceptual, 36–38; constitutive nature of, 36–39; for cosmos, 30; critiques of, 23–27, 35; definition of, 34; disease as, 31; emotive theory of, 26, 27n22; entailments of, 15, 26, 31; fossil-like nature of, 56–58; in mathematics, 28–29, 164–65; and religious thought, 97–98; in science, 27–31; source domains for, 97–98; substitution theory of, 26; and truth, 55–58; universality of, 35, 37n44; war on cancer, 31
metaphorics of sin: as burden/weight, 94–95; as debt, 95–96, 111; as infection, 64, 67, 74; as stain, 88, 94; as trespass, 96; as waywardness, 77–78
metaphorology. *See* Blumenberg
Miles, Jack, 83, 214
mind-body problem, 6
modernity, 4, 182–83, 197
Moltmann, Jürgen, 166, 168, 174–75, 180
monotheism, 32, 98
Moss, Lenny, 42n4, 42n6
mysterianism, 6
myth: and absolutism of reality, 52–53; and creation, 51; fundamental myths, 8, 9–10, 205; gnostic art myth, 205–6; Jungian, 192–93, 199, 195, 199, 203–6; and logos 10, 12, 27, 33, 52, 58; of redemptive violence, 117–18, 128, 141; work on, 52–53, 56, 58, 69, 71, 73, 189
naturalism, 5–6
nature and culture, 5
negative anthropology, 44, 52. *See also* Blumenberg
Nestorius, 180, 181
neurosis, 184–85
Newton, Isaac, 160–61
Nietzsche, Friedrich, 4, 6, 40, 49, 54–55, 56, 76, 120, 126–27, 213–14, 215
nihilism, 153–54, 156, 157
nominalism, 74–75, 154–55, 178–79
numinosum, 197

object-oriented ontology, 72, 75
On the True Religion (Augustine), 172
On Truth and Lies in an Extra Moral Sense (Friedrich Nietzsche), 40
O'Regan, Cyril, 183
Origen, 18–19
original sin, 10, 60–61, 75–76, 112, 118, 144, 146.
Ortony, Andrew, 26
Orwell, George, 20

Overmining, 72

paradigm shifts, 28
parousia, delay of, 83, 140
Pascal, Blaise, 49
Paul (apostle), 7, 60–61, 75, 162–64, 165–66, 170, 172
Pax Romana, 131
penal substitutionary atonement, 93, 113
Penrose, Roger, 165
Persian empire, 95–96, 102
personhood, language of, 165, 172n48
Philo, 134–35
philosophical anthropology, x, 3, 12, 15, 40–46, 52–53, 82, 160, 209
Philosophy of Rhetoric, The (I.A. Richards), 36
Plate, S. Brent, 7
Plessner, Helmuth, 40
positivism, logical, 24, 26–27, 33, 35, 38
postmodernity, 4
Power of the Sacred (Hans Joas), 14
Powers That Be (Walter Wink), 141
poverty, in Roman Palestine, 54n27, 75, 97, 130, 137
privatio boni, 187, 194
Process theology, 214
projection, theories of, 157
prosperity gospel, 97
principle of sufficient reason, 153, 157

ransom theory of atonement, 112–13, 120–21, 142, 148, 167
Rappaport, Roy, 13, 41, 43–44, 150
Rasmussen, Ulrik, 154n10, 155n14, 162
rationalism, 12
reason, 3, 58; principle of sufficient, 153, 157
Reason, Faith, Revolution (Terry Eagleton), 150
redemption, 10, 56, 112–13, 118–20, 128, 138, 141–42; Abelard's theory of, 148–49
reductionism, 5
reification, 56, 74
religion and science, debate, 5, 27, 194, 196–99

remembrance, 11
remythologizing of Christianity, 191–94, 196, 202
revelation, 3, 91; Book of, 89, 115, 123–24, 129, 141. *See also* violence
retrieval, 155
Richards, I. A., 36, 38–39
Roman Empire, 53–54, 103
Rorty, Richard, 39
Royal Society, 24

sacred canopy, 2–3
sacrifice, animal. *See* animal sacrifice
Samuels, Andrew, 202–3
satisfaction theory of atonement, 93, 113
scapegoat, 93, 95
scapegoating, 119, 215
Scheler, Max, 40
Schelling, Friedrich, 213–14
Schweitzer, Albert, 139–40
science: metaphors in, 27–31; and religion, 27, 194, 196–99
self-assertion. S distancing
Semiotics and the Philosophy of Language (Umberto Eco), 14
Septem Sermones ad Mortuos (Jung), 188, 190–91
significance, 22
sin, 59–76, 77–78, 104, 107–9; and atonement, 62; in Cain and Abel story, 64, 66–70, 73–74; as concept, 74–76; and collective punishment, 84–85, 107–9; and covenant, 80; and death, 62; and free will, 61; and guilt, 84, 94, 96, 147, 167, 210; metaphors of, *See* metaphorics of sin; ontologized 61, 74; and suffering, 108–9, 112; and *The Thing* (film), 63–69; transmission of, 75. *See also* original sin
Sloterdijk, Peter, 125
Snow, C. P., 27
social justice. *See* justice
solidarity, 180–81
Sontag, Susan, 30–31

soteriology, 173
soul, reality of, 21
Spiritual Problem of Modern Man, The (C.G. Jung), 182
Sprat, Thomas, 24, 34
startle response, 49–50
St. Matthew Passion (Hans Blumenberg), 82, 121, 167, 177, 181
Subjekt-Objekt (Ernst Bloch), 159
subjunctive spaces, 43
substitutionary atonement. *See* atonement
symbol-mindedness, 32–33

Taves, Ann, 7
Taylor, Charles, 4, 10, 4n7, 10n15, 39
Taylor, Richard, 152–53, 158
Teilhard de Chardin, Pierre, 217
Tertullian, 126–27
theodicy, 59, 83, 207, 210
theodrama, 177
theoretic culture, 38
Thing, The (John Carpenter), 63–69
Tillich, Paul, 146n47, 155, 157
trespass, 96
trinity, 165
trust, 157, 158. *See also* faith
truth: as viewpoint, 11; and metaphor, 55–58; urge to, 40, 54–55

Tyndale, William, 96

undermining, 71–72
universe. *See* cosmos
urge to truth, 40, 54–55
Ussher, James, 98–99

violence, 117–18, 121–29; divine, 80, 84, 115, 122–24, 128, 136, 146; myth of redemptive, 117–18, 128, 141; rhetorical and ideological, 122, 127–28; systemic, 127
Voegelin, Eric, 133, 182, 183
Voltaire, 1–2

White, Eric, 65–66
Williams, Rowan, 142
Wink, Walter, 141
Wizard of Oz (Frank L. Baum), 54
world-making, 7, 15
Work on Myth (Hans Blumenberg), 205
world openness, 46–48, 50, 52
Wright, N. T., 169

Yahweh, 66–69, 80–82
Yom Kippur (Day of Atonement), 94–95

Žižek, Slavoj, 209n75, 210n76, 216

Scripture Index

Hebrew Bible

Genesis

3	143
4:9	177
18	123
18:25	201

Exodus

3:14	116
32:14	214
32:26–29	122

Leviticus

20:45	133

Deuteronomy

7:1–2	122

Job

40:4	215
42:3	215

Joel

2:31–32	139

Hosea

6:6	214

Malachi

2:16	214

New Testament

Matthew

6:9–10	217
10:14–15	123
13:41–43	136
13:42	140
20:28	120
21:19	202
22:7	202
25	216
25:37–40	167
26:52	129
26:53–54	129

Mark

3:29	202
6:11	137, 202
9:43–48	202
10:45	147
14:39	171
15:34	175

Luke

3:15–18	123
3:15–17	141
13:23–28	124
14:12–14	168
19:27	202
21:9	140
21:32	140
23:34	120
24:13–35	217

John

1:14	173
3:18	125
3:36	125
6:53	124
6:53–56	125
10:18	174
13:8	125
13:15	146

Acts

17:24–29	163

Romans

1:4	170
3:25	146

1 Corinthians

1:18–25	152
5:7	146
8:5–6	170
13	165

Galatians

4:4–5	170
5:1	118

Philippians

2:5–12	170

Colossians

2:15	119

1 Timothy

2:5–6	120

Hebrews

9:14	147
9:22	128

1 Peter

1:19	146

Revelation

14:14–20	116

www.ingramcontent.com/pod-product-compliance
Lightning Source LLC
Chambersburg PA
CBHW031808220426
43662CB00007B/574